MARXISM AND MATERIALISM:

A Study in Marxist Theory of Knowledge

MARXISM AND MATERIALISM:

A Study in Marxist Theory of Knowledge

NEW AND REVISED EDITION

DAVID-HILLEL RUBEN

Department of Philosophy, University of Essex

THE HARVESTER PRESS · SUSSEX

HUMANITIES PRESS · NEW JERSEY

This second edition published in Great Britain in 1979 by
THE HARVESTER PRESS LIMITED

Publisher: John Spiers

17 Ship Street, Brighton

and in the USA by
HUMANITIES PRESS INC.,
Atlantic Highlands, New Jersey 07716

First published in 1977 by The Harvester Press Limited
Revised and with new material, 1979 (second edition)

© David-Hillel Ruben 1977, 1979

British Library Cataloguing in Publication Data

Ruben, David-Hillel
Marxism and materialism. – 2nd ed. – (Marxist theory and contemporary
capitalism).
1. Knowledge, Theory of
2. Communism
I. Title
121   BD161

ISBN 0-85527-766-1
ISBN 0-85527-776-9 Pbk

Humanities Press Inc.
ISBN 0-391-00966-4
        0-391-00965-6 Pbk

Printed and bound in Great Britain by
Redwood Burn Limited, Trowbridge & Esher

CONTENTS

FOR EIRA

PREFACE

It may well be that one of the kinder things that will be said about this book is that it is one which lacks an audience. It is intended to be a book of Marxist philosophy, both in the sense that it is *about* Marxist philosophy and in the sense that it is itself meant to be an instance or example *of* Marxist philosophy. For this reason, the book has two faces: a Marxist face and a philosophical face. I do not myself find the slightest difficulty in combining both aspects in one piece of work, but the difficulty with anything's having two faces is that it doubles the chances that everyone will find something about its appearance to dislike. Philosophers may find that the book is 'insufficiently philosophical'. At various points in the argument, certain remarks are taken as assumptions, or discussions are pursued only up to a point. Topics such as meaning, induction, reference and language, truth, reduction, necessity, correspondence, essence, and many others, would receive, in a book with only a philosophical face, a far more elaborate treatment. All of the points in Chapters IV and V—causality, theory and observation, the nature of scepticism, naturalism, foundationalism—would have been given a much fuller and more extensive development. But this book is, first and foremost, intended to have a polemical effect within Marxism, and in particular on Marxist thought. This has meant that I have tried to tailor the contents of the book to meet the intellectual needs of, and be readily comprehensible to, those Marxists who have a high degree of theoretical consciousness and understanding of their Marxism. This audience will have, as often as not, a very profound and sophisticated grasp of certain crucial theoretical questions that bear on Marxism, and a genuine feeling for some of the basic problems of Marxist philosophy, especially as those problems have been discussed by philosophers and theoreticians such as Gramsci, Lukacs, Althusser, or various representatives of the Frankfurt school. But this audience is not composed of professional philosophers, and I have attempted to bear this in mind, since the book is primarily addressed to them. As much as possible, I have tried to argue with, and speak in the terminology of, various thinkers within the Marxist tradition. Thus, I have not attempted a general discussion of the various anti-idealist arguments within orthodox philosophy, but have more or less restricted myself to the realist-idealist debate as it is situated within Marxism, since it is that debate which has been my real concern. Naturally, I still hope that professional philosophers will find the book both competent and philosophically interesting.

Whereas professional philosophers may find the book 'insufficiently philosophical', a converse but more serious problem is that many of the Marxists for whom the book was written may find the book 'overly philosophical'. In part, this is a deceptive appearance. Most Marxists have at least a passing familiarity with philosophy 'in the style of' Lukacs, Althusser, or Gramsci. Much of the language, jargon, and style of this continental Marxist philosophy is deeply imbued with the influences of Hegelian and other bourgeois philosophical traditions which were or are current on the continent. The style of this book is a product of the influences of other traditions and discussions. However, I do not believe that these stylistic differences, between continental Marxist philosophy and the Marxist philosophy which this book attempts, ought to be very important. In so far as the effects of continental and Anglo-American bourgeois philosophy do make some difference to the nature of the Marxist philosophy produced in their respective intellectual environments, I think that the difference is favourable to the kind of Marxist philosophy attempted here. But these differences should not be stressed unduly. Lukacs is of greater interest to us as Marxists than either the contents of *Mind* or of the *Revue de Metaphysique et de Morale*. However, familiarity of philosophical style does not breed contempt, and the unfamiliarity of style of this book may well put off many Marxists. I think that it would be disappointing if this did happen.

It is a pleasure to pay intellectual debts, both those of a general and of a special nature. On the general side of the ledger I wish to express my gratitude to two of my 'teachers', one who has helped me to appreciate philosophy and the other who helped me learn the meaning of my Marxism. As an undergraduate student of philosophy I had the opportunity to have Willis Doney as teacher. From him I learned those standards of clarity, rigour, and intellectual persistence which I have attempted to make my own. Whether or not I have learned his lesson well, he remains a far better judge than I. A further debt I wish to pay belongs to Hillel Ticktin, a former colleague at the University of Glasgow, and a present comrade on the editorial board of *Critique*. I went to Glasgow in 1970 a Marxist, but a very ill-educated one. Almost everyone seemed to be a Marxist in those heady days, as was then the fashion. Fashions changed, but from Ticktin I learned much of what I know of Marxist economics. Even more importantly, I learned by his example that not only is orthodox Marxism not necessarily dogmatic, as many erroneously believe, but on the contrary that intellectual rigidity and dogmatism are deeply inimical to any authentic Marxist approach or method. Ticktin's ability to see and state the problems in what he believed, his flexibility of approach, and his willingness to follow a thought wherever it leads, makes him a paradigm of what a Marxist thinker should be like. I have tried, as best I could, to follow his example.

I have many special debts connected with this book, due to all of which this book is far less bad than it might otherwise have been. I wish to thank, first of all, many of my comrades around *Critique,* who have discussed the ideas of this book with me from time to time, and who printed early versions of some of these ideas in *Critique* Nos. 2 and 4. Professor Roy Edgley, of Sussex University, kindly read over an early draft of the book in its entirety, and made very many helpful comments and suggestions. Eva Schaper, a former colleague in the Department of Logic, Glasgow University, and N. F. Bunnin, a present colleague at the University of Essex, read over the chapter on Kant, and made numerous recommendations. Richard Norman of the University of Kent commented on the chapter on Hegel. Mark Sainsbury of Bedford College, London, read over, and discussed at length with me, many of the ideas in Chapter IV. His comments on Chapter IV were extensive, detailed, and profoundly influenced much of my own thinking. He will no doubt recognise his influence in places, and I wish to acknowledge that influence and thank him for it. John Mepham, general editor of the series in which this book appears, is also to be thanked for his advice and help. Geoffrey Hellman, of Indiana University, made suggestions and comments on the earlier version of some of the ideas found in this book that appeared in *Critique* 4. I profited by Scott Meikle's reply to that article in *Critique* 6, and also from a letter from Adam Buick, which brought criticisms against some of these points I made there. The realism I try to state in this book differs greatly from the rather foundationalist position I took in *Critique* 4, and it was much of this criticism of my earlier article which led me to change many of my views on this point. Michael Dummett, in *Frege: Philosophy of Language,* claimed that it was unnecessary to say that others are not responsible for one's own mistakes, for if they were, they would not count as one's own mistakes at all. It is worth adding, however, that these people were not even causally responsible for my mistakes. I feel certain that all of their suggestions improved the quality of the work immensely.

I do not wish to lay claim to much original thinking. The basic theme of Chapter I, Kant's inconsistency, was already a theme that Lenin had developed, a theme discussed in different ways by Lukacs, Josef Maier, and others. My judgements about Hegel and Feuerbach in Chapter II are standard for those Marxists who do not engage in any special pleading on Hegel's behalf. Chapter VI is merely a reminder of those assets of Lenin's *Materialism and Empirio-Criticism* which are very often overlooked. It is only in Chapters IV and V that I try to make (what I think are) some new remarks about Marxist philosophy. It is with these two chapters that I am least satisfied. I make such remarks tentatively, well realising that much of an erroneous character will be detected in them. Yet, I hope they do occasion much criticism, for with criticism a fuller discussion of the nature of a Marxist philosophy can begin. The purpose of this book is to begin just such a discussion among Marxists.

Finally, I wish to thank F. Cioffi and N. F. Bunnin, professor and senior lecturer in philosophy respectively, at the University of Essex, for the personal encouragement and support they have given me during the writing of this book. I found their sympathy and help extremely valuable in the preparation of this book.

David-Hillel Ruben

PREFACE TO THE 2nd EDITION

This edition includes a postscript and an index. The postscript enables me to critically comment on the book. The index fills a major lacuna in the first edition of the work. I have also been able to make minor corrections in the text itself. I would also like to take this opportunity to thank my father, Blair Ruben, for his help on Chapter XI, which was never completed.

David-Hillel Ruben
January 1979

INTRODUCTION

'Repeatedly, and with quite understandable passion, I
have expressed the opinion that any unclarity in ideology
brings great harm. I think that ideological unclarity is
especially harmful for us now, when idealism of all
varieties and shades, under the impact of reaction and the
pretext of revising theoretical values, is holding veritable
orgies in our literature, and when some idealists,
probably for the sake of spreading their ideas, proclaim
their views to be Marxism of the latest model.'

G. Plekhanov, *Materialismus Militans*

It is an irony of history that Marxism, born from the decomposition of the
Hegelian Absolute Spirit and the death throes of German Idealism, and
whose intention it was to provide a materialist theoretical basis for the
struggle of the working class, stands in need of the very same purge that its
inception was meant to provide. Although for the first fifty years of its life
Marxism may have been subjected to positivist distortions, it has in its
second fifty years found itself beset with idealist tendencies. Those
positivist distortions, as they arose within the theory and practice of the
discredited Second International and especially within German Social
Democracy, are now well documented and understood. But the nature and
importance of the idealist tendencies within Marxism have not been
equally understood. Why should they have arisen? What were the material
conditions, either of capitalist society after the first world war, or more
particularly of the workers' movements during that period, which were
responsible for the appearance of those idealist tendencies? We do not yet
have a full answer to those important questions.

But even in the absence of those full answers, it seems salutary now to do
what one can to point out and describe those idealist distortions that have
managed to find their way into the theory and practice of Marxism. There
are at least two related ways in which such distortions arise. Materialism is
an ontological thesis about the nature of reality. But materialism is not a
blind act of faith. It needs a theory of knowledge which underpins it and
gives it plausibility, just as any ontological doctrine does. Materialism
needs a materialist theory of knowledge, and hence we can discern two
points of entry for idealist distortions in Marxism. First, and most directly,
a materialist ontology may be denied and the attempt made to substitute a
more 'refined' ontological basis upon which to build Marxism. The history
of Marxism has been littered with such attempts, often inspired by a

philosophical creed, whether Hegelian, Kantian, or Machian, with which Marxism is allegedly to be made compatible. Second, and less directly, an idealist theory of knowledge might be wedded to a materialist ontology, generating a theoretical tension which I shall want to describe in this book. It is especially this second sort of idealist distortion, in which epistemology becomes inconsistent with the materialism that is espoused, on which I shall focus in some detail.

Thus, the central contention of the book is that the acceptance of materialism places constraints on what can, with consistency, be accepted as an adequate theory of knowledge. Briefly, the argument will be that a materialist ontology demands a 'reflection' or 'correspondence' theory of knowledge, and I shall discuss Lenin's *Materialism and Empirio-Criticism* in this connexion in the last chapter of the book. That materialism does require a reflection theory of knowledge may not surprise professional philosophers—'Whatever else realists say, they typically say that they believe in a Correspondence Theory of Truth'[1]—but it may well come as a surprise to many Marxists, weaned on a diet of denunciation of *Materialism and Empirio-Criticism* for a host of alleged sins. The great virtue of that much maligned book is that in it, Lenin saw more clearly than any other Marxist before or since that such a connexion between materialism and the theory of knowledge often called a 'reflection theory' did exist. We may, with our arrogant sophistication with regard to the philosophical auto-didacticism of Lenin, prefer some more refined name for such an epistemological theory. Perhaps 'correspondence theory' is closer to the mark. But that in substance the theory of knowledge which Lenin defended, however named, is correct must be upheld by anyone who is a materialist.

I have said that the central claim of the book will be that materialism has a need, an affinity, for a reflection or correspondence theory of knowledge. I do not assert that the need or affinity is one of logical consistency. Suppose we adopted an interpretive, non-reflective theory of knowledge, according to which we are bound to impose certain *a priori* structures or beliefs on the world, rather than a reflection theory according to which our beliefs or conceptual structures *reflect* reality. Further, one could claim that one of the *a priori,* imposed beliefs that our minds brought *to* reality was the belief that there are mind-independent objects, a reality which was independent of the *a priori* structures which we inevitably foisted upon it. Such a view would certainly be formally consistent, however implausible and however little we could see any reason to believe it.

Rather, the need or affinity is one of something which I call epistemological implication. The argument, put schematically, runs like this: Materialism asserts the essential independence of reality from all thought. On an interpretive theory of knowledge, as I shall try to argue later, every object in reality which is *known* has an essential relation to thought. Hence, if we are to have any *knowledge* whatever of the reality to which materialism commits us (and hence the requirement is essentially *epistemological*), then a materialist must reject the interpretive theory of knowledge which I associate with Kant. What materialism needs then, epistemologically speaking, is a correspondence or reflection theory of knowledge, on which the relationship between a belief or a thought and the objects or real states of affairs which the beliefs are about is a contingent relationship.[2] If the theory of knowledge adopted does not preserve the contingency of the relationship between known objects and the knower, the credibility of materialism is undercut, since no known object could then be essentially independent of mind. There may be such objects, but they would be unknowable.

My discussion of reflection theory in chapters IV and V will explain why it is that reflection theory, carefully stated, avoids the standard objections brought against it by many Marxists, and in particular has nothing whatever in common with the positivism with which it is often wrongly identified. Indeed, reflection theory has been accused of many things— Stalinism, political passivity, mechanical materialism, state capitalism, denial of dialectics, and positivism are only a few of the charges levelled against it. Thus, my main line of defence of reflection theory will be to show why it is that these standard objections miss their mark. We shall take care that the reflection theory which we defend is not associated with misleading political or epistemological metaphors of passivity.

It is the question of political passivity which suggests at least some of the political importance that attaches to the abstract problems in the theory of knowledge which I intend to discuss. The connexion between positivist methodology and inevitabilist doctrines of historical change, which tended to lead either to political quiescence or reformism, is part of our well-documented understanding of the Marxism of fifty years ago. But how shall we comprehend that opposite deformation, voluntarism, which can come to characterise the political activity of revolutionaries? One suggestion may be that idealism, or 'idealist Marxism', given the nature of its comprehension of history and man's place within history, tends toward revolutionary voluntarism. Thus it is that any revolutionary activity which is able to avoid the dual dangers of quiescence and wishful thinking, of reformism and the terrorism of the exemplary act, must be founded on a theory of knowledge which is neither idealist nor positivist. Contrary to several generations of misinterpretation, Lenin provides us, in *Materialism and Empirio-Criticism,* with an *initial* statement of that theory of knowledge. Thus, there is a political importance, perhaps even urgency, in using Lenin to combat some of the idealist distortions which we described as arising from the adoption of an idealist theory of knowledge. We are looking for a materialist theory of knowledge, and hence for an adequate formulation of a reflection theory.

I have used 'idealist' and 'materialist', notoriously protean words, and 'correspondence' or 'reflection' theory, without saying what doctrines I have in mind. Let us begin by asking what a reflection theory is a theory of? First, I should like to say that I take 'reflection theory' and 'correspondence

theory' to be equivalent expressions for the same thing, just as Lenin did. It
is true that 'correspondence' has less misleading associations connected
with it than does 'reflection', and a far greater familiarity to the
professional philosopher, but I prefer to use the latter term, since that term
is the one chiefly used by Marxists in the debate about Marxist theory of
knowledge that has taken place since the publication of Lenin's
Materialism and Empirio-Criticism. Second, for professional philosophers
a correspondence theory is principally a theory about truth. Following the
formulations that have become current within Marxism, I prefer to speak
of a correspondence (or reflection) theory of knowledge. I do not think that
this amounts to any substantial difference, since, on most analyses, truth is
itself one of the conditions of knowledge, and clearly the one for which
correspondence would be a relevant consideration. Finally, in Chapter I,
when I come to discuss Kant I shall talk about thought or concepts
reflecting or corresponding to their objects. This is—intentionally—
ambiguous, for a thought could be said to be *true* when it corresponds to
reality, but a concept isn't capable of truth or falsity at all. The problem I
wish to trace through Kant has to do with the *a priori* or interpretive versus
the *a posteriori* or reflective nature of concepts (or categories). But I take it
that if a proposition is true because it corresponds to reality, then at least
some of the concepts used in that proposition must be *a posteriori,* must
also correspond to their objects, although the converse may not be the case.
Thus, a correspondence theory of truth presupposes a correspondence
theory of (at least some) concepts, and it is with the status of the concepts
used in expressing truths that I begin.

How am I using 'idealist' and 'materialist'? Since the whole of what
follows can be read as a commentary on just what such labels imply, I
cannot anticipate the results of what will follow by attempting a definition
of them at this point. However, there is one essential clarification I should
like to make here, since confusion is bound to arise unless it is born in mind
throughout all of what follows. I am using 'materialism' roughly in the
same sense which both Lenin and Engels give to it. Lenin says that 'the
fundamental premise of materialism is the recognition of the external
world, of the existence of *things* outside and independent of our mind . . .
for materialism, the object exists independently of the subject and is
reflected more or less adequately in the subject's mind . . .'[3] Lenin's
insistence on the 'materiality' of things is bound up with his attack on
Berkeley, Hume, and the tradition of (what contemporary philosophers
would call) phenomenalism. Generally, the hallmark of that tradition is the
analysis of physical objects into sets of actual and possible experiences
(speaking in the material mode) or the translation of statements about
physical objects into sets of counterfactual statements about experiences
(speaking in the formal mode). The denial of the reduction of the world to
mental experience is usually called 'realism' by contemporary
philosophers, and hence it would perhaps be less misleading to
philosophers to speak of realism rather than materialism, and perhaps less

misleading for Marxists as well, since Lenin's materialism or realism has little in common with the reductive materialism or physicalism associated with such philosophers as the Greek atomists, Hobbes, the eighteenth century French materialists, or the contemporary school of Australian materialists, which professional philosophers and many Marxists would not unnaturally associate with the label, 'materialism'. Put rather schematically, Marxist materialism, or realism, asserts the existence of *something* other than the mind and its contents, whereas reductive materialism claims that everything, including the mind and its contents, can be reduced to matter, or the physical. Indeed, one of the distortions of Marxism so common during the period of the Second International was to assimilate Marxism to a form of reductive materialism. Bernstein, for example, defines Marxist materialism thus:

To be a materialist means, first and foremost, to reduce every event to the necessary movements of matter . . . The movement of matter takes place, according to the materialist doctrine, in a necessary sequence like a mechanical process.

It is sometimes argued that Engels himself is at least partly responsible for the entry of this reductive materialism into Marxism, although I think it would be difficult to sustain such an accusation when one looks not just at isolated quotations but at the overall philosophical thrust of Engels' work.[4] Still, however we may decide about the relationship between Engels and the reductive materialism that is expressed, for example, in Bernstein's definition of 'materialism', it would not be seriously contested, I think, in the present climate of Marxist theory, that reductive materialism has very little to do with Marx's own materialism. Reductive materialism in the nineteenth century had as its spokesmen natural scientists like Büchner, Vogt, and Moleschott. Not only does Marxist materialism not commit one to reductive materialism, but throughout their lives Marx and Engels actively polemicised against its popularisers. In *Ludwig Feuerbach,* Engels criticized Feuerbach for conflating materialism in general with

the shallow, vulgarised form in which the materialism of the eighteenth century continues to exist today in the heads of naturalists and physicians, the form which was preached on their tours in the fifties by Büchner, Vogt and Moleschott.[5]

Engels calls them 'vulgarising pedlars', and Marx wrote a tract against one of their company, *Herr Vogt*. In *Capital* vol. I, Marx specifically rejects 'the abstract materialism of natural science, a materialism that excludes history and its process'. I shall, then, henceforward use 'materialism' only in the sense in which Lenin defined it, the assertion of the existence of some non-mental things, and never in the reductive sense of the denial of any (irreducibly) mental things whatever. Those Marxist writers who remained closest to the authentic spirit of Marxism have always appreciated the non-reductive nature of Marxist materialism, and thereby appreciated the integrity and reality of the social world which is, in a sense, the 'embodiment' of consciousness. Thus, Franz Jakubowski, for example, in his splendid *Ideology and Superstructure,* first published in 1936, comments:

In order to combat a widespread misunderstanding, it must be stressed that the superstructure is real . . . The superstructure is no less real than its base . . . There are in fact two forms of reality: the material reality and the 'ideal' reality (i.e. the reality of human ideas).[6]

Engels' own formulation of philosophical materialism is often in terms of 'primacy': 'those who asserted the primacy of spirit to nature . . . comprise the camp of idealism . . . The others who regarded nature as primary belong to the various schools of materialism'.[7] Lenin's and Engels' formulations are roughly equivalent, though, since (in the way in which Engels intends 'primary') what is primary relative to another thing can exist without that other thing. Although I will in subsequent chapters use 'materialism' and 'realism' interchangeably, in the first chapter I need to make (what will prove to be) an arbitrary distinction between them in order to discuss certain problems as they arise in Kant's theory of knowledge.

Once we begin to say clearly what is involved in Marxist materialism, there is a danger that it may begin to look wholly uncontentious.[8] Reductive materialism, however wrong-headed it may be, is at least an interesting and contentious doctrine which deserves discussion. But is materialism in the sense I wish to use it interesting or contentious? It is true that the philosophical attempt to build the ontology of the world from the parsimonious materials of actual and possible experience and only experience, as well as the philosophical denial of the intelligibility of such an attempt, has occupied centre stage for much of the life of post-Cartesian philosophy. But most contemporary philosophers simply take realism for granted. Not since the phenomenalism of the logical positivists died a welcome death some decades ago have many orthodox philosophers argued that external reality is mind-dependent or questioned that, in Lenin's phrase, 'the object exists independently of the subject'. But what may be uncontentious to the orthodox philosopher is, unfortunately, not always uncontentious, or clearly understood at any rate, within the Marxist camp. Encumbered with a Hegelian jargon whose implications are not always fully appreciated, many Marxists are, perhaps unconsciously, involved in a denial of materialism. This is the first and most direct way, as I earlier called it, in which Marxism has been subjected to idealist distortions, and I shall want to point out, in the course of what follows, those instances in which Marxists have been involved in an outright denial of materialist ontology. Moreover, if materialism in this sense *is* relatively uncontentious, it becomes even more crucial to understand what sort of theory of knowledge materialists must adopt, to what kind of theory of knowledge materialism commits us.

Why did Marx think it worthwhile bothering to assert the essential independence of things, of nature, from mind or thought? The answer is, as everyone knows, that the independence of things from thought was not uncontentious in the theoretical milieu in which Marx wrote. That milieu had been dominated by German Idealism, by Fichte, Schelling, Hegel, and others, as it arose out of reaction to and development of the Kantian critical philosophy. That miliéu was also marked by the philosophical attempt to give substance and credibility to Christianity or some form of Christian-like theism, an attempt which often closely identified mind with Mind and Mind with God. That milieu set, for Marx, a problematic, a set of intellectual parameters in which certain questions became 'live' questions. That intellectual milieu may no longer exist for us, and it may be difficult for us to understand *what Marx says* because we can no longer understand what questions he was trying to answer. Indeed the problem is even more acute for many contemporary Marxists, who 'know' the answers without understanding the questions to which the answers are answers. In order then, to understand the importance and content of Marx's materialism, we must think ourselves back into the philosophical context which Marx inherited, a context in which the central issues and problems may seem strange and unfamiliar to us now, but a context which does set the issues and problems within which Marx formulates his own materialist position, and through the understanding of which we can come to deepen our understanding of what Marx says. In short, to understand Marx, it is necessary to understand the philosophical parameters of the debate in which Marx was situated. We can begin to re-enter that philosophical environment by posing for ourselves the Kantian question concerning the two 'sources' of our knowledge, thought and reality, and it is to a discussion of that question and its location within German philosophy from Kant to Marx, to which I now turn.

Notes: Introduction

[1] Putnam, Hilary, 'What is Realism?' *Proceedings of the Aristotelian Society,* New Series, volume LXXVI, 1975-1976, p. 177. See also Hooker, C.A., 'Systematic Realism', *Synthese,* 26, 1973-74, p. 439: 'The Realist is clearly committed to a Correspondence Theory of Truth'.

[2] It is worthwhile pausing to observe that reflection theory does not need materialism in the same way in which materialism needs it. For a correspondence or reflection theory of knowledge to be true, the object of a thought or belief must only be essentially independent of that *particular* thought or belief. But, even though essentially independent of that particular thought, the object might not be essentially independent of thought *tout court*. It might be, as far as reflection theory goes, that the existence of any object necessarily presupposes that some thought or other exist but not necessarily the thought of it, and hence reality would *not* be essentially independent of thought. We can imagine a non-materialist correspondence theory, which would preserve *only* the contingency of the relation between an object and *its* thought.

But the result is otherwise if we start with materialism rather than with reflection theory. Materialism asserts the existence of reality independent of all thought, and hence of *any* particular thought too. Thus, it requires (epistemologically) a theory which does not tie reality to any particular thought either. There cannot be a materialism without a reflection theory in the way in which there can be a non-materialist reflection theory, unless of course we agree that none of the objects asserted by materialism to be essentially independent of thought are ever known. Thus, materialism needs a correspondence theory in a way in which correspondence theory does not need it. My claim, then, is about the need materialism has for reflection theory, but not the converse claim about any need of reflection theory for materialism.

3   Lenin, V.I, *Materialism and Empirio-Criticism,* Progress Publishers, Moscow, 1970, p. 100.

4   On the nature of Engels' materialism, and its relation to Marx's, see Donald D. Weiss, 'The Philosophy of Engels Vindicated', *Monthly Review,* vol. 28, no. 8, January 1977, pp. 15-30. I agree with Weiss' distinction between non-reductive and reductive varieties of materialism, and agree with the thrust of his argument, which assigns to Engels as well as to Marx a non-reductive version of materialism.

5   Engels, F, *Ludwig Feuerbach and the End of Classical German Philosophy,* Progress Publishers, Moscow, 1969, p. 23. It is often said that Lenin, in *Materialism and Empirio-Criticism,* espoused a reductive form of materialism. I think there is little evidence of this; consider his following remarks: 'As regards materialism . . . we have already seen in the case of Diderot what the real views of the materialists are. These views do not consist in deriving sensation from the movement of matter or in reducing sensation to the movement of matter; but in recognising sensation as one of the properties of matter in motion. On this question Engels shared the standpoint of Diderot. Engels disassociated himself from the 'vulgar' materialists, Vogt, Büchner, and Moleschott . . .' (pp. 49-50). Elsewhere Lenin speaks of 'the physical world familiar to all' being 'the sole objective reality' (p. 291). There is no hint here of denying, in reductive fashion, the ultimate reality of everything but matter in motion.

6   Jakubowski, Franz, *Ideology and Superstructure,* Allison & Busby, London, 1976, pp. 56-57.

7   Engels, *op. cit,* p. 20.

8   Perhaps it is this which accounts for the bad-tempered review given to Sebastiano Timpanaro's excellent *On Materialism* by Professor Philip Pettit in '*The Times Higher Education Supplement*' (14.5.76). Pettit notes the wide sense in which Timpanaro uses 'materialism', a sense roughly similar to the one I am using, and then proceeds to comment:

If this strikes the reader as a somewhat expanded sense of materialism, he may be assured that I agree. By the definition offered, the anti-materialist must believe either that man (or life) was on earth from the beginning—God need not enter the picture—or that man is not conditioned by 'nature' . . . In other words the anti-materialist must be little short of a complete ass.

The fact seems not to worry the author for he is quite disposed to believe that he has very stupid opponents.

These remarks are especially depressing coming as they do from someone who, unlike many of his British philosophical colleagues, should be aware of the nuances and differences among different philosophical traditions. What is a problem for one tradition may be a closed issue for another, nor was it so long ago that anti-materialism was *not* a closed issue on this philosophical island, for phenomenalism certainly denied the 'priority of nature over mind' in one sense at least. It is true that phenomenalism thought itself compatible with science (including geology, presumably), but I take it that Timpanaro would not give the phenomenalist this sort of protective shield of doing (merely) conceptual analysis. Pettit may disagree about this, and such a disagreement would provide a substantial issue for discussion. It would certainly have provided a better review than one composed of insults and innuendoes.

CHAPTER I

KANT

'The Kantian philosophy is a contradiction, it inevitably
leads either to Fichtean idealism or to sensationalism.'
Feuerbach to Bolin, 26 March, 1858.

Kant: Thought as Interpretation

We can think of the knowledge we possess about the world as having two independent 'sources', as a joint product of how we, as creatures capable of conceptual thought, are bound to interpret or conceive of the world, and of what the world itself is like. One may come to think of the conceptualisation or interpretation as the *form* which shapes or fashions the world of our knowledge, and the world or reality as the *content* or *matter* which comes to bear the forms we press upon it. Like any metaphor, such an image of the ingredients necessary for knowledge is not without its pitfalls. It is, after all, *only* a metaphor. It was an attractive image for Kant, and an image certainly not without at least some truth in it. Thus, the theme of the dual sources of our knowledge is perhaps nowhere more clearly expressed than in Kant's *Critique of Pure Reason:* 'The understanding can intuit nothing, the senses can think nothing . . . But that is no reason for confounding the contribution of either with that of the other; rather it is a strong reason for carefully separating and distinguishing the one from the other.'

The knowledge that creatures like ourselves possess 'springs from two fundamental sources of the mind . . . Through the first an object is *given* to us, through the second the object is *thought* . . .'[1] The understanding contributes form, sensibility contributes the matter, of our knowledge, for 'in every cognition there is to be distinguished matter, i.e. the object, and form, i.e. the manner how we recognise the object'.[2]

Why would Kant have been tempted by the idea that our knowledge springs from 'two fundamental sources of the mind'? Perhaps the following remark by Kant about two of his philosophical precursors can motivate the dual sources idea for us: 'In a word, Leibniz *intellectualised* appearances, just as Locke . . . *sensualised* all concepts of the understanding, i.e. interpreted them as nothing more than empirical or abstracted concepts of reflection. Instead of seeking in understanding and sensibility two sources of representations which, while quite different, can supply objectively valid judgments of things only in *conjunction* with each other, each of these great men holds to one only of the two . . . The other faculty is then regarded as serving only to confuse or to order the representations which this selected faculty yields' (B327). In Kant's mind, then, only a dual sources claim about knowledge could take us beyond the rationalist and empiricist errors of his philosophical forbearers. If sensibility were the sole source of knowledge, how might we account then for those features of necessity and universality in our knowledge, features which classical empiricism has always been hard put to explain? It is to avoid the dual dangers of rationalism and empiricism, of intellectually over-rationalising the world and of sceptically under-rationalising it, that Kant presses upon us the need for a dual-sources account of our knowledge. It is worth noting here that it is because of the particular historical figures that Kant has in mind that he limits the idea of sense experience being the sole source of knowledge to a special, empiricist version of that idea. That classical empiricist version not only held that all knowledge was derived from experience, but also contained a special theory about the simple sense impressions which were the proper objects of that experience. Kant never distinguished these two, separable views.

It is indisputable that Kant took his own metaphors seriously. Features of our experience which are necessary, and which can be known *a priori,* are attributed to the cognitive faculty of the understanding, and are said by Kant to arise by a synthesis of the understanding. In an obvious sense, for Kant, such features as objectivity, causality, spatiality, and temporality are 'in us', contributed to our experience from out of ourselves. Because our principal object of interest in this chapter is the historical Kant, we have not attempted to divest Kant of those quasi-psychological images and metaphors. Recent critics of Kant, most notably P. F. Strawson in his *The Bounds of Sense,*[3] have criticised Kant for these metaphorical formulations, and have tried to recapture the central themes of Kantian philosophy without using them. Strawson claims about Kant that 'wherever he found limiting or necessary general features of experience, he declared their source to lie in our own cognitive constitution' (p. 15), because he regarded 'the necessary unity and connectedness of experiences as being, like all transcendental necessities, the product of the mind's operations . . .' (p. 32). 'Kant's idiom is psychological' (p. 20), and such idiom is treated not as metaphor but as literal truth: '. . . we may be tempted to interpret the whole model of mind-made Nature as simply a device for presenting an analytical or conceptual inquiry in a form readily grasped by the picture-loving imagination. All such interpretations would, however, involve reading into much of the *Critique* a tone of at least half-conscious irony quite foreign to its character . . .' (p. 32). Thus, whereas our historical Kant viewed 'the very possibility of knowledge of necessary features of experiences . . . as dependent upon his transcendental subjectivism, the theory of mind making Nature' (p. 22), Strawson proposes to offer a reformed Kant who can do without such 'transcendental psychology'.

There is no real conflict between Strawson's remarks, and the treatment of Kant attempted in this chapter. Unlike Strawson, our intention is to present an historically accurate picture of those specific features of the critical philosophy which were taken seriously by his immediate philosophical successors, and not necessarily to present the most philosophically plausible rendering of that philosophy. However, it is worth noting that there are two distinct levels in Kant which Strawson wishes to jettison. We can distinguish in Kant between the *specific* explanation of the 'necessary features of our experience' which he offers, and the more general requirement that some explanation or other is in order. I think that there can be no doubt whatever that Kant's particular explanation, formulated in the long out-dated terms of a faculty psychology, has nothing but an antiquarian interest. But, as Strawson himself points out, even after expelling such terminology, we might still insist upon an answer being given to the Kantian question, 'How is synthetic *a priori* knowledge possible?' (or, 'Why does our experience have certain necessary features?'). Strawson rejects not only the specific Kantian answer to the question, but also the very legitimacy of attempting an answer to this request for an explanation: 'To this I can only reply that I see no reason why any high doctrine at all should be necessary here ... it is no matter for wonder if conceivable variations [to our alternative ways of looking at the world] are intelligible only as variations within a certain fundamental general framework of ideas ... There is nothing here to demand, or permit, an explanation such as Kant's' (p. 44). However, from the fact that an explanation of the origins of necessity, or of the synthetic *a priori,* 'such as Kant's' is illegitimate, it certainly does not follow that no account of the origins of necessity is possible. Can we say nothing more about concepts such as conceivability, intelligibility, or a possible description, which Strawson invokes so freely in his own reformulation of Kant's point? There is nothing *prima facie* illegitimate in, for example, the current distinction between necessity *de re* and necessity *de dicto.* Do the necessities which limit the ways in which we can describe experience derive from *de re* necessities? Or are such 'transcendental' necessities logical, or linguistic necessities? Do they derive from the meaning and use of language? And, if the latter, what sort of account are we prepared to offer for linguistic necessities? Are they conceptual, or conventional? Do they derive from human conventions which govern the use of language? Do they express stipulations? These sorts of questions are not usually considered illegitimate by professional philosophers, and yet they are all, in a sense, questions about the 'source' of necessity. The general intent of Kant's story about the synthetic *a priori* is to both accept Hume's point that these necessities are not *de re* necessities and yet to find an account of them which does not render them 'mere tautologies'.

Thus, we do not need Kant's particular, out-dated psychology in order to give substance to a contrast between say, *de re* necessity and something else. Now, some of the attempted contrasts do not 'humanise' necessity, do not show that such necessity arises 'in us'. For example, Platonic theories of meaning and conceptual truth do not 'humanise' the necessity that might be contrasted to *de re* necessity. But there are, in the philosophical literature, many plausible accounts of a 'humanised' kind of necessity that might be contrasted to *de re* necessity. I am thinking here especially of Wittgensteinian, and so-called conventionalist accounts.[4] It is no part of my purpose here to attack or defend these 'humanised' accounts of necessity. But surely they do offer plausible answers to the sort of question which Kant tries to answer, and which Strawson all too quickly dismisses as a question of 'high doctrine'. On a conventionalist account, which might locate necessity within certain agreed human *institutions, practices,* or even within certain very general *facts* about human beings, there is a sense in which the source of necessity *is* 'in us', where that need not be given a sense by an out-dated theory of psychology. Necessity can still be conceived of as a human contribution, just as Kant considered it to be. *Pace* Strawson, we can easily 'think both sides of those limits' (p. 44), for we can ask, for example, whether the necessary features of our experience, whatever they might be, arose from natural necessity on the one hand, or from general facts about human beings, the meanings of words in our language, convention, the constraint of retaining the overall simplest conceptual scheme, or whatever, on the other. There are many possible answers on the 'human' side of the dilemma other than a synthesis of the understanding. Some sort of distinction between *de re* and *de dicto* necessity will permit us to draw a Kantian-like contrast between transcendental realism and transcendental idealism; the contrast between what is in reality and what is a 'human' (linguistic, conceptual, conventional) contribution retains enough cogency to allow the discussions in this chapter, and throughout the book, to hold a philosophical as well as an historical interest. We will still be able to draw some sort of acceptable contrast between 'two sources', and we can ask about the essential independence of the world from language, convention, conceptual schemes, or whatever. Nor do we share Strawson's aversion to the possibility that this contrast may itself rest on empirical knowledge. Strawson criticises Kant's transcendental psychology on the grounds that it rests on matters of fact. Perhaps this accusation should have bothered Kant. It does not bother us, for it may turn out that the underpinning we give to necessity does have a factual basis. Necessities may derive from general facts about men and their situations. Whether or not this is so remains an open question at this point, but I do wish to mark it as a genuine philosophical possibility.

Thus, in this chapter, I continue to use, quite unashamedly, Kantian metaphors and images. I have no doubt that the particular filling that Kant gave to 'synthesis', 'understanding', 'sensibility', and so on are no longer adequate. But I do not accept that the enterprise of talking about two sources or stems of our knowledge is similarly outmoded, and I believe that there are many ways in which this talk might be fleshed out which contemporary philosophers might find wholly acceptable.

I have spoken in the first paragraph of this chapter of 'interpretation', as well as the more Kantian sounding 'conceptualisation', since 'interpretation' seems to me to catch rather well the *a priori* flavour of the Kantian dual sources claim concerning the role of the categories (and forms of intuition) in structuring our knowledge and experience of the world. Essential to any dual sources claim is not just the banality that in order to have knowledge we must think or 'capture' the world in thought, but more strongly that thought provides an independent (and hence *a priori*) second source or 'element', to use Kant's own phrase, for knowledge or experience, in addition to the source provided by what the object of thought is itself like. Thus, Kant's dual sources claim is a rejection of the classical empiricist understanding of thought since, for the classical empiricist tradition generally, thoughts (ideas), far from being an independent second 'source' of our knowledge, must themselves be traced back to experience, to the impressions (phenomenal objects) on which they depend, if they are to be meaningful. For the empiricist tradition, we could say that thoughts, concepts, ideas are reflective of the world or correspond to the world of objects, even though such objects are only phenomenal, rather than interpretive (with the *a priori* implications associated with that term) of it. Hence, the empiricists' concern to show how our most general concepts or ideas, like space, time, unity, infinity, can be got by abstraction from the objects of our experience, understood as impressions. For them, and their reflective understanding of thought, knowledge of the external world has ultimately but a single source. As Hume says: '. . . Let him ask from what impression that idea is derived? And if no impression can be produced, he concludes that the term is altogether insignificant';[5] and in *The Treatise:* '. . . all our simple ideas in their first appearance are derived from simple impressions, which are correspondent to them, and which they exactly represent'.[6] There are, of course, complications and sophistications to this picture, for the empiricists always allowed for 'truths about the relations of ideas'. But these complications are not important to the issues I wish to trace out. It is useful then, to speak of 'interpretive thought' and 'reflective thought' in order to mark the difference I want to indicate between the two theories or traditions, the Kantian and the Empiricist, the *a priori* and *a posteriori,* about the possibility of an independent role for conceptualisation in our knowledge.

I referred earlier to the banality that in order to have knowledge we must think, or that we must 'capture' the world in thought. Even this banality has been denied, for example by those after Kant who, influenced by the Romantic movement, glorified emotion and intuition and raised them to the epistemic status of providing a kind of non-conceptual understanding of the world. For them, a kind of knowledge was possible in which concepts played no mediating role of any sort. But what I wish to stress here is that someone who rejects a dual sources claim, as did the empiricists in their rejection of the claims by the rationalists on behalf of reason or innate ideas as an independent source of knowledge, is *not* thereby holding that there is no conceptual component necessary to thought. We are not interested in the claim that it would be perfectly possible to conceive of someone who could 'think' without the mediation of concepts or categories, or who could somehow mentally 'grasp' the world without some conceptual intervention. The possibility of non-conceptual comprehension is simply not at fundamental issue in the confrontation of these two traditions. Rather, the issue between them is whether concepts or thought can be adequately understood as entirely a 'reflection of' or in correspondence with the world, or whether thought must be assigned an independent, *a priori* role to play in the acquisition of knowledge, as both Kant and the rationalists (and some of the structuralists) have presumed. Both traditions, the interpretive and the reflective, can agree that concepts have an integral role to play in thought and knowledge.

Kant's dual sources claim is not just that, in our knowledge as a whole, some concepts have an *a priori* role to play. Kant's dual sources claim applies to each individual 'piece' of our knowledge, to every judgment, and says that, in each individual 'piece' of knowledge, in *every* judgment, thought makes an independent, second contribution along with that made by reality. I will henceforward refer to this as Kant's 'interpretation claim':

(IC) To make a judgment or claim to knowledge necessarily presupposes the activity of interpretive thought.

Again, it is the presence of 'interpretive' here that saves (IC) from being a banality. It may be banal to claim that making a judgment or claim to knowledge presupposes thinking (in a wide sense), simply because of the meaning of 'to claim' or 'to judge'. But it is not banal to claim that doing these things presupposes interpretively thinking, and this is the claim that (IC) is intended to make.

(IC) brings out the basic epistemic assymetry of thought and reality for Kant. Ontologically, they are for him a duality of 'equals'. Epistemologically this is not so, for not every claim to knowledge has, for Kant, being or reality as one of its sources. There are for Kant, as is well known, pure synthetic *a priori* truths which owe nothing to experience. So all synthetic truths have, necessarily, a formal element, and some have only a formal element. But no truth, synthetic or otherwise, can have only a material element.

Although there may be quibbles about the way in which I have formulated the Kantian interpretation claim, I do not think that it will be disputed that Kant held something at least very much like the claim as I have expressed it. This can be seen in his doctrine of transcendental synthesis of the understanding. Kant's basic premise is that the consciousness, whose contents are diverse and multifarious, displays a fundamental unity—'It must be possible for the "I think" to accompany all my representations, for otherwise something would be represented in me which could not be thought at all, and that is equivalent to saying that the representation would be impossible, or at least would be nothing to me' (B 131-132). What Kant seeks to demonstrate is that for the unity of representations to be possible, for the 'I think' to accompany a representation, those representations must be synthesised according to the categories of the understanding, which amount to the most general *a priori* rules of synthesis. Thus, a necessary condition for any content to be admitted to consciousness, and hence to knowledge, is that the content, the representation, be synthesised by the *interpretive* concepts of the human mind, the categories. No representation which has not been so synthesised is either experiencable or knowable. There must be an *a priori* 'totality of rules under which all appearances must stand if they are to be thought as connected in an experience', Kant reminds us in the *Prolegomena* (section 36).

Let us look again at (IC). It might be supposed that one could, through some procedure of phenomenological analysis, determine what the interpretive element was in any knowledge claim, and then by 'subtracting' just that element and no more, one could discover and describe the bare matter, or uninterpreted content, behind the knowledge claim. Such a supposition would be an illusion. Since (IC) is a claim about all knowledge claims, it asserts that, however much analytical pruning away of interpretation one were to engage in, one would never be left with a knowable but uninterpreted remainder, the pure given of the empiricists. Suppose someone, after engaging in such epistemic trimming finally asserted that he had reached some bedrock knowledge about an uninterpreted 'given' in experience, some wholly unvarnished truth. Such an assertion would be contradictory for anyone like Kant who also held an interpretation claim. In no judgment or claim to know something could there be an absence of interpretative thought and hence no one could ever know anything whatever about that which isn't interpreted *qua* uninterpreted. Thus (IC) is a form of denial of the empiricists' idea of a knowable, 'unvarnished' given, which was meant to serve for them as an epistemic foundation stone for the intricate structure of our knowedge. It is true that some passages, especially in the first edition of *The Critique of Pure Reason,* suggest such an empiricist account of given but uninterpreted data of experience. But it is generally accepted that Kant has an alternative account, which he uses especially in the second edition, on which no *knowable* or *experiencable* datum could be unsynthesised by the *a priori* rules and concepts of the understanding, and it is only this alternative account of the data of experience which is consistent with his overall theory of knowledge.[7] On his most plausible account, then, there can be no knowable uninterpreted given, and only such an account is compatible with his insistence on the part that both *a priori* concepts and intuitions play in the acquisition of human knowledge.

We have already seen why the empiricists, with their reflective understanding of thought, would reject any interpretation claim about all judgments, since for them there is at least one class of judgments, those about the uninterpreted given, for which (IC) does not hold. I have already mentioned how a controversial (IC) can get confused with the banal claim that thought is involved in all knowledge. Philosophers who accept some version of (IC) are sometimes guilty of expressing their substantial claim in a way that does make it seem equivalent to this banality. For example:

What is immediate can never reach the threshold of utterance—any attempt to utter the immediate by means of *any* symbols is a relinquishment and a falsification of it[8]

Sometimes it may look as if such a position is merely asserting that one cannot *describe* the object without using symbols, or a language, which is trivially true because of what 'describe' means. Perhaps partly because such claims are often expressed in such a misleading way, Nelson Goodman has taken interpretation claims to be banal. In particular, he argues that anyone who raises a question about *uninterpreted* entities is 'covertly demanding . . . that I describe what I saw without describing it'.[9] But if it is so obviously impossible to make any claim about uninterpreted entities, then the Kantian assertion that all our knowledge is knowledge of interpreted entities must be banal. If Kant, or Lowenberg, is merely saying that to know implies to think symbolically, how could it be other than trivially true that we cannot think about the pre-symbolic?

Leszek Kolakowski, in his essay 'Karl Marx and The Classical Definition of Truth,' has a similar argument.

. . . one can admit the validity of the idealists' traditional argument: 'A situation in which one thinks of an object that is not thought of is impossible and internally contradictory.'[10]

Kolakowski wishes to argue against the empiricist notion of an uninterpreted given, and does so by arguing that it involves the alleged logical absurdity of thinking about that which is not thought of.

Goodman's questioner and Kolakowski's empiricist are not committing such obvious mistakes. Suppose a philosopher holds that it is impossible to describe the uninterpreted, on the basis of holding (IC). Thus, the impossibility of describing the uninterpreted rests on the substantial tie between knowledge, judgment, or description on the one hand, and interpretation on the other—the link which (IC) asserts—and this, even if true, is certainly not a triviality. There is no immediately obvious analytic connection between 'description' and 'interpretation', for there is nothing obviously contradictory about the notion of reflective thought, or of a description which reflects its object. Goodman, before he could reduce (IC) to the banal demand for a description of the undescribed, would have to assume that an uninterpreted entity is necessarily an undescribed one, which is precisely what a reflection theory would deny, since it claims that we can describe an 'uninterpreted' reality, whether given in experience as empiricism assumes, or discoverable only by theory. The philosopher who attempts to describe the uninterpreted is not trying to describe something without describing it (as Goodman would have us believe) or trying to think about that which isn't being thought about (as Kolakowski appears to think), but is trying to describe or think without interpreting. The argument here is substantial, and one simply cannot dissolve it by seeing either assertion or counter-assertion as trivially true or contradictory.

The Kantian claim we have labelled as (IC) cannot be reduced to the assertion that all knowledge involves thought, or concepts, or to the Goodmanesque triviality that one cannot describe without using symbols, or Kolakowski's banality that you cannot think about something without thinking about it. It is, rather, a claim about the role interpretation plays in all knowledge, a claim whose denial is significant. Kant's interpretation claim is close to an assertion of what is sometimes referred to as conceptual idealism, although I shall show later why his position falls short of a full conceptual idealism in a rather puzzling way.[11] And the last thing one should say about conceptual idealism is that it is trivially true, that its denial is an absurdity.

Kant: The Objects of Thought

Also implied in Kant's dual sources claim, in addition to (IC), is that there is something which is essentially independent of thought, essentially independent of the synthesising operations of the mind. I shall call this Kant's 'independence claim', '(IpC)'. That there is something other than thought, whose existence does not imply the existence of thought or mental activity of any sort, is ground shared between Kant and the empiricists.[12] I am not now thinking of the difficult and problematic conception in Kant of *noumenon,* of the thing-in-itself, for even if we read Kant with the *noumenon* jettisoned, there still must remain, in addition to thought, whatever it is that sensibility contributes, that second source of our knowledge. Kant says that these objects spring from one of the 'two fundamental sources of *mind*' [my emphasis], so presumably they are not to be conflated with noumena. I shall refer to these objects, which are essentially independent of all thought, 'pre-conceptualised intuitions'.[13] Kant contemplates the possibility of appearances not bound together by the process of conceptualisation, and says of such appearances that they 'might indeed constitute intuition without thought, but not knowledge; and consequently would be for us as good as nothing' (A111), because we could have no possible experience or knowledge of such appearances. Kant also remarks about them: '. . . appearances can certainly be given in intuition independently of functions of the understanding' (A90); 'Objects may, therefore, appear to us without their being under the necessity of being related to the functions of understandings' (B122); 'That which, as representation, can be antecedent to any and every act of thinking, is intuition' (B67); and 'That representation which can be given prior to all thought is called intuition' (B132). Thus, there are for Kant pre-conceptualised intuitions, and Kant seems equally committed to their *existence* in both the first and second editions of *The Critique.*

Wolff, in his *Kant's Theory of Mental Activity,* claims to find a shift in Kant's views on this point. Wolff admits that Kant, at A90, says that there is a possibility of appearances 'given in intuition independently of functions of the understanding'.[14] He follows this with a series of supposedly increasingly conflicting statements by Kant, that the categories 'relate of necessity and *a priori* to objects of experience' (A93), that such appearances 'would be for us as good as nothing' (A111), that such perceptions would be 'merely a blind play . . . even less than a dream' (A112), and finally 'for it is only because I ascribe all perceptions to one consciousness . . . that I can say of all perceptions that I am conscious of them' (A122). But in fact there does not seem to be any shift within the passages that Wolff cites. Kant is apparently distinguishing *the having of an intuition* and *the being conscious of or experiencing of an intuition* (i.e. their being something 'for us'). Kant's position is, then, that although there are such preconceptualised intuitions, as such they cannot be admitted to the unity of consciousness and so I cannot be *aware* of them. There cannot be, for Kant, an uninterpreted given of which I can be conscious or aware, but it does not follow from that that there cannot be an uninterpreted given *at all* which if it did come into my awareness, would become interpreted. We argued in the previous section that Kant's considered view must be a denial of the empiricists' uninterpreted given in experience. But it would not necessarily follow that Kant denied the existence of uninterpreted (but unexperiencable) given *tout court*.[15] We noted earlier that there is a shift between the first and second German editions concerning the *knowability* of the uninterpreted, and we said that only the position which seems to dominate in the second edition, the denial of the *knowability* of any uninterpreted given, is compatible with Kant's theory of knowledge. But there is no accompanying shift, as far as I can see, in *The Critique*, either within an edition or between editions, concerning the *existence* of pre-conceptualised or uninterpreted intuitions. Kant seems quite committed to them throughout. Existence seems here to be one question, knowability quite another.

Kant, then, seems committed to intuitions which cannot be experienced or thought about or expressed in judgments. Since both consciousness and experience are clearly on the side of thought—'For experience is itself a species of knowledge which involves understanding . . .' (B XVIII)—Kant is committed to phenomenal intuitions which are not possible objects of consciousness or experience. This seems to resolve any appearance of inconsistency among the quotes that Wolff cites. It is true that Kant does say that 'It must be possible for the "I think" to accompany all my representations', which might suggest that there could be *no* representation independent of the unity of consciousness and hence no representation independent of conceptualisation, no pre-conceptualised intuitions. It is, however, worth noting that Kant's argument for the 'I think' accompanying all my representations is that if it did not accompany a representation, that 'representation would be impossible, or at least would be nothing to me' (B132). But the effect of the final qualification, 'would be nothing to me', is to change 'accompanying all my representations' to 'accompanying all the representations which are something to me', i.e. 'accompanying all the representations of which I am conscious', and thus would allow once again for the possibility of pre-conceptualised intuitions, although not ones of which I could be aware or conscious. I doubt whether *everything* Kant says in *The Critique* is consistent with interpreting him either as saying that there are (or can be) pre-conceptualised intuitions or as saying that there cannot be such things. But I think the most plausible interpretation of the matter is the one I have given, and this is reinforced by seeing how Wolff's opposition to the idea of 'an unsynthesised manifold' as 'an obvious incompatibility with his [Kant's] central argument'[16] is a confusion, since on Wolff's own understanding, Kant's central argument is that 'the validity of the categories is a necessary condition of *consciousness itself*'. [my italics]. That is, Wolff patently conflates the existence of an unsynthesised manifold, which is not incompatible with Kant's central argument, with the *consciousness* of such an unsynthesised manifold, which is incompatible. The interpretation I have adopted also seems to be confirmed by what Kant says about consciousness in his *Logic*: 'all our cognition has a twofold relation, first to the object, second to the subject. In the former respect it is related to presentation, in the latter to consciousness, the general condition of all cognition in general. (Actually, consciousness is a presentation that ånother presentation is in me).'[17] Kant's remarks here seem to allow for the possibility of presentations which are not presented to me, i.e., of which I am not aware. Kant then proceeds to describe a case in which two men see a house, one man who knows that it is a house and the other, a savage, who does not recognise what he sees. In the case of the savage, Kant asserts that he is having 'mere intuition'. Whatever we make of this peculiar example, it does show us that Kant was willing to conceive of intuitions without concepts, for it is only the first man who according to Kant has 'intuition and concept at the same time'.

Therefore, I ascribe to Kant the independence claim, that something *exists* independently of thought. In what follows, I will depart from *The Critique* terminology by calling such an independent thing an 'object', as I have already been doing. For Kant, experience of objects is the result of the joint operation of the two sources of knowledge, sense and understanding. But I will use 'object' as that which is essentially independent of thought, thereby eschewing Kant's own, more technical terminology even when I am discussing Kant. Let me, then, formulate Kant's independence claim thus:

(IpC) There are objects essentially independent of all thought, or of all interpretive mental activity.

In (IpC), the sense of 'independent' is 'not in necessary or essential relation to'. As I shall argue in the next section, objects which do exist within synthesised experience are *essentially* related to thought or mental activity, in the straightforward sense that the existence of such experienced objects, objects of awareness, are necessarily the results of mental activity or interpretive thought and hence *imply* the existence of that activity or thought. The relation between thought and object in those cases is a necessary or internal relation. (IpC) asserts that there are some objects about which this is not true.

In (IpC), we are not interested in causal or contingent independence. Even if (IpC) were true, it would leave open the logical possibility that everything in the universe does as a matter of contingent fact stand in some causal relation to thought. It is plainly the case that there are things which bear no causal relation to, or no relation of contingent dependence on, thought, but (IpC) makes no claim about this fact one way or another. Even if everything were contingently dependent in some way on thought—suppose for example man had in fact laboured on every bit of matter in the universe—it would not thereby be true that everything was *essentially* dependent on thought, that it couldn't have been otherwise.

It is easy to confuse the Kantian independence (from mental activity) claim with another, and apparently similar, claim about the independence of objects from *mind*.[18] Claims about the essential independence of objects from thought or mental activity, which are the ones we have been discussing, and claims about the essential independence of objects from the mind, are far from identical, as one can see in considering the cases of an empiricist or of Kant. This is not a familiar distinction in contemporary philosophy, yet it is one with which we shall have to work, whatever its ultimate plausibility, in order to comprehend properly the theories of knowledge of both Kant and Hegel.

For an empiricist, all objects of consciousness are impressions, and hence have a phenomenal or mentalistic existence. In that sense, they are essentially dependent on the mind. But imagine that there are impressions which do not have corresponding ideas. Many empiricists allowed for unsensed sensa data, sense data of which I was in fact unaware, unconscious. Indeed, since Hume, for example, argues that 'all distinct ideas are separable from one another' and since the idea of an impression and the idea of an idea are distinct, then 'the actual separation of these objects is so far possible, that it implies no contradiction nor absurdity'.[19] Hume, then, must allow for the possibility of phenomenal mind-dependent impressions, upon which no 'mental activity' had been performed in order to obtain a corresponding idea. Such impressions would be mind-dependent and thought-(or idea-) independent, for there would in fact be no corresponding idea on which they might depend.

Similarly for Kant, since we can only know things as they appear to us, never as they are in themselves. *All* the ingredients of knowledge are phenomenal, or have a phenomenal status, both form and content, structure and matter, of knowledge. This can be seen by Kant's referring to the pre-conceptualised intuitions as 'intuitions' or 'representations', which suggests a phenomenal status for them. As I argued earlier, Kant is committed to intuitions of which a man is *not* aware or conscious. Thus, Kant's pre-conceptualised intuitions are phenomenal, or mentalistic, in the sense that they necessarily relate to how things appear; they are 'appearances given in intuition' as Kant described them. Although they can exist independently of our consciousness of them, and therefore independently of any mental activity or synthesis, of the categories of the understanding, they remain phenomenal and cannot exist apart from the way in which they are related to human sensibility. In short, the pre-conceptualised intuitions, thought-independent as they may be, are still *de mente*. They are, at one and the same time, perceptual—they are, after all, intuitions—and yet essentially independent of thought. In both the cases of Hume and Kant, one can distinguish thought-independence and mind-independence.

What, for Kant, is *both* thought—and mind-independent? The noumena are both. Thus, the conception of noumena and of pre-conceptualised intuitions are *distinct* problems in Kant, the former being both thought and mind independent, the latter thought (or mental activity) independent only. Whatever sense we can make of this distinction, it is one that we need to make in coming to understand Kant's theory of knowledge. I do not think that the distinction can ultimately be maintained and I shall say why that is so when I come to discuss Marx. But I think that it is crucial to appreciate that the problem which Marx inherited from Kant and Hegel was formulated in terms of the relation between thought (or mental activity) and reality. That is not the same problem as the problem of the relation between the mind (or mental things) and reality, as it was discussed by the classical empiricists, or latter day phenomenalists for example, and with which contemporary philosophers will be far more conversant than with the rather strange sounding formulation of thought and reality.

Lucio Colletti's recent Kantian interpretation of Marx is muddled on just this point.[20] Colletti rightly stresses Marx's disagreement with Hegel, and alliance with Kant, on the question of the duality of thought and being. But for Kant the 'being' in this pair of contrasts, although thought-independent since it is being contrasted with thought, need not thereby be mind-independent as well. The confusion arises from Colletti's unfortunate tendency to treat 'mind' and 'thought' as synonyms, and indeed from Colletti's generalised tendency to treat sets or pairs of oppositions as equivalent.[21] If we distinguish, as I think we can, between thought-independence and mind-independence in Kant's theory of knowledge, we can see why Kant's acceptance of the independence claim is not yet, for him, materialism, in the sense that Lenin and Engels gave to that term. We shall, for the present, call the acceptance of the independence claim 'realism', since it asserts the *reality* of objects (whether the objects are mental or material) essentially independent of thought, rather than 'materialism'. In this terminology one could either be a materialist realist (Marx), if the objects independent of thought exist independent of the mind as well, or a non-materialist realist (Hume or Kant) if the objects independent of thought, namely impressions, do not exist independently of mind. However, when we come to discuss Marx, I will, as I have already said, show why for Marx this distinction cannot be drawn, and, thus, for Marx there can be no distinction between realism and materialism.[22]

Conversely, the position that rejects the independence claim is, we can say, 'idealism'. For idealism in this sense, no object exists which is essentially independent of thought.[23] This is Hegel's own definition of idealism in *The Phenomenology of Mind*: 'But *qua* reason . . . self-consciousness is . . . certain its self is reality, certain that all concrete actuality is nothing else but it. Its thought is itself *eo ipso* concrete reality; its attitude towards the latter is thus that of Idealism . . . The subsistence of the world is taken to mean the actual presence of its own truth; it is certain of finding only itself there'.[24] It is true that 'realism' and 'idealism' are often used differently from this, but this is no matter for concern as long as we are clear about the sense in which we intend those terms. In my terminology, for example, Hume is a non-materialist realist, whereas Hegel is an idealist. This is, I submit, a welcome conclusion. For the tendency to lump philosophies as alien as Hegel's and Hume's under a single rubric, 'idealism', even when qualified by 'subjective' and 'absolute', is to be avoided. At any rate, on the question in which we are interested, the relation of thought and object, Hume and Hegel offer us wholly different answers, and that our terminology allows us to distinguish them so readily permits us to focus our question all the more perspicaciously. Hegel did not maintain that reality was composed of mental objects as many philosophers assume by wrongly conflating his idealism with the phenomenalism of the empiricists. Objects, for Hegel, are creations of thought or Idea, and are, as the 'other' of thought, essentially dependent on it. In my sense, Hegel denies realism by denying (IpC). But, once created, such objects are as material or non-phenomenal as anything could be. To put the point rather paradoxically Hegel is a non-realist materialist, since he accepts both that there are irreducibly material objects, but that they are essentially related to Idea or Thought. Indeed, Hegel himself distinguishes his philosophy from Berkeley's on just this issue of whether there is something thought-independent. Berkeley is criticised for allowing something 'alien' to (essentially independent of) thought, namely sensations or impressions:

. . . by pointing out that in all being there is this bare consciousness of a 'mine', and by expressing things as sensations or ideas, it fancies it has shown that abstract 'mine' of consciousness to be complete reality. It is bound, therefore, to be at the same time absolute Empiricism, because for the filling of this empty 'mine' . . . its reason needs an impact operating from without in which lies the *fons et origo* of the multiplicity of sensation or ideas . . . But it fails to link up its contradictory statements about pure consciousness being all reality while all the time the alien impact or sense—impressions and ideas are equally reality.[25]

Hegel criticised Berkeley for allowing thought-independent entities. Hegel, then, I call an 'idealist' and Berkeley a 'realist', to capture this important difference between them, of which Hegel was so conscious. Phenomenalism, in our terminology, is a form of non-materialist realism. Hegel's idealism is a much more vigorous and radical thesis than phenomenalism: there is nothing—phenomenal or material—which is independent of thought or Idea, no object essentially independent of concept.

Indeed, Hegel's problematic takes the problematic of the empiricists and stands it on its head. For Locke, Berkeley and Hume, what is given, what is obvious, is the object, albeit as an impression and therefore in the form of a non-material object. Thought is the problem—either to be reduced to its object (ideas are the pale reflection of impressions) or to be somehow comprehended independently on its own (Kant's *a priori* categories of the understanding). For Hegel, the object constitutes the problem. The given, the immediate is thought, and somehow the object is to be comprehended by it. 'Reason', says Hegel, 'is the conscious certainty of being all reality.'

My intention here, though, is not to enter into a discussion of Hegel, which I shall do in the next chapter. I have merely wanted to suggest the historical accuracy of my use of 'realism' and 'idealism', and to justify the distinction between materialism and realism which I have drawn in discussing Kant's theory of knowledge.

Kant: Epistemological Inconsistency

Let us call two propositions or claims, p and q, strongly epistemologically inconsistent if (a) p and q are logically consistent and (b) the truth of p implies that there can be no possible evidence for believing that q is true. A person can be said to be strongly epistemologically inconsistent when he believes both of a strongly epistemologically inconsistent pair of propositions.

It would be to make no mistake in formal logic to believe an epistemologically inconsistent pair of propositions. Rather, the mistake is epistemological, and we have for that reason called the inconsistency *epistemological.* I have defined the notion for a pair of propositions, but it is easy to see how to extend the notion to cover the case of an epistemologically inconsistent set of propositions.

There is a somewhat weaker form of such inconsistency. We can say that p and q are weakly epistemologically inconsistent if (a) p and q are logically consistent and (b) the truth of p implies that there is in fact no evidence for believing that q is true. Thus, the following two propositions are weakly epistemologically inconsistent: 'unicorns exist' and 'there is no evidence of any kind which suggests that unicorns exist'. From the truth of the second proposition it follows that there is in fact no evidence for believing the first proposition.

Theists are committed to strong epistemological inconsistency if they believe that God exists and that there is no *possible evidence* for belief in God's existence. Indeed in the sense in which faith is juxtaposed to reason, faith *is* strong epistemological inconsistency, somehow conceived as a virtue. They believe a proposition, that God exists, and they believe another proposition, that there is no possible evidence for God's existence, which implies that it is impossible to know that the first proposition believed is true.

Kant's theory of knowledge contains within it just such a strong epistemological inconsistency. I will argue that his independence claim (IpC) and his interpretation claim (IC) are inconsistent in just this way. Now, it is a commonplace criticism that Kant, on the basis of his theory of knowledge, has no justification for believing that there are noumena. It would be, in our terminology, strongly epistemologically inconsistent of Kant to believe both that there are noumena and that all possible knowledge is of phenomena only. Of course, Kant himself realised that those two beliefs were strongly epistemologically inconsistent, and so, for Kant, noumena are posited by reason in its practical rather than theoretical employment, in fact an article of faith. Indeed, my earlier example of a strong epistemological inconsistency, belief in God, was deliberate, for the natural consequence of believing an epistemologically inconsistent pair of propositions is *faith* in that for which one can have no possible evidence. The fate of the noumenal realm in German philosophy after Kant is well-known. Either, like a social pariah, it was soon dropped from most respectable speculative systems, or its inconsistent opposite number was dropped, so that *knowledge* of noumena was accepted (by intuition, for example) as possible.

I want to stress that the question of the knowability of noumena is not the epistemological inconsistency I am referring to, although it does raise parallel epistemological problems. The inconsistency in Kant's philosophy goes much deeper than is generally appreciated. It is inconsistent epistemologically to hold that there are noumena and that all possible knowledge is of phenomena. But even if, as I suggested earlier, we read Kant's *Critique* with the noumena already discounted, there is still an epistemological inconsistency between the interpretation and independence claims. This inconsistency arises wholly *within* the phenomenal realm, and hence is a much deeper and more significant inconsistency than that which arises from the Kantian problem of the noumena. Giving Kant a so-called 'one realm' as opposed to 'two realms' interpretation does not allow him to escape the sort of inconsistency I claim to find in his theory of knowledge. Kant's (IC) and (IpC) are certainly inconsistent in the sense which I have explained. They are formally consistent, for it could be the case, unbeknownst to us, that there is some thought-independent reality. But we can bring out the epistemological inconsistency involved in such a supposition in the following way.

Suppose Kant's interpretation claim were true, *viz:* 'To make a judgment or claim to knowledge necessarily presupposes the activity of interpretive thought.' The nub of the tension between (IC) and (IpC) centres around the nature of the relationship between any experienced or known object and interpretive thought. What I claim is that, on (IC), any known object is *essentially* related to thought and, hence, if (IC) is true, we can never know any objects of which (IpC) would be true, objects which would be essentially independent of thought.

For any object, there are an indefinitely large number of descriptions which are applicable to it. Consider one such description, 'the thing which caused the explosion to occur', a description which makes use in an obvious way of at least one of the *a priori* categories of the understanding, causality. Can we say that, under that description, the relationship between object and interpretive thought is a necessary or essential one? Does the existence of the object described as 'the object which caused the explosion to occur' imply the existence of a synthesis using the *a priori* concept of causality?

It would not be accurate to say simply that, for Kant, the existence of the object under such a description implied the existence of interpretive thought. It is certainly logically possible that noumena, for instance, really do enter into causal relationships, although we could never know whether or not this was so. It is possible that causal descriptions are true of noumena, and noumena are essentially independent of thought. Kant never says, or ought to say, that this is not possible. But what Kant does say is that the *a priori* categories of the understanding have *legitimate* application only within experience, to phenomenal objects. They may have a logically possible application to noumena, but not a legitimate one, not one to which we could ever be entitled.

Once we restrict our scope to phenomena, to objects which are objects of knowledge and experience, we can be assured that their causal properties arise from the application of the *a priori* category of causality. What descriptions, if any, may or may not be true of unexperienceable and unknowable things can only be a matter for speculation. But the descriptions true of phenomena which assign causal properties to them arise from the workings of the understanding. So, the upshot here is that although the existence of objects correctly described as 'the thing which caused . . .' does not logically imply the existence of a synthesis of the understanding using the category of causality, what we can say is that, under *that* description, the implication does hold if the object is phenomenal, one which is an object of our knowledge. Thus, for all objects which we experience or know, their existence under causal descriptions *implies* the existence of interpretive thought. For a causal object in the realm of phenomena to exist, it is necessary and not contingent that there be a synthesis of the understanding.

Now, because of (IC), what is true for the causal description I have been using as an example must also be true for any possible description available to us, *as long as the description is restricted in application to phenomena*. If there were a description available to us such that, under that description, the existence of the object did not imply the existence of interpretive thought, a synthesis of the understanding, then (IC) would be false, since we could make a judgment about an object such that the activity of interpretive thought was not necessarily presupposed. So, if (IC) is true, it must be the case that no description, no knowledge, is available to us about any object whose existence does not necessarily presuppose the existence of a synthesis of the understanding. The existence of any object which is an object of knowledge, under any description available to us, *implies* the existence of interpretive thought. Or equivalently, for all objects about which we have some knowledge, their existence *implies* the existence of interpretive thought.[26] We can drop the qualification, 'under any description available to us', since any object which only failed to imply the existence of interpretive thought when described in a way unavailable to us would, to that extent, be unknowable and hence not a phenomenal object at all. So, we can say that for *all* objects of knowledge, their existence *implies,* for Kant, the existence of interpretive thought.

Finally, if my argument thus far is valid, its conclusion means that we *cannot* know or experience an object which is not essentially related to interpretive thought. But this is just to say that we *cannot* know that (IpC) is true, even though it may be: 'There are objects essentially independent of interpretive thought'. Holding (IC) undermines any possibility of knowing that (IpC). They are, then, epistemologically inconsistent. There might be, as Kant says, two distinct sources of our knowledge, thought and sensibility, form and content, consciousness and being, 'two stems', as Kant says. We could never come to know this, since we could never know or experience one stem which did not show it to be in essential relation to the other. We might then wonder if there were really two independent sources of our knowledge at all.

That it is the interpretation claim which generates the unknowability not just of noumena but of any reality essentially independent of thought can be seen by reminding ourselves of a correspondence theory account of the relations been thought and reality. Once again it would be a banality to assert that one cannot come to know or judge an object without bringing it into some relation with thought, just as one cannot describe an object without using words or symbols. But because of the nature of correspondence or reflection, the relation between an object and thought is a contingent relation. Even for all objects which are in fact known, on a reflection theory their existence does not necessarily presuppose the existence of the thought in which they are reflected or to which they do correspond. Known or experienced objects under reflective (rather than interpretive) descriptions stand in no *necessary* dependence to thought; the object as it is reflected could exist apart from the contingent relation it may come to have to reflective thought. So we can hold onto (IpC), at the price of abandoning (IC), with which it is epistemologically inconsistent, in favour of a reflection theory. On a reflection theory, an object's being *in fact* known does not put it into an *essential* relation to thought. It is interpretive thought only which is responsible for tying known objects to thought with this necessary or internal relation.

There is, then, no special difficulty for the empiricists in knowing what the object is like independent of thought, for one has every reason for supposing that the object one knows would be essentially the same if one were not engaged in the act of knowing or thinking about it. Ceasing to actively think about it or know it, on a correspondence theory, does not essentially change the object; it only removes one accidental relation in which it stands. More graphically, since thought on a correspondence theory is not interpretive, there is no reason to suppose that the thinking is making an essential difference, as it were, to the object of knowledge.

But for Kant the matter is otherwise, and this difference springs from the interpretive, *a priori* nature which thought has for him. The relation of thought to object is *essential* for any object of knowledge or experience. It is *essential,* for any object about which we judge or about which we claim to know, that there be a synthesis of the understanding. Thus, known objects stand in essential relation to thought and cannot be independent of mental activity. Kant's interpretive claim is epistemologically inconsistent with realism, with the belief in a thought-independent reality, in a way in which a reflection theory is not. Both noumena and pre-conceptualised intuitions, as equally interpretive-thought independent, are therefore equally consigned to unknowability.

Kant's Materialism: Independence versus Creation

In the section of *The Critique of Pure Reason* called 'Anticipations of Perception', Kant refers to sensation as 'the matter of perception', and says that it is sensation which 'can never be known *a priori* and which therefore constitutes the distinctive difference between empirical and *a priori* knowledge' (B209). And so here, if anywhere, we should be able to find what it is about our experience that should convince us that it has two sources rather than a single source. Now, Kant tells us that sensation itself is capable of a further internal analysis. There is the intensity of the sensation, and the quality of the sensation. Thus, 'Every sensation, therefore, . . . has a degree, that is, an intensive magnitude . . .' (B211), and 'The *quality* of sensation, as for instance in colour, tastes, etc., is always merely empirical, and cannot be represented *a priori*' (A176). Wolff[27] suggests that the intensive magnitude and quality are related as form and matter, and thus, since knowledge is always of form and never of matter, 'there would appear, therefore, to be a possibility that even the subjective content of perception might have cognitive significance, in its degree of intensity, if not in the quality'. If this is so, as it transpires, even the matter of perception has a form and matter.

Intensity, or intensive magnitude is treated as form, for it is a constitutive, *a priori* concept of the understanding, and it is for Kant a synthetic *a priori* truth that all sensation has intensive magnitude. Kant finds his own results surprising. One would think, he says, that *a priori* knowledge about sensation ought to be impossible. 'For it does indeed seem surprising that we should anticipate experience precisely in that which concerns what is only to be obtained through it, namely its matter. Yet, none the less, such is actually the case' (B209). Since all *a priori* knowledge comes by way of a synthesis, Kant even invents a bogus synthesis for 'generating the magnitude of a sensation from its beginning in pure intuition = 0, up to any required magnitude' (B208), and he tells us that we can 'determine *a priori,* that is, can construct, the degree of sensations of sunlight by combining some 200,000 illuminations of the moon' (B221).

Sensation is the matter of perception, but it turned out to be matter only relativity, for it too had a form and matter. With the *quality* of the sensation, though, we seem to have arrived not just at matter relative to some form, but at what Kant took to be bedrock matter epistemologically, the substratum of our knowledge. This ought to be what, out of all else, we do not just inject into or project onto our experience of reality; it ought to be what reality is itself like. '. . . in all quality (the real in appearance) we can know *a priori* nothing save their intensive quantity . . . everything else has to be left to experience' (B128). The quality of the sensation—that it is a certain colour or taste—cannot be anticipated and is in that sense *a posteriori.*

Thus, not every feature or item of our knowledge is put there, or created, by the understanding. Kant does not lack a concept of the 'purely empirical'. 'If we remove from our empirical concept of a body, one by one, every feature in it which is merely empirical, the colour, the hardness or softness, the weight even the impenetrability . . .' (B6), its '. . . existence cannot be constructed . . .' (B222). But although the 'purely empirical' is not a *creation* of thought, it is not in Kant something that is *independent* of thought either. The quality of the intuition, Kant tells us, is its matter, and is not brought into being or created through a synthesis of the understanding in the way in which the intensive and extensive magnitudes of the intuition are generated.

But this quality as the matter of intuition, the purely empirical, is not thought-independent either, for Kant provides us with some knowledge of it, and we have already shown that, on the basis of (IC), where we have an object which is known (or experienced), in this case the *quality* of the intuition, then the existence of that object stands in a necessary relation to thought, to the synthetic activity of the mind. This shows, I think, that Kant's concept of matter plays a peculiar role in his theory of knowledge, although it may well play a different role in his philosophy of science.[28] The hallmark of matter is, for Kant, that it is the 'purely empirical'. It is not *created* or *generated* or *produced* by the understanding in the way in which he claims causality or intensive and extensive magnitude are. But because such sensory qualities are knowable, they are not *independent* of thought. Thus, the role matter plays in Kant's theory of knowledge is by itself insufficient to make Kant a realist and *a fortiori* insufficient to make him a materialist. For any object which is known or experienced, its existence under the description 'This is heavy' or 'This is hard' implies the existence of thought just as much as it does under the description 'This was the cause of the explosion'. There is no judgment we can make about an object which does not necessarily presuppose the application or involvement of the *a priori* categories of the understanding, and hence no description available to us of what pre-conceptualised intuitions might be like. We do not put 'heaviness' or 'hardness' *into* what we experience in the way in which, for

Kant, we do put 'causality' there. But even though not put there by us, it is not essentially independent of our putting things there either. Matter must be distinguished, then, from pre-conceptualised intuition. Unlike the latter, matter is knowable and hence not essentially independent of the synthesis of the understanding.

Some commentators of Kant have misunderstood the nature of the Kantian intuitive sensory qualities, wrongly identifying them with the subective appearances or sense data of the empiricists, which are essentially independent of thought or mental activity. Stefan Körner, for example, argues that Kant's central aim is to show the conditions which are necessary if we are to have objective experience.[29] According to Körner's interpretation of Kant, it is the application of the categories which is the necessary condition for the possibility of objective experience, for their unifying function upgrades subjective experience to objective experience. But if this were accepted it would allow for the possibility of subjective experience, e.g. this *seeming* heavy to me, to which the categories have not been applied. 'This seems heavy to me' could then be a judgment about the pre-conceptual intuitions, a judgment made wholly in terms of reflective rather than interpretive concepts. If Körner were right our interpretation of Kant would be seriously wrong.

Körner's evidence for this as Kant's position is taken primarily from the *Prolegomena:* 'This, of course, conforms to Kant's view, a view expressed most clearly in the *Prolegomena,* that the Categories which are embodied in the logical forms of judgment are not applied in merely perceptual judgments'.[30] Körner interprets Kant as saying that the only concepts which are contained in perceptual judgments about subjective experience are those 'which are abstracted from sense-perceptions',[31] and thereby excludes all *a priori* categories. Clearly, if Körner were right, objects under those 'perceptual' descriptions would not, even when known, imply the existence of interpretive thought. Such 'perceptual' objects could be described and known, and yet their existence would not *necessarily* imply the existence of a synthesis of the understanding.

The difficulty with this interpretation is that it cannot account for Kant's central and singly most important claim that the 'I think' must be able to accompany all the contents of my consciousness, and that a necessary condition for this being so is that the categories have been applied to all those contents. It is legitimate to ask, then, of Körner's interpretation: Can the 'I think' accompany subjective presentations? If so, then on Kant's own argument the categories must apply to them, and Körner then would be wrong in holding that these presentations are experiences minus the *a priori* or interpretive categories. If not, if the 'I think' does not accompany these presentations, then such presentations cannot enter the unity of apperception and hence are not such that I can be *conscious* of them. If I cannot be conscious of them, then I cannot make judgments about them— whether these judgments be objective or subjective, or whatever. Körner is inclined to answer the question in both ways at once: 'A manifold without synthetic unity might be perceivable but could not be thinkable—at least not in objective terms.'[32] But such an unconnected manifold could not be thinkable (and hence not experiencable in the full sense in which for Kant that does imply thought) in any sort of judgment. Since Kant does clearly make judgments about these sensory qualities, the ultimate matter of all intuition, i.e., since for Kant these sensory qualities are clearly thinkable, then they cannot be independent of the application of categories and hence, *pace* Körner's interpretation, they cannot be the same as the subjective appearances of the empiricists, a notion wholly inimical to the central thrust of Kant's theory of knowledge. Unlike the subjective appearances, the sense data of the empiricists, Kant's qualities are not category-independent entities, since Kant, unlike those empiricists, denies the possibility of any experienced or known object—whether an objective or subjective 'object'—whose existence is not necessarily related to the activities of the understanding. Happily, most commentators do not share Körner's interpretation.[33] Körner's interpretation rests on the distinction between judgments of experience and of perception, the latter of which do not demand the application of the categories. Kant makes this distinction in *The Prolegomena* of 1783, and such a problematic distinction should not be transposed to the Kant of *The Critique* without more ado, especially since it makes nonsense of the main thrust of Kant's argument, which demands a necessary link between the application of the categories and the making of any judgment whatever, in short, the interpretation claim.[34] As we have argued previously there are, for Kant, pre-conceptualised intuitions. The point to mark here is that these are not the same as the quality or matter of sensation, which are necessarily related to the synthesis of the understanding. Such pre-conceptualised intuitions, unlike sensory qualities, are unknowable and unexperiencable because they stand in no relation to a synthesis of the understanding. As I said earlier, they are as unknowable as things-in-themselves.

Finally, we might permit ourselves to speculate that Körner has not yet separated sufficiently in Kant the question of what thought *produces* from the question of what is *independent* of thought, and that his failure to do so might be what accounts for this misinterpretation of the presentations which serve as the matter of perception and on which the categorial forms are imprinted. Sensibility, for Kant, is the source of what is 'other than' thought. Insofar as we can judge or make claims about this 'other', it can only be an *other* in the sense of being the empirical element which thought does not *put* there. But it cannot be 'other' in a fuller sense of being essentially independent of thought. Failure to draw this distinction may be what is responsible for mis-attributing to the Kantian empirical element in sensation the sort of thought-independent status which sense data have for the empiricist.

It may be difficult to understand how something, matter in this case, could be dependent in its existence on thought but not created by the thought or mental activity on which it essentially depends. I referred earlier to Kant's (IC) as falling somewhat short of 'conceptual idealism'. For if it is to be called 'conceptual idealism' then it is one of a peculiar sort. If we think of conceptual idealism as either the position that (put formally) all of the categories or concepts which we employ to organise and structure our experience are put there by us, or as the position that (put materially) all known objects or objects of which we are conscious arise from our conceptual projection onto raw experience, then Kant is not a conceptual idealist. Sensory qualities are *there,* unlike causality, and not there *because* of our mental activity; presumably the category of heaviness or hardness, to rehearse Kant's examples, is not an *a priori* concept, but a wholly *a posteriori* one. But, on the other hand, the interpretation claim is still true about heaviness or hardness or about judgments about them, for such 'matter' of experience stands in essential relation to the synthetic activity of the mind, and judgments about it presuppose necessarily the existence of the *a priori* categories of the understanding. Perhaps we should call Kant's position not one of conceptual idealism, which has built within it the notion of thought putting everything into reality, but conceptual dependecism. Many critics of Kant conflate conceptual idealism proper with the Kantian conceptual dependecism I have described. Gareth Stedman Jones, for example, in his article on the early Lukacs,[35] claims that 'critical philosophy based itself on the idea that thought could only grasp what it itself had created and strove to master the world as a whole by seeing it as self-created'. But this is, as I have argued, to misunderstand the *given* (but concept- or thought-dependent) role that matter as the quality of sensation plays in Kant's theory of knowledge. In short, it confuses creation and dependence. If it is difficult to understand how something can be dependent for its existence on thought, but not put there or created by thought, this is Kant's difficulty, and one which German philosophy after Kant had to face, as we shall soon see.

One of the few Kantian commentators to have discussed this particular problem in Kant's philosophy is W. H. Walsh, in his recent *Kant's Criticism of Metaphysics.*[36] How are we, after all, to account for the epistemic role of sensation in Kant's philosophy? Walsh notes that sensation cannot play for Kant the same role as it did for the empiricist, for whom sensation is 'a species of knowledge'. Kant did toy with such a view, but 'it was clear even then that the main theory of knowledge advocated in *The Critique,* according to which knowledge demands both a sensory and an intellectual component, must rule out any doctrine of immediate knowledge . . . and so would exclude thinking of sensation as a form of knowledge by acquaintance'.[37]

What is Walsh's alternative suggestion for understanding sensation in Kant's philosophy?

To fit in with the rest of *The Critique,* sensation must be conceived of as a form of experience which is *sui generis.* There can be no knowledge . . . without sensory input, but sensation is an experience to be enjoyed rather than a matter of contemplating objects: bare sensing conveys no knowledge, but simply qualifies the subject . . . Sensation without judgment is not a form of awareness. *A fortiori*, it does not involve awareness of an object which is essentially private . . .[38]

and earlier, in a similar vein,

. . . sensation is not strictly a form of awareness, since it has no true objects, but a mode of experience which is *sui generis;* without it experience of particulars would be impossible. though it is false to describe it as presenting particulars for description. Sensory content— 'intuitions', as Kant calls them—are not objects of any sort, public or private.[39]

Walsh takes seriously Kant's dictum that there are 'two stems of human knowledge'. He sees that Kant holds a 'doctrine of the separate nature of concepts and intuitions', and correctly concludes that such concept-independent intuitions would not provide 'a form of awareness'. As we have maintained throughout, they would be as unknowable as noumena. My only objection to Walsh's discussion is that he tends to collapse sensation into pre-conceptualised intuitions. I think that one has to admit that Kant's sensations, the matter of experience, *are* possible objects of awareness and hence do not have a 'separate nature' from concepts at all since they are essentially dependent on the *a priori* concepts of the understanding. Insofar as Kant does insist on there being something with a 'separate nature' from concepts, these can only be the unknowable and unexperiencable pre-conceptualised intuitions, and these latter are not the same things as those odd Kantian sensory qualities, features of an experience essentially dependent on a thought which is not itself responsible for having put them there. But Walsh is correct in insisting that whatever it is that the 'other' source of knowledge provides us, it must be, in its independence of the *a priori* categories, something which cannot be an object of awareness.

Kant: Concluding Remarks

I have tried to show that (IC) and (IpC) are strongly epistemologically inconsistent. Kant then is faced with an obvious dilemma. Let us return to the preconceptualised intuitions of which (IpC) speaks. Either we can be conscious of, or have some knowledge about, such intuitions as they exist apart from synthesised experience, or we cannot. Each form of the dilemma shows how there is a deep tension within the very heart of the Kantian critical philosophy.

To take the first horn of the dilemma, suppose that we could have such knowledge, make some judgements about, be conscious of or experience (in the full Kantian sense), these pre-conceptualised entities whose existence is essentially independent of interpretive thought. On this horn, we could retain the epistemological credibility of the independence claim. We could be realists, but we would have to sacrifice the interpretation claim, for we could make at least one judgment or claim about entities which are not essentially related to the activity of the mind even though, of course, they would have to stand in at least a *contingent* relation to the mind if we were to make a judgment or claim about them, and we could make also at least one judgment which did not necessarily presuppose an interpretive, *a priori* contribution. We would have to sacrifice the heart of Kant's epistemological insight. Since some knowledge or some judgments would not arise as a result of a synthesis, some knowledge would therefore lack an interpretive element. Behold, it transpires that not all intuitions without the *a priori* concepts of the understanding would be blind (B76). Short-sighted perhaps, but not totally blind. In a sense, it would not be true that 'the senses can think nothing', for one could *know* something about these pre-conceptualised intuitions apart from the occurrence of any synthesis of the understanding. If we could know about something which did not stand in essential relation to thought, then it is not true that 'only through their [*a priori* understanding and sense] union can knowledge arise' (B76), for we would have achieved some knowledge without the employment of the *a priori* understanding. Indeed, on this horn, Körner's empiricist interpretation of Kantian presentations would have been correct, but of course at the price of jettisoning the interpretation claim, and jettisoning the necessary condition for the transcendental unity of apperception, the application of the *a priori* categories to all the contents of consciousness. Kant's epistemology would in this respect become indistinguishable from that of an empiricist, whose foundational knowledge comes by direct acquaintance with the objects of perception. In short, some of our knowledge would be *reflective* of reality rather than *interpretive* of it. Finally, if we admit to getting knowledge of some sort about these preconceptualised intuitions directly from experience, it raises the possibility that other knowledge might also arise from the senses without any contribution from the understanding. Perhaps Kant has been overparsimonious in his cognitive allotment to sensation and overly generous in what he has given to the *a priori* understanding. The object which exists, essentially independent of thought, may be fuller and richer than Kant has allowed. Once our realism is allowed a toehold, Kant may find it difficult to prevent its expansion. We retain (IpC) but only by paying the price of jettisoning (IC). We can be realists, but with a correspondence or reflection theory of thought.

On the other hand, to take the second horn of the dilemma, suppose that we can have no knowledge of what exists apart from the synthetic activity of the mind, from thought. We continue to take Kant's epistemological programme seriously by retaining (IC). What is independent of thought, such as pre-conceptualised intuitions, must be as unknowable as the noumenal realm itself. Retention of (IC) is epistemologically inconsistent with (IpC). We retain our interpretive claim about knowledge, but jettison realism. What is perhaps alone surprising in Kant's position is that Kant, on the one hand, so readily admits when he is thinking of noumena that there can be no possible knowledge of even the existence of that which exists independent of our synthesis of the understanding and forms of intuition, and yet on the other claims to *know* that our experience of the world has two separate sources, is the product of our interpretation of pre-conceptualised intuitions which as the second of the 'sources' exist independently of thought. When Kant discusses the thing-in-itself, he denies the possibility of *knowing* that it exists. However, when he mentions the pre-conceptualised intuitions, that second source of our knowledge, Kant speaks as if we could *know* that this second source existed. Yet the problem of the thing-in-itself and that of the pre-conceptualised intuitions raise substantially the same epistemological difficulty, namely the problem of how one could even *know* that such a thing exists, let along what it is like. Since both are independent of the concepts of the understanding and forms of intuition, there could be no possible experience or knowledge of either the one or the other. Kant faces up to this problem with the thing-in-itself by denying the possibility of any knowledge of it whatever, but he never came to similar terms with the doctrine that there is something in our experience independent of thought, the second 'source' of our knowledge, although that doctrine ought to share precisely the same fate as the thing-in-itself at his hands. Kant's epistemology gives him no right to be a realist, empirical or transcendental. It seems simply inconsistent of Kant to resort to a form of fideism about the existence of things-in-themselves and at the same time to assert with such confidence that our knowledge has two independent sources. Indeed, one can take Hegel's many explicit criticisms of the Kantian thing-in-itself and apply them outright to the problem of the second source of knowledge, since they raise, as I have already said, the same epistemological difficulty.

We can surmise that perhaps some implicit feeling for this inconsistency led Kant to add the suggestive but wholly unexplored qualification to his two-sources theme: '. . . there are two stems of human knowledge namely, sensibility and understanding, which perhaps spring from a common, but to us unknown root' (B30). Kant may say that '. . . our empirical knowledge is made up of what we receive through impressions and of what our own faculty of knowledge . . . supplies from itself' (B2), but it is difficult to see how, on his own programme, Kant could be entitled to such claims. It may be worth saying again that Kant *is* entitled to speak of a form and a matter or our experience, matter being that which is not *created* by thought: 'That experience contains two very dissimilar elements, namely, the matter of knowledge from the senses, and a certain form for the ordering of this matter, from the inner source of the pure intuition and thought . . .' (B119). This matter of experience need not be collapsed into pre-conceptualised intuitions, as Walsh does. If that had been all that was implied by the two sources claim, neither source created by the other, there would not be the same objection to knowing that our knowledge has two sources. It is when the sources are conceived of as essentially independent of one another that epistemological difficulty develops, for at once one source becomes as unknowable as the noumenal realm, and one then wonders how Kant is entitled to suppose that our knowledge arises from two independent sources at all, unless it is by the same sort of act of faith to which he resorts in the case of the noumena.

The lesson I hope to have extracted from Kant is simple and clear. A realist (and *a-fortiori* a materialist) ontology, for example that expressed in Kant's (IpC), is epistemologically inconsistent with the interpretive understanding of all thought. To make realism epistemologically plausible, one needs a 'reflection' or correspondence theory of thought or knowledge. Kant's own critical philosophy was never able to overcome this deep tension. The following judgment by Josef Maier, from his *On Hegel's Critique of Kant*, accurately summarises quite succinctly that tension:

The greatness, the tragedy, and the paradox of Kantian philosophy consist in the fact that he did not allow the given to disappear behind the grim architectonic of rational forms produced by the understanding, but, on the contrary, posited and held to the irrational character of all content (the given) and yet, in spite of this, strove to erect a system.[40]

Maier's remarks correctly evaluate, I think, the importance and the lesson of Kant's philosophy from the point of view of Marxist materialism. There can be no 'return' to Kant's materialism (or realism), as many have urged throughout the history of Marxism, without serious re-evaluation of Kant's theory of knowledge, with which materialism (or realism) is epistemologically inconsistent. Lenin too, long ago, spoke of a tension within Kantian philosophy, although he was speaking of the tension between Kant's theory of knowledge and his retention of the idea of noumena. But, as I have said before, although the problems of noumena and pre-conceptualised intuitions are different, the tensions they generate for Kant's critical philosophy are the same. Hence, it is worthwhile to recall Lenin's evaluation as a fitting conclusion to a discussion on Kant which I hope will have a relevance for Marxists:

The principal feature of Kant's philosophy is the reconciliation of materialism with idealism, a compromise between the two, the combination within one system of heterogeneous and contrary philosophical trends . . . Recognising experience, sensations, as the only source of our knowledge, Kant is directing his philosophy . . . towards materialism. Recognising the apriority of space, time, causality, etc., Kant is directing his philosophy towards idealism. Both consistent materialists and consistent idealists . . . have mercilessly criticised Kant for this inconsistency . . .[41]

Lenin recognised Kant's attempt to wed materialist ontology to idealist epistemology, and it is 'this inconsistency' which we too, in this chapter, have tried to underscore.

Notes: Chapter I

[1] Kant, Immanuel, *The Critique of Pure Reason*, Macmillan and Co. Ltd., London, 1929. Translated by Norman Kemp Smith. B 75 - B 76. References in *The Critique* will be made using only the standard 'A' and 'B' notation following the quoted passage, which indicates pagination in the first and second German editions respectively.
[2] Kant, Immanuel, *Logic*, Bobbs-Merrill, Indianapolis, 1974. Translated by R. Hartman and W. Schwarz, p. 37.
[3] Strawson, P. F., *The Bounds of Sense*, Methuen, London, 1976. The following six page references in the text refer to this book.

4   There is ample literature on this. See especially some of the 'Wittgenstein' literature on the
    nature of necessity: Barry Stroud, 'Wittgenstein and Logical Necessity', *Philosophical
    Review*, Vol. LXXIV, 1965; Michael Dummett, 'Wittgenstein's Philosophy of
    Mathematics', *Philosophical Review*, Vol. LXVIII, 1959; Charles S. Chihara,
    'Wittgenstein and Logical Compulsion', *Analysis*, Vol. XXI, 1960-61; Jonathan Bennett,
    'On Being Forced to a Conclusion', *PASS*, Vol. XXXV, 1961; O. P. Wood, 'On Being
    Forced to a Conclusion', *PASS*, Vol. XXXV, 1961. The first three articles are collected in
    G. Pitcher, ed., *Wittgenstein: A Collection of Critical Essays*, Anchor Books, Doubleday
    & Co., Garden City, New Jersey, 1966.
5   Hume, David, 'An Abstract of A Treatise of Human Nature' in *Hume on Human Nature
    and the Understanding*, ed. by A. Flew, Collier Books, New York, 1962, pp. 291-292.
    Hume is speaking of himself in the quotation.
6   Hume, David, *A Treatise of Human Nature*, Oxford University Press, Oxford, 1965,
    edited by L. A. Selby-Bigge, p. 4.
7   For a discussion of this shift in Kant's position between the two editions, see Walsh, W. H.,
    Kant's Criticism of Metaphysics, Edinburgh University Press, Edinburgh, 1975, pp. 11-16
    and pp. 88-96.
8   Lowenberg, J. 'The Futile Flight from Interpretation', in *Meaning and Interpretation*,
    University of California Publications in Philosophy, Volume 25, 1950.
9   Goodman, Nelson, 'The Significance of *Der Logische Aufbau der Welt*', in Schilpp, Paul
    A., ed *The Philosophy of Rudolph Carnap*, Open Court Publishing Company, La Salle,
    Illinois, 1963.
10 Kolakowski, L., 'Karl Marx and The Classical Definition of Truth', in *Marxism and
    Beyond*, trans. Peel, J. Z., Pall Mall Press, London, 1969, p. 64.
11 For an interesting account and defense of conceptual idealism, see Rescher, Nicholas,
    Conceptual Idealism, Basil Blackwell, Oxford, 1973.
12 Obviously, I am distinguishing *mind* from *mental activity*. All objects for the classical
    empiricist tradition and especially for Hume, are 'mental'. But the existence of such objects
    does not necessarily imply the existence of thought (ideas), or mental activity.
13 This point has been much discussed and is controversial. For an interpretation different
    from the one I adopt, see Wilfred Sellars, 'Some Remarks on Kant's Theory of
    Experience', *Journal of Philosophy*, vol. 64, 1967, pp. 633-647, and chapter I of his
    Science, Perception and Reality, Routledge and Kegan Paul, London, 1963. In reply to
    Sellars, see Jonathan Bennett, *Kant's Dialectic*, Cambridge University Press, Cambridge,
    1974, p. 30. I am following Bennett's interpretation, which is also the one of D. P. Dryer,
    in *Kant's Solution for Verification in Metaphysics*, Allen & Unwin, London, 1966, pp. 66-
    67.
14 Wolff, R. P., *Kant's Theory of Mental Activity*, Harvard University Press, Cambridge,
    1963, pp. 156-159.
15 Dryer, D. P. *op. cit.*, pp. 125-127, footnote 6, who makes a similar distinction.
16 Wolff, R. P., *op. cit.*, p. 157, subsequent quote from p. 156.
17 Kant, I., *Logic*, p. 38.
18 See my remarks in footnote 12.
19 Hume, David, *op. cit.*, pp. 79-80.
20 Colletti, Lucio, *Marxism and Hegel*, New Left Books, London, 1973. Chapter VIII, 'Kant,
    Hegel, and Marx', is especially relevant.
21 I develop this remark in a review of Colletti's *From Rousseau to Lenin* in *The
    Philosophical Quarterly*, vol. 23, October, 1973, pp. 377-379.
22 This distinction does not apply to Feuerbach either. He calls his philosophy indifferently
    both 'materialism' and 'realism'.
23 The standard use of 'realism' and 'idealism' is different in contemporary philosophy.
    'Idealism' is usually the name given to phenomenalism, whereas on my usage
    phenomenalism is a species of non-material realism. For an example of this standard
    usage, see for example Joel Kupperman, 'Realism vs Idealism', *The American
    Philosophical Quarterly*, vol 12, No 3, July 1975, pp. 199-210. My own usage comes close
    to Kant's. Kant calls himself a transcendental idealist but empirical realist. If we accept

that Kant affirms the existence of pre-conceptualised intuitions, he is a realist in my sense. They exist independently of thought (and hence are *real*). But he is a non-materialist realist, since they do not exist independently of mind. To be a materialist in my sense, he would have had to have been a transcendental realist as well as an empirical one. Kant's famous 'Refutation of Idealism' in *The Critique* is an attempted refutation of empirical idealism only, not a refutation of the transcendental idealism which Kant makes so central to the critical philosophy.

[24] Hegel, G. W. F,, *The Phenomenology of Mind,* trans. by J. B. Baillie, George Allen and Unwin Ltd., London, 1966, p. 273.

[25] *Ibid,* pp. 278-279.

[26] The result about essential dependence will be trivial if, in each possible description of the object, is included some reference to the object's being known. Under such descriptions, 'is in fact known', etc., any object trivially implies the existence of thought. I therefore exclude these and similar epistemic references from the descriptions under which the existence of the object *implies* the existence of thought, in order to make the result non-trivial.

[27] Wolff, R. P., *op. cit.,* p. 234.

[28] The problem of the status of matter in Kant's philosophy has been underdiscussed in the English language literature. See Ralph C. S. Walker, 'The Status of Kant's Theory of Matter' in Lewis White Beck, editor, *Kant's Theory of Knowledge,* Reidel, Dordrecht, 1974, pp. 151-156 and G. Buchdahl. *Metaphysics and Philosophy of Science,* Basil Blackwell, Oxford, 1969, chapter VIII, where the question is also touched on. Judgements about the matter of experience would be, on Kant's theory of knowledge, reflective (because we don't *put* heaviness there), even though materialism is denied, since such qualities are not essentially independent of thought.

[29] Körner, Stefan, *Kant,* Penguin Books Ltd, Harmondsworth, Middx., 1960, chapter 3.

[30] *Ibid,* p. 53.

[31] *Ibid,* p. 48.

[32] *Ibid,* p. 61.

[33] See for example Jonathan Bennet, *Kant's Analytic,* Cambridge University Press, Cambridge, 1966, pp. 132-134; Norman Kemp Smith, *A Commentary to Kant's Critique of Pure Reason,* Macmillan & Co. Ltd., London, 1930, pp. 288-289; and W. H. Walsh, *op. cit.,* pp. 11-16 and pp. 88-96.

[34] See for example B 140, B 142.

[35] Jones, Gareth Stedman, 'The Marxism of the Early Lukacs: An Evaluation', *New Left Review,* 65, (1971), pp. 27-64. Ian Craib in 'Lukacs and the Marxist Critique of Sociology' is involved in a similar misreading of Kant on this point: on Kant's philosophy, '. . . we can only know what we create; the object 'in-itself' remains unknowable and the world that we know is the 'product' of rational mind' (*Radical Philosophy* 17, Summer 1977, p.29).

[36] Walsh, W. H. *op. cit.,* pp. 94-96.

[37] *Ibid,* p. 95.

[38] *Ibid,* p. 95.

[39] *Ibid,* p. 14.

[40] Maier, Josef, *On Hegel's Critique of Kant,* AMS Press, Inc., New York, 1966, pp. 65-66.

[41] Lenin, V. I., *Materialism and Empirio-Criticism,* Progress Publishers, Moscow, 1970, pp. 260-261.

CHAPTER II

BETWEEN KANT AND MARX

In this chapter I want to describe and discuss two very different responses within post-Kantian German philosophy to the tensions I have referred to within Kant's critical philosophy. The responses are those of Hegel and Feuerbach. I do not want to give the impression that I believe that it was only Hegel and Feuerbach who are to be distinguished for their response to Kant within the German philosophical environment of the early nineteenth century. On the contrary, the whole of the German idealist tradition, for example, was in part at least a development in reaction to Kant's philosophical influence. The philosophies of Fichte and Schelling, Schlegel and Novalis, Jacobi and Schleiermacher, are part of this general movement that set itself the task of working through the problems and difficulties bequeathed by Kant. Each represents a different and unique resolution of some of those Kantian difficulties. I have chosen Hegel, for example, rather than Fichte and Schelling, to represent an example of the 'idealist' response to Kant. Naturally this is not in the least to suggest that Fichte and Schelling are not interesting or important in their own right. But the chapter is not intended as a short excursion into the history of German philosophy during this intensely interesting period. Rather, it is only intended to portray two examples of different responses to Kant's philosophy.

This chapter is not historical in another sense. I am primarily interested in Kant, and the two responses to Kant, as a way of situating the thought of Marx. In the next chapter I shall argue that, with regard to the specific philosophical questions I shall be and have been discussing, Marx follows Feuerbach in being a realist. Thus I shall argue that Marx, from at least the period of *The Critique of Hegel's 'Philosophy of Right'*, rejected the alternative, idealist response to Kant. I am, then, less interested in what the real, historical Hegel said than I am in what Marx's Hegel said. In a sense, this chapter could just as well be about Feuerbach's and the pseudo-Hegel's response to Kant. In fact, however, I claim something more than this, since I think that Marx's interpretation of Hegel is essentially correct. Therefore, I am willing to offer what I say as an accurate portrayal of what the real Hegel (and the real Feuerbach) had to say in response to the Kantian philosophy. But it is still worth remarking, I think, that my real interest in this is the comprehension of Marx, and for that reason I am less interested in the historical accuracy of the Hegel I present and more interested in the Hegel that Marx imagines, even though in fact I think these are the *same* Hegel. In order to understand Marx, it would be more important to understand what Marx thought Hegel had said, rather than what he really did say, should these be different things. Happily, I do not think that they are substantially different.

Hegel, as is well known, read Kant and expelled, banished, the Kantian unknowables. Hegel's critique of unknowability in the critical philosophy is directed against the whole conception of the noumenal realm. Kant denied the possibility of knowledge of things in themselves, and limited knowledge to knowledge of phenomena, of things as they appear. But, asks Hegel, by what right do we call knowledge of phenomena *knowledge* at all?

Since . . . this knowledge knows itself to be only knowledge of appearances, it admits to be unsatisfactory. Yet, it is assumed at the same time that things, though not rightly known in themselves, are still rightly known within the sphere of appearances, as though only the kinds of objects were different, and one kind, namely things in themselves, did not fall within knowledge, but the other kind, namely appearances, did. How would it be to attribute accurate perception to a man, with the proviso that he was not able to perceive truth but only untruth? As absurd as that would be, a true knowledge which did not know its object as it is in itself would be equally absurd.[1]

To know something is to know what it truly is. But to 'know' something only as it appears is to fall short of this, and thus to fall short of knowledge. According to Hegel, the Kantian philosophy is a refined version of epistemological scepticism, for it in fact denies the possibility of knowledge.

What, asks Hegel, are noumena, knowledge of which is being denied? No qualities can be attributed to them. But this is to make noumena *unqualified*. But that which cannot be qualified, determined, in any way is mere abstraction, unreal. Thus we cannot have knowledge of noumena because there *is nothing* more about them to know, for they are merely ideal.

. . . it is indeed impossible to know what the thing-in-itself is. For the question 'what' demands that determinations should be indicated; and since it is postulated that the things of which these are to be predicated must be things-in-themselves, that is, indeterminate, the question, in sheer thoughtlessness, is so put as to render an answer either impossible or self-contradictory . . . Things in themselves . . . are mere abstractions, void of truth and content.[2]

Hegel's criticism of the unknowability of noumena would apply in equal measure against the unknowability of the pre-conceptualised intuitions. They, too, could have no determinations, and must therefore be 'mere abstractions'. But abstractions are concepts, and so pre-conceptualised intuitions, like noumena, as only concepts, are 'only a product of thought'.[3] Hegel was aware that, according to Kant, there is something which is not necessarily related to thought: 'there is a surplus . . . which is . . . foreign and external to thought, namely the thing-in-itself', and that, on the Kantian theory of knowledge, to be 'external' to thought was a passport to unknowability. What is knowable is internally or necessarily related to thought. Hence, both noumena *and* pre-conceptualised intuitions, on Hegel's argument would be equally unknowable, since both are 'external' to thought.

I am not claiming that Hegel ever dealt explicitly with the problem in Kant's critical philosophy of the pre-conceptualised intuitions, but only that, had he done so, they would clearly have been dispatched to the same fate as the noumena. Hegel's arguments about the noumena can be transposed to the question of pre-conceptualised intuitions. Whatever is 'foreign' to thought is unknowable. In *The Phenomenology of Mind,* at the end of 'Reason's Certainty and Reason's Truth', Hegel criticises those doctrines, presumably including Kant's, that hold that reality can be divided into 'the unity of apperception and a "thing" as well, whether a thing is called an alien impact, or an empirical entity, or sensibility, or the "thing in itself". . .'. Hegel *may* here be distinguishing between Kant's noumena and preconceptualised intuitions, and including them both in his critique, although this is not a distinction he elaborates or explains elsewhere.

What then, Hegel may have asked, remains for us if we do read the Kantian philosophy with unknowables banished? Hasn't Kant left us in an unsatisfactory position? Thought, for Kant, can have an 'other' only in the attenuated sense that there is something in our experience which the understanding does not itself create. We distinguished, in our discussion of Kant, the 'matter' of our experience, the 'purely empirical' element from pre-conceptualised intuitions. If we banish the unknowable pre-conceptualised intuitions, 'matter' still remains. But we also saw that this Kantian matter of our experience has a peculiar status. It is necessarily related to thought, internally related to thought (simply because it *is* knowable) without having been created or put there by thought. Unlike the pre-conceptualised intuitions, it is not even supposed to be an 'other' to thought in the full sense in which it might be supposed to exist even if there were no thought to which it could be related. But how, Hegel might have asked, can we understand the idea that there might be something uncreated by thought but necessarily related to it? Hegel ties unknowability not just to whatever is *external* to thought (noumena and pre-conceptualised intuitions), but to whatever is not a product of thought: 'there is in Kant's philosophy a surplus . . . which is not posited and determined by thinking self-consciousness and is foreign and external to thought . . .'[3] So, for Hegel, even matter would turn out to be an unknowable if it were not ultimately a determination or product of thought. What is necessarily related to thought fares, for Hegel, no better than what is wholly foreign to thought, unless its being necessarily related indicates that it is thought's creation. What Gareth Stedman Jones earlier mistakenly accused Kant of *is* true of Hegel: thought can only know what it itself has created.

Thus, if the matter of our experience is not fully independent of thought, if it is necessarily related to thought, might this not be because it is thought's creation? Of course even if, following Hegel, matter is conceived of as a creation of thought, it might still be what yields *a posteriori* knowledge. We might accept, perhaps, that there is *a posteriori* knowledge, *and* that even matter is created by thought, for some creation may be 'unconscious', non-deliberate, executed by Spirit working behind the mental backs of finite consciousness. For those elements in our knowledge which thought creates in such a way, knowledge of them must remain *a posteriori*. But a creation of thought nonetheless. All of the elements in our experience must have *some* source or principle of explanation. We cannot on Kant's philosophy give matter or sensibility a source or principle of explanation *independent* of thought, and so it would seem that, ultimately, thought itself must be the source or principle of explanation of matter. We may well begin to doubt that there really are two independent sources or constituents of our knowledge at all. In a sense, then, matter would remain 'purely empirical', since it provided us with *a posteriori* knowledge, but not in any way inconsistent with its being a thought-creation. Hegel would explain its knowability by its being a product of the thought which knows it.

We agree, then, with Richard Norman's recent discussion of Hegel on this point:

It is in this context, I think, that we can also understand what Hegel means by 'that point where knowledge is no longer compelled to go beyond itself, where it finds its own self'. I would interpret this too as an essentially Kantian claim: Hegel accepts Kant's view that the pure *a priori* concepts are the product of the intellect, so that in encountering them 'knowledge . . . finds its own self'; and if Kant's residual 'things-in-themselves' are eliminated, it will then be the case that 'knowledge is no longer compelled to go beyond itself'. In knowing reality, the intellect knows itself, because it knows what it has itself put there.[4]

Although Norman's account of Hegel's position, that the intellect can only know what it creates, seems to us correct, Norman does not appreciate the extent to which Hegel's position moves beyond Kant's, even apart from the question of noumena. For Kant the intellect can *know* what it does not itself put into reality, namely the matter of experience, the 'purely empirical' element of sensory qualities. For Kant the intellect can only know what is necessarily related to it, and *that* might not be what it has created. For Hegel, there is no longer any distinction one can draw here. Whatever is knowable *is* a thought creation. Hegel's philosophy moves from Kant's conceptual dependicism, as we earlier called it, into being a conceptual idealism in the fullest sense. Insofar as Hegel banishes unknowables, he banishes *everything* except thought and its creations.

We can pose this problem for Kant, not in a way which he would have countenanced, but using his terminology all the same. Kant toyed with the idea of an intellectual intuition. Sensible intuition is intuition in which 'the subject's faculty of representation is affected by the object'. Sensible intuition is that appropriate for creatures whose knowledge has dual sources or constituents. But intellectual intuition, the awareness of things-in-themselves, is a creative awareness in which thought produces its own objects, a kind of awareness, as Kant says, that 'can belong only to the primordial being'.[5] In God's mind concepts 'would be self-specifying down to the level of individuals: the concepts themselves would determine what particulars fell under them, rather than wait around for application to any suitable particulars that might turn up'.[6] Such concepts would be, as Kant calls them, 'synthetic universals' since such concepts particularise themselves, or synthesise or manufacture their own application, rather than merely wait around—in Walsh's metaphor—for their application in the manner of the analytic universals which feature in our non-divine understanding.

It is true that Kant says that we are wholly incapable of comprehending even the possibility of such a sort of awareness, and so clearly Kant is not himself going to tolerate an attempt to answer many questions about the nature of intellectual awareness, or synthetic universals. But suppose we asked Kant: how can we be so sure that we are not just that sort of creature whose thought creates its object? How is Kant justified in his claim that only a 'primordial being', but not we, have an awareness such that it is capable of intellectual intuition? It is true that not all our universals could be synthetic ones, since some of our concepts have no instances. But consider all those concepts of ours which do have instances or application to something. Perhaps *those* concepts are synthetic. Perhaps they have created their own application. How could we tell the difference between those concepts with application which have and those which have not created their own instances, particularised themselves? Perhaps the difference between God and us is just that all of his concepts are synthetic ones, and only some of ours are.

If we were such creatures, some of our knowledge at least would be single-sourced, for those objects which fell under synthetic universals would have their source in thought and hence another, independent source would not be needed in order to account for knowledge of them. Would the experience of creatures with intellectual and those with sensible intuition have any differences at the phenomenological level? Could any of us tell whether any of our concepts which did have instances had them because the concepts were analytic or synthetic? If both kinds of experience, the intellectual and the sensible, both kinds of knowledge, that which arises from analytic and that which arises from synthetic concepts, had just the same 'feel' to it, how could any of us ever tell which kind of creature he was? Am I a sensible or an intellectual intuiter? Are my instanced concepts analytic or synthetic? Perhaps I have no knowledge about an object apart from any essential or internal relation to thought because all objects are products of thought. Perhaps knowledge has but one source, and not two sources after all. Maybe thought creates its own objects.

Kant never took such questions seriously. But Hegel did, and this leads us on to certain difficulties and controversies in interpretation of Hegel's philosophy. We have seen how, in Kant, any knowable object is essentially related to thought or concept. It is easy to show that Hegel, too, accepted *at least* this, for it was the task of the Hegelian philosophy to demonstrate the internal, necessary connections between that which we might have otherwise taken to be related only inessentially, contingently. Indeed, this constitutes the very heart of that strange sounding Hegelian formulation, identity-in-difference. If two 'things', a and b, are internally or essentially related, then each is necessary for the existence of the other. Thus, in an obvious but metaphorical sense, one can say that part of the very being or essence of a is in b, and conversely. In this Hegelian sense of identity, subject and object are shown to be identical. 'It is ordinarily supposed that the subjective and objective are blank opposites; but this is not the case. Rather do they pass into one another'.[7] Clearly, Hegel has rejected the Kantian independence claim (IpC), and he explicitly states this to be the case. He says:

Since, then, everything material is overcome by the action of the mind implicit in Nature, this triumph being consummated in the substance of soul, the latter emerges as the ideality of everything material . . . so that everything called matter, no matter how much it conveys to ordinary thinking the illusory appearance of independence, is known to have no independence relatively to mind.[8]

What is startling and novel in much of post-Kantian German philosophy, and in Hegel's philosophy in particular, is not just the thesis of the essential connection between subject and object. As we have already seen, this is something to which anyone who holds fast to an interpretive thought claim is committed willy-nilly, as the status of matter in Kant's philosophy should have convinced us. What is novel is that Hegel, and others, offered some sort of account or explanation of this essential connection. Why *should* the matter of knowledge be essentially related to thought, to form? In what sense can we retain a dual-sources account of knowledge if the two 'sources' are in essential connection? Can we find a single unifying principle to account for these two essentially connected elements of our knowledge, form and matter? How could we know something unless we ourselves had created it?

Hegel seeks to provide us with an answer: '. . . the emptying of self-consciousness itself establishes thinghood . . .'[9] For Hegel, thought, in being related to matter, is only being related to what is essentially its own creation, as I have already claimed. It is the creative or productive function of thought which is to account for the essential relation that holds between producer and product. Thus, like others in the German idealist tradition which followed Kant, Hegel takes subject or consciousness as the single, unifying, explanatory principle to account for both subject and object. There remains no irreducible duality, no external datum or given, no irrational surd inexplicable by the principles of form and system alone.[10] For Hegel, this means that content or object must itself be a creation or projection of the subject. The object is in essential relation to the subject because it *is* the subject in its otherness; it is a projection or creation by the subject.

Mind is the only reality. It is the inner being of the world, that which essentially is, and is *per se;* it assumes objective determinate forms and enters into relations with itself—it is externality, and exists for itself, yet in this determination and in its otherness, it is still one with itself . . .[11]

Why should creation suggest *essential* relation between creator and created? We do not normally think of creation in this way. If I create a painting or build a chair, or produce a book, the painting, chair or book is not essentially connected to *me*. Each can continue to exist when I cease to exist. But we must understand the peculiar nature of Hegelian creation.[12] Creation must be taken together with the notion of identity-in-difference. It is not that one thing, a subject, creates another thing, an object. It is rather that something, a subject, creates 'itself in otherness'. The object created by the subject *is* only the subject taken in apparent externality. The relations of the creator to the created are, ultimately, relations to itself. But everything is *necessarily* identical to itself. Now that is not the 'abstract identity' of orthodox philosophy. For Hegel, necessary self-identity applies to identity-in-difference also, and thus there is a necessary relation between creator and created, since the created is just the self-same creator in its otherness. Creation then, for Hegel, is a kind of continuous self-impelled development. The creator cannot, before creation, be fully itself, since its full development and completion is only achieved through its creative acts; what it creates is itself in its full development or fulfillment. It exists, but only inadequately, before its creative acts; it exists fully adequately only when its inner dynamic, its self-impelled creative tendency, has finally been worked out. But since what it is related to in its creations is only itself, it is necessarily or internally related to its creations, and for Hegel this would be so whether the creations were mundane objects like tables and chairs or were of rather more cosmic proportions, like the universe as a whole.

The creation of object by subject occurs in the Hegelian system both at the human, phenomenological level, and at the metaphysical level. It is true that Hegel does not intend that these two levels be ultimately distinct or different. Hegel's philosophy is in intention an immanentist one, in the sense that he thinks that absolute Idea, or Spirit, or Mind, *Geist,* only exists in and through the thoughts, minds, ideas, spirits of historical individuals. It is controversial whether or not Hegel's philosophy is susceptible of a purely immanentist reading, whether he does manage to dispense with transcendent elements altogether. Regardless of which side of this debate we choose, the transcendental or immanentist reading of *Geist,* it will be useful to discuss creation at the phenomenological and metaphysical levels separately.

First I should like to discuss the human level, the level of what things are like *for us. The Phenomenology of Mind* is the logical history of the consciousness of men. It is divided into three principle sections, 'Consciousness', 'Self-consciousness', and 'Reason'. In the early stages of consciousness objects are taken to be particular, external existences. Hegel describes and comments upon the progression of consciousness through increasingly sophisticated stages of its attitude toward the object of its awareness. In 'Self-consciousness' consciousness, frustrated in its attempts to grasp and explain the object, is turned back on itself. The objects of consciousness are now the self, and other selves. In this sphere, too, the self is confronted with contradictions, divisions, which result finally in 'the unhappy consciousness'. So it is then only in the sphere of Reason that the self can find the reconciling and satisfying truth. What is that truth, the truth of the subject and its objects, toward which *The Phenomenology* has been moving? What is Reason, this synthesis of the objectivity discussed in 'Consciousness' and the subjectivity investigated in 'Self-consciousness'? It is the absolute knowledge achievable in its most adequate form by the philosopher:

The surmounting of the object of consciousness in this way is not to be taken one-sidedly as meaning that the object showed itself returning into the self. It has a more definite meaning: it means that the object as such presented itself to the self as a vanishing factor; and furthermore, that the emptying of self-consciousness itself establishes thinghood . . . self-consciousness knows this nothingness of the object because on the one hand self-consciousness itself externalises itself; for in doing so it establishes itself as object, or, by reason of the indivisible unity characterising its self-existence, sets up the object as itself. On the other hand, there is also this other moment in the process, that self-consciousness has just as really cancelled and superseded this self-relinquishment and objectification and has resumed them into itself, and is thus at home with itself in its otherness as such.

This totality of its determinate characteristics makes the object *per se* of inherently a spiritual reality; and it becomes so in truth for consciousness when the latter apprehends every individual one of them as self . . .[13]

That truth, achievable only at the level of Reason and, in its most fully adequate form, only by philosophy, is that the object of awareness *is* the self, is a something created by the self or subject and which is only the self in its other appearance. This is the reconciling truth, the satisfying truth, for nothing remains that is alien to the self. The self is fully at home because it has domesticated all strangeness. This 'makes the object *per se* or inherently a spiritual reality'. Consciousness then 'apprehends every individual . . . [object] as self . . .'.

In an earlier part of the third division, 'Reason', entitled 'Reason's certainty and Reason's Truth', Hegel specifically criticises Kant and Fichte, and describes something which we might call the 'mechanics' of such a creation, for he offers a description of how it is that content or object is produced by thought or concept.[14] Hegel's criticism of Kant in this passage shows, I think, that Hegel takes what he is doing as an alternative account of the dual sources of knowledge claim that one finds in the critical philosophy. 'To put it otherwise, the category means this, that existence and self-consciousness are the same being, the same not as a matter of comparisons, but really and truly in and for themselves. It is only a onesided, unsound idealism which lets this unity appear on one side as consciousness, with a reality *per se* over against it on the other.' Hegel is clearly involved in a rejection of any sort of epistemological dualism.

What has Hegel to say about Fichte? For Fichte, all experience must be accounted for by the subject, the Ego or I, which produces that experience out of itself. In intellectual intuition the pure ego *posits* itself as pure ego and as non-ego. Pure ego establishes itself and its other from itself.

Moreover, pure ego posits a plurality of finite selves and non-selves within itself. But the single principle for all of this (individual selves, individual things (non-selves), and the pure non-ego) is the spontaneous activity of pure ego. Now, as we shall also see later when we come to discuss intellectual intuition, Hegel's principle criticisms of Fichte do not concern matters of substance but rather concern matters of methodology. For Fichte, this activity of pure ego is expressed in undemonstrable presuppositions. Fichte begins his philosophy with an account of the activity of ego. Herein lies his methodological divergence from Hegel. For Hegel, knowledge of the spontaneous, self-generating activity of the self is the *result* of *The Phenomenology of Mind,* the truth at which the book ends and not from which it begins. Phenomenologically speaking, consciousness initially apprehends reality as *otherness*. It feels certain that its object is other than itself. This is why Hegel begins *The Phenomenology* from that level of apprehension. 'The consciousness which is the truth, has forgotten the process by which this result has been reached; the pathway thereto lies behind it . . . It merely gives the assurance of being all reality; it does not, however, itself *comprehend* this fact.' There is, in all this, no intimation of a substantive disagreement between Fichte and Hegel. Hegelian and Fichtean views of creative thought are substantially the same; they differ only on whether creative thought is a starting-point or result in philosophy.

Thus, Hegel takes us through a logical history of the development of consciousness, from its 'certainty' that the object is other, to its absolute Knowledge that the object is only itself. It is in the section 'Reason's Certainty and Reason's Truth' that Hegel offers an account of the 'mechanics' of this spontaneous creative act. In ordinary, finite consciousnesses, there appears to be an 'other' to thought, a given which is different than thought. This is a phenomenological *fact* about our awareness. How can idealists explain this? Self-consciousness is 'the category bare and simple'. But reality is a determinate reality, complex, with many determinations. How are we to account for this complexity and richness by an abstract concept, which is 'bare and simple'?

Hegel explains that there is negation in the pure concept—there is nothingness in being. But to negate is to determine, make more determinate, and thus within the pure concept are 'many', a plurality of determinate concepts: '. . . the many categories are species of the pure category, which means that the pure category is still their genus or essential nature and not opposed to them'. Yet this plurality of concepts is all that one needs to account for the phenomenon of otherness in our experience. These many concepts '. . . are indeed that ambiguous being which contains otherness, too, as opposed to the pure category in its plurality'. Strictly speaking, 'we can no longer talk of things at all', since the plurality of concepts are not truly other than thought. Thus, it is merely the differentiating activity of concept into a plurality of concepts, and finally into the concept of individual singleness, which makes for the appearance of otherness. But there remains nothing which is truly other to thought. 'Difference, therefore, *is,* but completely transparent, a difference that is at the same time none. It appears in the form of a *plurality* of categories . . .' In truth, 'Consciousness . . . qua essential reality, is the whole of this process of passing out of itself qua simple category into individuality, and the object, and of viewing this process in the object, cancelling it as distinct, appropriating it as its own, and declaring itself as this certainty of being all reality, of being both itself and its object'. *Of being both itself and its object.* This recognition appears at the level of Reason to man's consciousness. It is the truth at which philosophy aims, for all true philosophy is idealism. In the Introduction to *The Science of Logic,* Hegel summarises the results he has already achieved in *The Phenomenology* thus:

The concept of pure Science, and the Deduction of it, are assumed in the present treatise so far as this, that the *Phenomenology of Spirit* is nothing other than the Deduction of this concept. Absolute knowledge is the *Truth* of all modes of consciousness, because . . . it is only when absolute Knowledge has been reached that the separation of the *Object of Knowledge* from *Subjective Certainty* is completely resolved . . .

So pure Science presupposes deliverance from the opposition of Consciousness. Pure Science includes *Thought insofar as it is just as much the Thing in itself as it is thought, or the thing in itself insofar as it is just as much pure Thought as it is the Thing in itself.* Truth, as *Science,* is pure Self-consciousness unfolding itself . . .'[15]

Secondly, we can discuss this creation, or creative activity, at the metaphysical level, although much of what Hegel says at the human phenomenological level cannot be ultimately understood or made intelligible without presupposing this metaphysical level of interpretation of creativity and concept as well. There are passages throughout Hegel's philosophy in which he makes metaphysical points which parallel the ones which I have already quoted. For example, in *The Science of Logic* Hegel remarks: 'this definiteness (of concept) . . . is what appears as content', and '. . . it is Form itself which changes only into the show of a content, as also into the show of *a* something external to the show.'[16] Again, in the Introduction to *The Science of Logic* Hegel is arguing that logic is a logic of matter as well as a logic of concepts: 'But Logic is not on this account a mere formal science . . .'. Why is not Logic merely formal? How does Hegel's logic come to be a logic of reality as well? 'The content which we miss in the logical forms, is nothing other than a solid foundation and concreting of those abstract forms . . . But it is just logical Reason which is that substantial or real, which holds together in itself all abstract determinations, and is their solid, absolutely concrete reality. Thus, we do not need to seek far afield for what is usually regarded as a filling or content; it is not the fault of the subject-matter of Logic if it is supposed to be without content or filling, but of the way in which Logic is conceived'.[17] Dialectical logic, for Hegel, is a logic of thought and matter, *because* matter is an expression of thought and, as such, obeys whatever laws thought obeys.

Nowhere is Hegel's treatment of self-creating thought or concept at the metaphysical level in sharper focus than in his overall plan in *The Encyclopaedia of the Philosophical Sciences:*

... philosophy is subdivided into three parts:
I. Logic, the science of the Idea in and for itself.
II. The Philosophy of Nature, the science of the Idea in its otherness.
III. The Philosophy of Mind: the science of the idea come back to itself out of that Otherness.[18]

Hegel views these divisions as stages in the advance of the Idea. Consequently at the end of the *Logic,* the Idea has reached its fullest, richest stage as 'Idea', namely absolute Idea. Hegel then tells us that:

The Idea which is dependent or for itself when viewed on the point of this its unity with itself, is Perception or Intuition, and the Percipient Idea is Nature. But as Intuition the Idea is, through an external reflection, invested with the one-sided character of immediacy or negation ... The Idea ... resolves to let the 'moment' of its particularity ... go forth freely as Nature.[19]

This is something which Hegel repeats elsewhere. He anticipates this result, for example, in the opening section of *The Science of Logic:* '. . . we see that absolute Spirit . . . at the end of its evolution freely passes beyond itself and lapses into the shape of an immediate being; it resolves itself to the creation of a world which contains everything included in the evolution preceding that result . . .'[20]

Thus, both in the overall plan to Hegel's philosophy, and in numerous passages, Hegel takes seriously what were only suggestions in the Kantian philosophy. In the company of others in the post-Kantian German philosophical milieu, thought or concept has the logically prior and generative role to play in the explanation of matter, reality. Principally in *The Phenomenology,* this is considered at the human, phenomenological level, the level of individual and social consciousness. But the underpinning for the doctrine about man's consciousness is given by Hegel's parallel metaphysical position: Idea or Concept produces nature from itself, and is thus capable of a genuine creative act.

The problem of interpreting what Hegel meant by Thought creating Nature, Creation at the metaphysical level, has occasioned a great deal of controversy within Hegelian scholarship. Many commentators and critics of Hegel, Feuerbach and Marx foremost amongst them, have interpreted Hegel's views in the obvious theological way, and understood 'Idea passing over into Nature' as a disguised way of talking about God's creation of the world. Nor is there any doubt that sometimes Hegel himself offers this interpretation. Hegel ascribes divinity to the Idea:

The divine Idea is just this: to disclose itself, to posit the Other outside itself and to take it back again into itself in order to be subjectivity and spirit.[21]

In an early work, Hegel is even more explicit:

The absolute ever plays with itself a moral tragedy in which it ever gives birth to itself in itself in the objective world, then in this form gives itself over to suffering and death and raises itself to glory from its ashes.[22]

At the end of the discussion of the 'materiality' of his logic, from which I have already quoted, Hegel concludes:

Logic is consequently to be understood as the System of Pure Reason, as the Realm of Pure Thought . . . One may therefore express it thus: that this content shows forth God as he is in his eternal essence before the creation of Nature and of a Finite Spirit.[23]

Finally, again in the *Philosophy of Nature,* Hegel tells us:

God has two revelations, as Nature and as Spirit. Both these divine formations are temples of God that He fills by His presence. God as an abstraction [the Idea in itself—DHR] is not the true God: only as the living process of positing His other, the World (which conceived in divine terms is His son) and first in the union with His other, as spirit, can He be subject.[24]

But *must* we take what Hegel says at the metaphysical level concerning the creative relation of thought to being in this literal, and hence theological, sense? Even if Hegel sometimes weakened his own case by introducing such elements of theological interpretation, the possibility still remains that we could offer, on his behalf, a more plausible, non-theological elucidation of what he means. Various writers have in fact argued that this is so, that it is not necessary to read Hegel in the way in which I (following Feuerbach and Marx) read him, and have suggested alternative accounts of Hegel's views on the 'transition' from thought to being in Hegel's philosophy.

I want to discuss three such examples of Hegel interpreters who attempt to offer some sort of non-theological interpretation. None are, I think, successful in the sense that none of the accounts are plausible as expositions or interpretations of what Hegel *said.* I do not dispute that such accounts have a sort of Hegelian 'feel' about them, nor that they do represent some *part* of what Hegel was attempting to say. I do dispute them as accurate accounts of Hegel's own philosophy. These accounts may be sympathetic ways of stating a Hegelianesque message, but they are simply not accurate accounts of Hegel.

J. N. Findlay is known for his non-theological interpretation of Hegel's philosophy. How does Findlay interpret the transition from Idea to Nature? In particular, what permits Findlay to conclude that 'In spite, therefore, of much quasi-theological mystification, there is nothing but the utmost intellectual sobriety in Hegel's transition from the Idea to nature.'[25] Findlay seems, at least in his essay 'Hegel's Use of Teleology', to rest his case on the following sort of argument:

Infinite teleology is therefore the central notion of the Hegelian *Logic.* How does it operate in the *Philosophy of Nature* . . . Here it might seem that the transition from the Absolute Idea to the Concrete sphere of Nature and Spirit was precisely not teleological, for does not Hegel say that the Absolute Idea freely releases its moment of particularity, thereby giving rise to the concrete, intuitive idea of Nature and does not all this suggest the generation of the world by a ready-made, pre-existent perfection, which generation has all the purposeless gratuitousness of Thomistic creation. Hegel certainly tried hard in this passage and in some others to mislead his readers into believing that he held something like Christian theism, a doctrine that is not through and through teleological, that explains things by their origins rather than by their ultimate goal. He provides however, the materials for his own demythologization . . . He there makes perfectly plain that the transition at the end of the *Logic* really involves the breakdown of an abstraction rather than a creative advance to anything more comprehensive. We simply see that the idea of infinite teleology to which we have advanced is so far a *mere* idea, an abstract *logical shadow,* rather than an actual concrete achievement, and that it is only insofar as it can *also* be a concrete achievement that it can be a genuine idea at all.

Hegel tells us that the realm of logic is the realm of shadows, of though-forms stripped of sensuous concretion. The Absolute Idea may be the noblest shadow in the realm of shadows . . . It is however nothing at all except as worked out in the realm of Nature and Man.[26]

Findlay is without any doubt right in stressing this teleological aspect in the transition from Idea to Nature. In order to *be,* Idea must become instantiated or concretised in a world. In part, Hegel is making the perfectly plausible point that there can be no ultimately complete or actual Idea or Spirit without a world, a material world, which bears or instantiates it. In order to *be,* there must be a nature for Idea to be *in.*

But where Findlay errs is his assumption that a theological and teleological point of view are mutually exclusive. It is true that orthodox Christian doctrines of creation are not teleological, for on those accounts God is perfect *before* creation and hence does not 'need' the created world for any purpose whatever. But Hegel's theology is not orthodox, and Hegel's doctrine of creation is not the same as 'the purposeless gratuitousness of Thomistic creation'. What Hegel envisions is a theology in which God needs the world in order to complete or perfect himself. God before creation is not truly or fully God. Thus, in a passage from the *Philosophy of Nature* which Findlay cites: 'God as an abstraction is not the true God, but is only as the living process of positing his other, the world . . .' What we can attribute to Hegel then, in order to make sense of the transition from Idea to Nature, is not a Thomistic doctrine of creation, but rather a highly unorthodox, teleological doctrine of creation, a teleological theology

In his foreword to Hegel's *Philosophy of Nature,* Findlay explicates the transition again thus:

The Absolute Idea leads on to the greater concreteness of Nature and Spirit, because instantiation, concrete embodiment is part and parcel of its sense: it would not *be* the Absolute were it not thus instantiated and embodied, and it may in *this* sense be credited with a power of self-release, of ideal or formal causality.[27]

This short recapitulation of the transition by Findlay shows, I think, that in the end Findlay too ascribes an unorthodox theology, but a theology nonetheless, to Hegel. The teleological strand in Findlay's interpretation is clear. In order to *be,* the Absolute Idea is necessarily instantiated. But Ideas, normally understood, even if they are necessarily embodied, do *not* have the power of self-release or of ideal or formal causality. There are *no* ideas which embody themselves. Thus an accurate interpretation of Hegel must include both the elements of teleology and of self-creation, and this can only be done, I submit, by ascribing to Hegel a very unorthodox (by Christian standards) theological doctrine. The reader must then decide for himself whether Findlay's judgement can stand: 'In spite, therefore, of much quasi-theological mystification, there is nothing but the utmost intellectual sobriety in Hegel's transition from the Idea to Nature.'

Copleston also argues for a non-theological reading of Hegel. Copleston acknowledges that Hegel himself sometimes preferred theological interpretations of what he was doing, but he concludes:

But consideration of the Hegelian system as a whole suggests that this passage represents an intrusion as it were, of the way of speaking which is characteristic of the Christian religious consciousness, and that its implications should not be pressed. It seems to be clear enough that according to Hegel the doctrine of free creation by God belongs to the figurative or pictorial language of the religious consciousness.[28]

Once Copleston has de-theologised Hegel's message, what by way of an alternative does he offer us? What Copleston seems to find objectionable in the 'theological' interpretation of Hegel is the notion that the creation, or derivation, as he begins calling it, of Nature is portrayed as 'free' and accomplished *in time*. Thus, Copleston wishes to replace the idea of *free* creation by the idea of *necessary* manifestation:

From the strictly philosophical point of view, the Absolute in itself manifests itself necessarily in Nature. The necessity is an inner necessity of Nature.[29]

Further, this *necessary* derivation of Nature from Idea must be understood, he claims, *non-temporally:* 'and from this it follows that from the philosophical point of view there is no sense in speaking of the absolute in itself as existing "before" creation. If Nature is derived ontologically from the Idea, the latter is not temporally prior to the former.'

But what is not clear on Copleston's account is what sense can be made of the idea of a necessary, non-temporal derivation of Nature from Idea, if a theological interpretation of this is forbidden us. If Idea freely creating nature in time is theological, how is Idea necessarily manifesting itself as Nature non-temporally any more acceptable? This too seems to need a theological interpretation, although once again we can see that it will be an unorthodox one. It is true that Hegel, as Copleston interprets him, will have abandoned a Christian God who freely creates the world, but abandoned it in favour of an unorthodox God who necessarily does so.[30]

When Copleston then tries to explain Hegel's conception of the relation between Idea and Nature in a way which does not rely on any theological doctrine, he does so by producing a doctrine which simply fails to capture Hegel's philosophical intentions. Copleston claims that on his non-theological interpretation 'it is perfectly reasonable to speak of the *Logos* as expressing or manifesting itself in finite things'. How does *Logos* express or manifest itself in finite things? Simply in the sense, Copleston informs us, that *Logos,* Spirit, is 'the universal of universals; even though it exists only in and through the particulars, it itself persists whereas the particulars do not. Hence it is perfectly reasonable to speak of the Logos as expressing or manifesting itself in finite things.'[31] Thus, the universal, or *Logos,* 'is in a certain sense logically prior to its manifestations'.

But if this interpretation of the Idea-Nature relation as one between universals and particulars is plausible, it buys this plausibility only by abandoning Hegel. What Copleston omits from his account is essentially the same point which was omitted by Findlay. The point is that, for Hegel, the Universal is self-particularising, it particularises itself. This is no ordinary universal. What Copleston imagines is that if the connection between Idea and Nature is taken as one of necessity, rather than 'free' contingency, then this will itself provide an adequate interpretation of self-particularisation. Thus, 'The Idea concretises itself' would simply be taken as 'The Idea necessarily implies a material embodiment'. I do not wish to deny that this is a not unreasonable reinterpretation of Hegel, but I do deny that this accurately captures all of what Hegel, the historical Hegel, intended. Hegel insists not just that Idea necessarily implies that there is a nature, but that the 'existence' of nature can be accounted for, explained by, Idea. Indeed, in the *Philosophy of Nature* Hegel stands Copleston's interpretation on its head by elucidating universal-particular talk by means of a theological model:

How does the universal determine itself? . . . A more concrete form of the question is: How had God come to create the world?[32]

Of course, what Hegel would claim is that, in such a passage, he was merely 'elucidating' in the sense of rephrasing a philosophical truth in a religious, more popular, and hence more readily comprehensible, manner, but that the philosophical formulation must be intelligible in its own right, without depending on a translation into religious language. Such is, no doubt, Hegel's position. But what I am asserting is that, whatever Hegel's position on the relation between religious and philosophical language may be, the latter does not in fact carry its own intelligibility, and Hegel's tendency to reformulate the remark about the self-determining universal into religious language, in the above quote, is itself symptomatic of the difficulty involved in giving such a formulation independent sense. Thus, Hegel does not just claim that the existence of Idea necessarily implies the existence of a material embodiment. Hegel asserts more strongly that Idea determines, or produces its own material embodiment. The necessary relation which arises between Idea and object is itself explained as an outcome of the Idea's self-determination, and is not therefore a full and adequate rendering of what Hegel intends the relationship between Idea and Nature to be. Finally, we can ask Copleston, then, what sense are we to give to the notion of a universal concreting or instantiating *itself* if not a theological one?

We noted in our opening remarks about Copleston's interpretation that he stressed two features: the necessity of the transition from Idea to Nature, and its non-temporality. It is worthwhile mentioning that the question of time is irrelevant in deciding whether Hegel's message is ultimately theological or not. Copleston imagines that temporal creation is a necessary part of the 'myth of creation. It is not. At least one theological tradition holds that God as eternal exists outside time. No act of his can be temporally dated, and hence creation did not happen at a time either. Creation of nature explains in some non-temporal way the beginning of time, but the creation itself stands in no temporal relation to that beginning. Thus, Copleston's argument that the ontological derivation in Hegel is a non-temporal one goes no distance at all in distinguishing the Hegelian derivation from (some) theological creations, as Copleston appears to assume.

All such 'plausible' but 'anemic' interpretations of Hegel, such as Findlay's and Copleston's, in the end come to grief on precisely the same point: the self-creative or generative power of Idea. Both Findlay's teleological and Copleston's universal-particular interpretations of the transition from Idea to Nature omit this and hence both, although they stress ideas which are genuinely at play in Hegel's philosophy, cannot pretend to be accurate accounts of what Hegel himself intended. I have argued that nothing short of a theological reading can account for the creative or generative power of Idea to effect its own transition, but I have also admitted that this theological reading commits Hegel to a very unorthodox deity, who creates and perfects himself by effecting this transition. Findlay is right then to say that Hegel rejects a Thomistic or neo-Platonic doctrine of creation, which assumes a perfect God who creates an inescapably 'other' nature which is not needed to accomplish his perfection. Copleston is right to stress the element of necessity in the transition from Idea to Nature, since in any case by 'free' Hegel meant only 'self-necessitated' or 'not necessitated externally'. But both Findlay and Copleston are wrong to conclude from any of this that Hegel is not to be interpreted theologically. It is God who provides, for Hegel, the unifying explanatory principle which accounts for form and matter, Idea and Nature. It is God who ultimately justifies Hegel in rejecting an epistemology committed to dual sources of knowledge.[33] Again looking back at Kant, one can see just how apt this theological interpretation of Hegel's philosophy proves to be. In intellectual intuition, thought does literally bring forth its object out of itself. Kant restricted such activity to the Primordial Being and Hegel too is speaking not so much of the intellectual activity of individual men, but rather of the intellectual activity or movement of God, or Idea, and of men only secondarily insofar as they are manifestations of Idea. Hegel's philosophy is a quasi-philosophical cloak for an unorthodox version of the religious myth of creation, and both Marx and Feuerbach saw the theological import of Hegel's philosophy although they do not seem to have appreciated its highly unorthodox nature.

Richard Norman's recent book on Hegel's *Phenomenology* comes surprisingly close to this theological interpretation of Hegel, but then quickly shies away from its own conclusion. Norman begins by recognising that:

> Hegel . . . is a more consistent idealist than Kant. The difference between the two could be formulated as follows. Although I have suggested that Hegel is akin to Kant in being a *transcendental* idealist he would not follow Kant in asserting his idealism to be a purely *formal* idealism. The suggestion that the categories determine only the 'form' of experience immediately invites talk of some independently specifiable 'matter' to which the categories are applied . . . Hegel calls it a 'onesided unsound idealism', an 'abstract empty idealism'. . .[34]

Norman then proceeds to describe some of the 'acceptable' features involved in Hegel's idealism. He notes, however, that there *might be* a further strand in Hegelian idealism which is less 'favourable':

> So far I have been presenting Hegel's idealism in what I would regard as a favourable light. I have been focusing on that strand in his thought which seems to me to constitute a plausible and indeed attractive form of idealism—a position which could be described as 'Kantianism, minus the thing-in-itself, plus a social theory of mind'. It has to be admitted, however, that there is another important strand in Hegel's idealism, and one which I regard as much less attractive . . . But there is also a much stronger sense which could be given to the assertion that the world is the work of reason, so that Hegel would then be saying something like this: 'The world is created by God, it is the product of divine reason' . . . and the notion of divine creation would be further elaborated by giving a stronger sense to the talk of mind 'objectifying itself'; the divine mind, it would be said, *creates* the world by *thinking* it. On this interpretation, then, Hegel's idealism would be a form of theism.[35]

Norman concludes that he is 'reluctant to attribute such a position to Hegel', although there is no doubt that Hegel does, sometimes, lapse 'into an acceptance of the misleading model'.

Where Norman goes wrong, I think, is in his belief that it is 'acceptable' to describe Hegel as an idealist of both form *and* content, and 'unacceptable' to ascribe a theological interpretation to him. What *could* it mean to say that the categories, for Hegel, unlike for Kant, determine both the form *and* matter of experience, if we do not understand this as a way of speaking of God's creation of the world? Form, normally understood, cannot create or determine the material for its own application. We must, then, go back to intellectual intuition and synthetic universals, and I cannot see what sense we can possibly give to this if not a theological one. Part of Norman's problem here is that he, like so many other commentators on Kant, conflates noumena and the content of experience. It is one thing to say that Hegel is Kant minus the unknowable thing-in-itself, but quite another to say that Hegel is a Kant who permits his idealism to be an idealism of form producing its own content. The former claim may be unobjectionable; the latter is a philosophical rendering of theological creation. If it is acceptable to Norman that Hegel is an idealist of form and content (and not just that Hegel dispenses with Kant's noumena), then it must also be acceptable that Hegel holds 'a pantheistic view of reality as the emanation of a divine mind.[36]

It is true that when Hegel comes to discuss intellectual intuition he appears dismissive of it. His treatment of intellectual intuition in the *Preface to the Phenomenology of Spirit,* and in *The Science of Logic* might suggest that he did not take intellectual intuition as seriously as I have suggested.[37] Hegel's remarks on intellectual intuition evidence the nature of his disagreements with Fichte, a problem which I have already mentioned in passing. These disagreements do not in the least suggest that he did not take intellectual intuition seriously, for they are ones of method but not of substance. Like Fichte, Hegel accepts intellectual intuition. Thus, Hegel remarks:

The absolute principle, the one real foundation and firm standpoint of philosophy is, in the philosophy of Fichte as in that of Schelling, intellectual intuition or, in the language of reflection, the identity of subject and object . . . Fichte's philosophy, therefore, is a genuine product of speculation.[38]

But methodologically, Hegel insists that the truth of intellectual intuition is a philosophical *result* and not a place at which one *begins* philosophical argument. This is the general point which Hegel makes at both of the places in which he explicitly discusses intellectual intuition. Hegel rejects intellectual intuition as a starting point, as a beginning in philosophy, for it is something concrete, mediated, 'something which contains within itself diverse determinations'.[39] In philosophy one begins with what is simple and immediate, and since pure knowing, 'even in the shape of intellectual intuition', 'is not *immediately* present in the individual consciousness', it is a result and not a beginning in philosophy. Again,

. . . although the ego could in itself or in principle be characterised as pure knowing or as intellectual intuition and asserted as the beginning, we are not concerned in the science of logic with what is present only in principle . . .

In the Preface to *The Phenomenology* Hegel asks whether, on Schelling's view, 'this intellectual intuition does not fall back into that inert, abstract simplicity, and exhibit and expound reality itself in an unreal manner'. Hegel goes on to tell us that the truth is to be found in the subject, but only as *result* and not as beginning:

True reality is merely this process of reinstating self-identity, of reflecting into its own self in and from its Other, and is not an original and primal unity as such, not an immediate unity as such. It is the process of its own becoming, the circle which presupposes its end as its purpose, and has its end for its beginning: It becomes concrete and actual only by being carried out, and by the end it involves.[40]

Thus in both passages Hegel has in mind by 'intellectual intuition' the doctrine that this Ego is where one *begins,* and this he rejects as improper. Since intellectual intuition is the self which creates and contains its Other, it is a mediated result and not an unmediated simple beginning. The truth of philosophy may be intellectual intuition, but truth is a result and not a beginning.

Hegel's dismissive attitude, then, is not directed against intellectual intuition *in principle* ('an sich') but rather only against a certain philosophical use to which it may be wrongly put. Indeed, intellectual intuition *as result* is the final truth of his philosophy, the projection of the object by the subject, at first seen as an alien object but later recognised by that subject as merely its own.

In effect, Hegel's response to Kant's 'problem', the joint assertion of (IC) and (IpC), is to jettison the indepedence claim. There is nothing independent of thought, since nature or object is itself thought's creation. Hegel's greatness lies in his clear recognition that, on the Kantian picture of thought as interpretive, any belief in the independence of the object is undercut. If all thought is interpretive, then there can be no *knowledge* of an object independent of thought. Once 'interpreted', the object *qua* interpreted is in a necessary relation to thought. Hegel, in his respect for the Idea, preferred to reject the independence of the object rather than question the interpretive and ultimately for him, creative, role of Thought. Hegel resolved Kant's problem by rejecting the independence claim and accepting the interpretive claim. But since all thought is interpretive, and finally creative, what is *truth* for Hegel? Is not knowledge *true* when it corresponds to reality? Is not an idea *correct* when it corresponds to the object of which it is the idea? Not for Hegel, for Hegel rejects these essentially 'reflective' notions of truth and adequacy. It is not that notions are true when they reflect objects; rather, objects are what are true and they are true when they correspond to, or realise their notion. Hegel explicitly rejects any correspondence theory of truth, and that he did so is entirely consistent with the non-reflective role which he assigns to thought:

> . . . the object is regarded as something in itself finished and complete, something which, as far as its reality is concerned, could entirely dispense with thought, while on the other hand, Thought is something incomplete which has to seek completion by means of some material and indeed has to adapt itself to its material as if it were a form in itself pliable and undetermined. Truth is supposed to be the agreement of Thought with its object, and in order to bring about this agreement (for the agreement is not there by itself) thinking must accommodate and adopt itself to its object.

> These views . . . express the determinations which constitute the nature of our ordinary consciousness just as it appears; but these prejudices, translated into the sphere of reason . . . are errors.[41]

Hegel saw that idealism and classical correspondence theory were 'epistemologically' inconsistent.

Thus we have seen, so far, the epistemological inconsistency in Kant's joint espousal of (IC), the interpretive claim, and (IpC), the independence claim. We also noted Hegel's heroic abandonment of the independence claim and retention of the interpretive claim. It is in this light that we can begin to make sense of the importance of Feuerbach for German Philosophy, prior to Marx. Marx said of himself that he had stood Hegel right side up, but this reversal had already in essence been accomplished by Feuerbach. Feuerbach can be understood as resolving Kant's problem in a precisely opposite way to that of Hegel—a retention of the independence claim and a rejection of the interpretive claim. In his retention of (IpC), Feuerbach thereby establishes his credentials as a materialist.[42]

Feuerbach was not an especially deep or profound thinker. Nor was he overworried about consistency or careful development of his thought. His views are not consistent over time, and, more importantly, it is not clear that they are consistent at any one time. Various different themes run through and criss-cross his philosophy—for example, both a conventionalist and an objectivist theory of truth—and are never really satisfactorily resolved.[43]

Therefore, when I said that 'Feuerbach can be understood as resolving Kant's problem in a precisely opposite way to that of Hegel', I did not mean to do justice to the complexity (or confusion) within Feuerbach's thought. There may well be passages in Feuerbach which contradict other passages which I will cite. But I am claiming that what I am putting forward represents one important tendency in Feuerbach's philosophy, and indeed what I would consider its most progressive tendency, its fullest break with Hegelian idealism.

Feuerbach's retention of the independence claim, his belief in a world independent of thought, is perhaps what is best known, and least controversial, of all of Feuerbach's philosophy. 'I do not generate the object from thought, but the thought from the object, and I hold that alone to be an object which has an existence beyond one's own brain'.[44] Feuerbach insists repeatedly on the duality of subject and object—as did Kant—and rejects the Hegelian identification of the two, or anyway accepts it in name only, meaning thereby simply 'the sensory contemplation of man by man'.[45] Feuerbach criticised Hegel's famous chapter in *The Phenomenology of Mind* in which Hegel 'resolves' the particularity of 'here' and 'now' into universals: 'Hegel has not refuted the here which presents itself as an object of sense-perception distinct from an object of pure thought . . .'[46] In the *Logic* of Hegel thought is only 'in uninterrupted unity with itself; the objects of thought are only its determinations; they are entirely incorporated in the Idea and have nothing of their own which could remain outside thought',[47] Feuerbach claims. For Feuerbach, the world is essentially independent from thought: '. . . consequently, man's ideas of the sun, moon, and stars, and other beings of nature, although these ideas are products of nature, are yet products distinct from their objects in nature'.[48]

Feuerbach further argues—correctly, I think—that the rejection of the independence of the object from thought, can only lead to a theological point of view, and it is this which forms the nub of his critique of Hegel:

. . . we have the philosophy of identity . . . where the subject is no longer limited and conditioned by a substance existing apart from it and contradicting its essence. But the subject, which has no longer an object apart from itself and consequently is no longer limited, is no longer a 'finite' subject—no longer the 'I' opposite whom an object stands; it is the absolute being whose theological or popular expression is the word 'God'.[49]

Reject the independence of the object from thought, Feuerbach tells us, and one will end with a theology. 'The identity of thought and being is therefore only the expression of the divinity of reason . . . But a being that is not distinguished from thought and that is only a predicate or a determination of reason is only an ideated and abstract being, but in truth it is not being . . . the identity of thought and being, therefore, expresses only the identity of thought with itself'.[50] 'The Hegelian view that nature, reality, is posited by the Idea is only the *rational* expression of the theological teaching that nature is created by God, that material being is created by an immaterial . . . being. At the end of the *Logic* the Absolute Idea even contrives to come to a nebulous "decision", in this way itself documenting its origin in the theological heaven.'[51] Kant's version of idealism is tarred with the same brush: 'God is the creator of Idealism'; 'Idealism is nothing but rational or rationalised theism.'[52]

The nature of Feuerbach's materialism has been much discussed. Whether or not there is anything 'more' to reality than matter is, for example, something about which Feuerbach changes his mind. His earlier materialism, which he even referred to as idealism to distinguish it from 'absolute materialism', asserted that there was *more* than just matter, that thought was not reducible to matter, but both were components of reality ('Wo nur materie ist, da ist kein Begriff der Materie'). His later, vulgar or reductive materialism, on the other hand, treats everything as matter, or an 'expression' of matter, a tendency of his later thought often ridiculed by citing quotations from his writings such as the following: 'Everything depends upon what we eat and drink. Difference in essence is but difference in food.' But what is constant throughout the twists and turns in Feuerbach's materialism, or sensationalism as he also called his philosophy, was the acceptance of the existence of a real, independent of all thought. And this is the only element of his materialism which concerns us here.

Feuerbach's insistence on the independence of the object, nature, from thought or idea, which we have been calling realism, is coupled with a rejection of the theory of knowledge implicit in the interpretive thought claim, a theory on which objects come to express or realise their concepts rather than their concepts correspond with their objects. Feuerbach's realism is complemented, then, with a correspondence theory of knowledge, and that is why I have claimed that Feuerbach resolved Kant's 'problem' in a way precisely opposite to that of Hegel. Instead of the Hegelian resolution in terms of interpretive thought and object dependence, one finds in Feuerbach object independence and a correspondence theory of knowledge. Feuerbach is not always faithful to that rejection of an idealist theory of knowledge and acceptance of a realist, correspondence theory, but this does form the most important tendency in his theory of knowledge.

Hook, in *From Hegel to Marx,* calls Feuerbach's theory of knowledge 'an emphatic Aristotelian realism', and in many passages this is undeniably so. '*The Laws of Reality* are also laws of thought'[53] is not the slogan of a Kantian, who rather speaks of the Copernican Revolution by which '. . . the objects . . . conform to the concepts . . .' (Kant, *CPR* LXVII). It is true that Feuerbach had no carefully worked out and elaborated theory of knowledge, but from numerous passages one can gather that Feuerbach was thinking in terms of a reflective understanding of thought rather than a wholly interpretive one. First, there are remarks which show his explicit disavowal of the Kantian interpretive understanding of thought.

Kantian idealism in which the objects conform to the understanding and not the understanding to the objects, is therefore nothing other than the realisation of the theological conception of the divine mind, which is not determined by the objects but rather determines them.[54]

Then there are passages in which he describes the 'sensualism' of his theory of knowledge: 'I found my ideas on materials which can be appropriated only through the activity of the senses.'[55] He even refers to knowledge as a 'copy' of the independently existing object: 'Man's knowledge, which follows the objects as their copy, is . . . *a posteriori,* or empirical knowledge'.[56] Feuerbach never disentangles what precisely in our knowledge of reality comes from reality itself and what from the way in which our minds are structured to conceive it, but the direction of his thought is to be a realist about quite a lot in our knowledge. He makes fun of the Kantian dictum 'The understanding does not derive its laws (a priori) from nature, but rather it prescribes them to it'. Causality and natural kinds, for example, are features of our experience of the world not because they belong to the *a priori* structures of the understanding, but because that is how things really are. Our ideas, our knowledge, must come to 'correspond' to what exists in nature.

. . . The Book of Nature is not composed of a chaos of letters strewn helter-skelter so that the understanding must first introduce order and connection into the chaos. The relations in which they are expressed in a meaningful proposition would then become the subjective and arbitrary creations of the understanding. No, we distinguish and unify things through our understanding on the basis of certain signs of unity and difference given to the senses. We separate what nature has separated: we tie together what she has related; we classify natural phenomena in categories of ground and consequence, cause and effect because factually, sensibly, objectively, things really stand in such a relation to each other.[57]

What we find then, in Feuerbach, is an answer to 'Kant's problem' which is different from Hegel's resolution. We find a realist ontology and a 'reflective' or correspondence theory of knowledge rather than an idealist ontology and an 'interpretive' theory of knowledge. There is a recognition in both Hegel and Feuerbach that ontology and theory of knowledge must be made consistent—not in the strictly logical sense of 'consistency' but in the sense that they must support and render plausible one another. It was precisely the juxtaposition in Kant of realism (in my sense) and the interpretive understanding of thought which generated what I called an 'epistemological inconsistency', and I have attempted to read in Hegel and Feuerbach two entirely different responses to that inconsistency. Both try to put ontology and theory of knowledge into closer harness than did Kant, although in opposite harnesses. It is with Feuerbach's response, realism and a correspondence or 'reflection' theory of knowledge, that the philosophical stage is now set upon which to introduce Marx, for Marx, as I shall argue, took Feuerbach's criticism of Kant and Hegel and Feuerbach's elaboration of his own alternative for granted. Marx adds and amplifies, but in those additions to Feuerbach there is never any hint of rejection of those real accomplishments of Feuerbach in dealing with the Hegelian system.

Notes: Chapter II

[1] Hegel, G. W. F., *Science of Logic,* Vol. I. Trans. by W. H. Johnston and L. G. Struthers, George Allen & Unwin, Ltd., 1966, p. 57 in the Introduction.

[2] *Ibid,* pp. 133-134.

[3] *Ibid,* p. 73, for this and next quote.

[4] Norman, Richard, *Hegel's Phenomenology: A Philosophical Introduction,* Sussex University Press, London, 1976, p. 17.

[5] *The Critique of Pure Reason,* B 72. See also A 256. Here, if anywhere, the problems of the noumena and the matter or content of knowledge, which we have been keeping distinct, seem to coalesce, for the primordial being whose knowledge is single-sourced creates noumena by his intelligible intuition, and not just the matter or content of his knowledge and experience.

[6] Walsh, W. H., *Kant's Criticism of Metaphysics,* Edinburgh University Press, Edinburgh, 1975, pp. 12-13.

[7] Hegel, G. W. F., *The Philosophy of Right,* trans. by T. M. Knox, Oxford University Press, Oxford, 1952, p. 232, the addition to paragraph 26. In paragraph 26, p. 32, Hegel says of subject and object that '. . . they . . . pass over into their opposites as a result of their finitude and their dialectical character'.

[8] Hegel, G. W. F., *The Philosophy of Mind,* Oxford University Press, Oxford, 1971, supplement to paragraph 389, pp. 32-33.

[9] Hegel, G. W. F., *The Phenomenology of Mind,* trans. by J. B. Baillie, George Allen & Unwin, London, 1966, p. 789. See the extended discussion on pp. 789-791 in which Hegel develops this point.

[10] This deserves some measure of qualification. Hegel insists repeatedly that in his system some things retain their contingency and cannot be seen to follow with necessity from Absolute Idea. For example, Hegel says in *The Philosophy of Right* that although the division of society into three classes and the need for punishment to 'fit' the crime follow from the Idea by necessity, it cannot be determined with similar necessity the class position of each particular man, or precisely what the punishment should be. Such things have an ineradicable element of arbitrariness, capriciousness, chance, in their determination. W. T. Stace, in his *The Philosophy of Hegel* (Dover, USA, undated) tells the story of how a Herr Krug 'supposing Hegel to be attempting in the philosophy of nature to deduce all actual existent objects from the pure Idea, enquired whether Hegel could deduce the pen with which he, Herr Krug, was writing'. Hegel's reply was that 'philosophy has more important matters to concern itself with than Krug's pen' (Stace, p. 308). It is not clear how this should be reconciled with the interpretation of Hegel that Idea creates its 'other'— since particularity *is* the 'other' of universality. But this qualification does not seriously affect the point I am trying to make—namely, that for Hegel, the idea *has,* like God, generative powers. The qualification only affects the scope and range which we should assign to those generative powers. Perhaps one could distinguish here between what Idea generates and what men are able themselves to deduce from Idea, so that objectively Idea does create everything, including Herr Krug's pen, but that, subjectively, its creation of such particulars is not transparent to finite minds and hence does not permit us to follow its creations of particulars by our own deductive inferences.

[11] *The Phenomenology of Mind,* p. 86. See pp. 80-81 and pp. 85-86.

[12] For a discussion of the peculiarity of the Hegelian notion of creation, and its connections with the theory of expression in Herder, see Charles Taylor, *Hegel,* Cambridge University Press, Cambridge, 1975, Part I.

[13] *The Phenomenology of Mind,* pp. 789-790.

[14] *Ibid,* pp. 272-280 offer an extensive elaboration by Hegel of this point. This and the unnumbered quotes which follow are taken from this important section.

[15] *The Science of Logic,* Vol. I, p. 60.

[16] *Ibid,* p. 48, p., 47.

[17] *Ibid,* pp. 58-59.

[18] Hegel, G. W. F., *The Logic of Hegel,* Trans. by William Wallace, Oxford University Press, Oxford, 1972, section 18.

[19] *Ibid,* section 244.

[20] *The Science of Logic,* I, p. 83.

[21] Hegel, G. W. F., *The Philosophy of Nature,* ed. A. V. Miller, Oxford University Press, Oxford, 1970, p. 14.

[22] This quote, and an interesting discussion about de-theologising Hegel and the problem of accounting for the necessity in his system, are to be found in Raymond Plant, *Hegel,* George Allen & Unwin, London, 1973, p. 129-139 and *passim.*

[23] *The Science of Logic,* I, p. 60.

[24] *The Philosophy of Nature,* p. 13.

[25] Findlay, J. N., *Hegel: A Re-Examination,* George Allen & Unwin, London, 1959, p. 269.

[26] Findlay, J. N., 'Hegel's Use of Teleology', in his *Ascent to the Absolute,* George Allen & Unwin, London, 1970, pp. 102-103.

[27] Findlay, J. N., 'Forward', *Hegel's Philosophy of Nature, op. cit.,* p. XIII.

[28] Copleston, Frederick, S. J., *A History of Philosophy,* Vol. VII, Search Press, London, 1971, pp. 195-196.

[29] *Ibid,* p. 196 for this and the following quotation.

[30] Cf. Taylor, Charles, *op. cit.,* whose exposition of Hegel's unorthodox theology is unrivalled. See especially pp. 100-102. See also G. R. G. Mure, *An Introduction to Hegel,* which examines the roots of Hegelianism in Aristotle's philosophy and discusses the Aristotelian notion of God.

[31] Copleston, *op. cit.,* pp. 197-198.

[32] *The Philosophy of Nature,* p. 13.

[33] Cf. Josef Maier, *On Hegel's Critique of Kant,* AMS Press, New York, 1966, p. 37: 'Hegel intends his philosophy as an attempt to overcome this dualism . . . His contention is that since it is preposterous to say anything at all about an object that can have no relation to consciousness, in other words, to speak of a reality apart from a subject, the mind . . . must itself be proclaimed the ultimate, unconditioned reality, the only true and real being. In other words, if this entire world of our experience is the product of conscious processes working through form-giving principles of that consciousness, then the subject of rational knowledge, consciousness, or Mind, is the unconditioned reality . . . Mind . . . is the subject and object of knowledge.' I follow, generally, Maier's interpretation of both Kant and Hegel. Maier's book, which is written from a Marxist perspective, deserves to be more widely known.

[34] Norman, Richard, *op. cit.,* p. 111.

[35] *Ibid,* pp. 112-113.

[36] *Ibid,* p. 115.

[37] Both of these passages are mentioned, and the problem of intellectual intuition discussed, in Stanley Rosen, *G. W. F. Hegel: An Introduction to the Science of Wisdom,* Yale University Press, New Haven, 1974. See also G. R. G. Mure, *An Introduction to Hegel,* Oxford University Press, Oxford, 1970, especially chapter X.

[38] Hegel, G. W. F., *Werke,* ed. H. G. Glockner, Stuttgart, 1927-1939, Vol. I, pp. 143-144. Quoted in Copleston, *op. cit.,* p. 167.

[39] *Science of Logic,* I, pp. 89-90 for this and following quotations.

[40] *The Phenomenology of Mind,* pp. 80-81 for this and above quotes.

[41] *The Science of Logic,* I, pp. 54-55.

[42] In chapter I, I carefully distinguished materialism and realism in order to distinguish in Kant the problems of the noumena and the matter or content of experience or knowledge. In chapter III I shall collapse that distinction. In the meantime, in my discussion of Feuerbach, I will take the liberty of using 'materialism' and 'realism' interchangeably, since the raison d'être for which the distinction was introduced in discussing Kant no longer exists in dealing with Feuerbach. Feuerbach is both a materialist and hence a realist; the distinction is one Feuerbach would not have drawn, nor one that we need to draw for him in understanding his philosophy. Indeed, he calls his philosophy 'materialism', 'sensualism', and 'realism' indifferently.

[43] For a discussion of this and related matters see Sidney Hook, *From Hegel to Marx*, University of Michigan Press, Ann Arbor, 1962, Chapter 7.

[44] Feuerbach, Ludwig, 'Preface to the Second Edition', *The Essence of Christianity*, Frederick Ungar Publishing Co., New York, 1957, p. 2.

[45] Kamenka, Eugene, *The Philosophy of Ludwig Feuerbach*, Routledge & Kegan Paul, London, 1970, p. 103. As an example of his insistence on the duality of subject and object, and of the epistemological implications this has for Feuerbach, consider this criticism of Hegel: 'This unity of subject and object is a principle which is as unfruitful as it is pernicious for philosophy, especially because it overrides the distinction between the subjective and the objective, and frustrates any attempt to deal with . . . the problem of truth.' *Sämtliche Werke*, 1st edition, Band II, p. 195.

[46] Feuerbach, Ludwig, *Sämtliche Werke*, 1st edition, Band 2, ed. W. Bolin and F. Jodl, 10 volumes, Frommans Verlag, Stuttgart, 1903-1911, p. 214. Quoted in Hook, *op. cit.*, p. 230.

[47] Feuerbach, Ludwig, *Kleine Philosophische Schriften, 1842-45*, ed. M. G. Lange, Leipzig, 1950, p. 99.

[48] Feuerbach, Ludwig, *Sämtliche Werke*, Stuttgart, 1903-1911, Band VII, p. 516; quoted in Lenin, *Materialism and Empirio-Criticism*, Progress Publishers, Moscow, p. 150.

[49] Feuerbach, Ludwig, *Principles of the Philosophy of the Future*, The Bobbs-Merrill Company, Indianapolis, 1966, Translated by Manfred H. Vogel, p. 35.

[50] *Ibid*, p. 38.

[51] *Klein Philosophische Schriften*, p. 72.

[52] *Principles of the Philosophy of the Future*, p. 28.

[53] *Sämtliche Werke*, 1st edition, Band 2, p. 334.

[54] *Principles of the Philosophy of the Future*, p. 28.

[55] 'Preface to the Second Edition', *The Essence of Christianity*, p. 2.

[56] *Principles of the Philosophy of the Future*, p. 15. Feuerbach's argument, with which I am in agreement, is that 'the Hegelian philosophy can therefore be derived from Kantian and Fichtean idealism'. The salient feature of Kant's philosophy is that 'the subject which has no longer an object apart from itself and consequently is no longer limited . . . is the absolute being whose theological or popular expression is the word "God"' (pp. 34-35). On the other hand Feuerbach appreciated that Kant, unlike Hegel, retained in his philosophy an 'external', other element: 'But Kant's idealism is still a limited idealism—idealism based on the viewpoint of empiricism' (p. 28).

[57] *Sämtliche Werke*, Band 2, pp. 322-323.

CHAPTER III

MARX AND MATERIALISM

We have now traced the fate of 'Kant's problem' through its treatment by Hegel and Feuerbach. Essentially, the dilemma in Kant arises by trying to wed an idealist theory of knowledge to a realist ontology. We have seen how Hegel's response to that problem was the adoption of an idealist ontology, in order to suit the theory of knowledge. That is, the independence claim was dropped for the sake of the interpretation claim. Conversely, Feuerbach's reply was in favour of the retention of the realist ontology. For Feuerbach, the essential independence of nature is retained at the expense of the interpretation claim.

The stage is now set for Marx, for it must be remembered that it was upon the philosophical stage for which such problems formed the script that Marx began his intellectual life, and it is with such problems in mind that one can begin to understand the point of much that he says. The purpose of this chapter is two-fold. First, I want to show how Marx, following Feuerbach, worked within the assumptions of a realist or materialist ontology. Second, I want to discuss and criticise some of the large number of Marxists or Marx scholars who have disputed this point. It may come to many as something of a surprise that this point is disputed, since 'Marxism' and 'materialism' have become so commonly identified. But the materialism of Marx has been disputed: Marx 'himself never was a materialist'.[1] Naturally, some of this controversy is attributable to different senses of 'materialism' not being distinguished. But it will be recalled that the materialism which we have been discussing, and which I attribute to Marx, is not the 'strong' doctrine of reductive materialism, but only the weaker doctrine that something exists independently of thought (and mind). What is perhaps surprising is that some have even denied that Marx held materialism in this last sense. For example, Bertell Ollman, in his recent book *Alienation,* claims that Marx, following Hegel, Spinoza, and others, subscribes to a philosophy of internal relations, so that nothing is logically independent of anything else. Hence, it follows that 'if nature and society are internally related . . . an examination of any aspect of either involves one immediately with aspects of the other. The priority suggested above cannot exist if the parts are not logically independent.'[2] In our statement of materialism, or object independence, we were interested in essential independence, not the absurd notion of the causal independence of the world, with which it is sometimes conflated by those writing on Marxism. But this is just what Ollman's philosophy of internal relations seeks to deny, for according to it nature and society, or nature and thought, are *essentially related,* internally related. Hence, according to Ollman, Marx is not a materialist even in my sense. My purpose in this chapter will be to vindicate the claim that Marx is a materialist.

I do not claim that, in Marx, one also finds a well-developed theory of knowledge as such. There are occasional remarks and suggestions. Marx, for example, says in *Capital* Vol. I that, for him, unlike for Hegel, the ideal is 'nothing else than the material world reflected by the human mind, and translated into forms of thought',[3] and in his doctoral dissertation, 'On The Difference Between the Democritean and Epicurean Philosophy of Nature', there are some approving remarks about Epicurus who held that 'the concept depends on the sensuous perceptions', that 'the phenomenal world (is) real', and so on.[4] These phrases and remarks, snatched as they are from writings which are separated by a period of some twenty-five years or more, hardly constitute a theory of knowledge. But my strategy should be clear: if we are forced to admit that Marx's ontological position is materialist, then for the sake of epistemological consistency, Marxists must adopt a realist 'reflection' or correspondence theory of knowledge as well. For a development of that materialist theory of knowledge we shall have to wait for Chapters IV and V, and a discussion of Lenin's *Materialism and Empirio-Criticism* in chapter VI.

I distinguished materialism and realism in the first chapter, the former being a species of the latter. For the materialist, the object exists independently not only of thought but also of mind. The distinction was made to accommodate Kant's philosophy, as I understood it. But the distinction has already outlived its usefulness, as we noted when we came to discuss Feuerbach. Now that we are dealing with Marx I think it is time to explicitly collapse the distinction altogether. Indeed, unlike the classical German philosophers, Marx does not usually discuss 'thought' or 'mind' as such, but 'thinking human beings'. 'Real, active men' is his primary category, from which 'thought' or 'mind' are only abstractions. Thus, he says in *The German Ideology:* 'Men are the producers of their conceptions, ideas, etc.—real active men . . .', and 'The premises from which we begin are not arbitrary ones . . . but real premises from which abstraction can only be made in the imagination. They are the real individuals, their activity, and the material conditions under which they live . . .'[5] As we shall see, in criticising Hegel, Marx does speak explicitly of the independence of objects from thought. But he also speaks interchangeably of the independence of objects from subjects—from men—and this is because, for him, the person or subject rather than thought or mind is the basic category with which one begins, and what is essentially independent from subjects is going to turn out to be independent of thought, or mental activity, *and* mind. These formulations from *The German Ideology,* in which Marx and Engels were 'to settle accounts with our erstwhile philosophical conscience', do not have, to be sure, an explicit class orientation. These formulations speak of 'man', rather than in class terms. But this does not affect the point I wish to make; for Marx, from his earliest writings, what is rejected is the classical philosophical point of view, dictated by epistemological considerations, that takes mind or thought or even knowing subject as the primary epistemological category. For Marx, 'real, active men' plays that role. Marx criticises Hegel for this reification of thought from the human subject: '(Why Hegel separates thought from the subject we shall see later: at this stage it is already clear, however, that when man is not, his characteristic expression also cannot be human, and so neither could thought be grasped as an expression of man as a human and material subject endowed with eyes, ears, etc., and living in society, in the world, and in nature)'.[6]

Because of Marx's perspective, we can change the terms in which we discuss materialism or realism. Since for Marx 'person' or 'man' rather than 'thought' is the important, primary category, we can say that realism asserts the essential independence of nature from real, active men, from the activity of real individuals. Thus, Marxian realism (or materialism— I henceforth use these interchangeably) is the belief in an objective realm outside thought or mind *in the widest sense*. What is this 'widest sense'? An object which is mind-dependent need not exist 'in' the mind, in the sense in which the classical empiricists would give to that locution. Mind-dependence need not hold that reality is reducible to mental experiences. Rather, mind-dependence might be attributed to an object insofar as the existence of that object implies the existence of 'mind', by which we now mean recognisably human activity of any sort with its characteristic intentional and purposive features. As an example of such an object, think of a painting. Although paintings do not exist 'in' the mind of the subject, they are not mind-independent either, in the sense we are now giving to that expression. If there were no minds, no purposive, intentional activity on the part of men, there could be no paintings. Paintings must be painted, and painting is a purposive, human activity. If a canvas is laid outdoors and, from the action of wind, rain, etc., comes to have some sort of 'design' on it, we still do not have a painting, but rather an unusual natural object, such as a piece of driftwood thrown up by the sea and placed on display for its natural beauty. Driftwood, and natural 'paintings' are not artefacts. Paintings are the result of praxis or human labour, and praxis indicates the presence of mind. A mind is manifested by purposive activity, and Marx took purposive activity as an indication of that which is special about men:

A spider conducts operations that resemble those of a weaver, and a bee puts to shame an architect in the construction of her cells. But what distinguishes the worst architect from the best of bees is this, that the architect raises his structure in imagination before he erects it in reality. At the end of every labour-process, we get a result that already existed in the imagination of the labourer at its commencement . . . he also realises a purpose of his own that gives the law to his *modus operandi,* and to which he must subordinate his will.[7]

Paintings, as one sort of cultural object, could no more exist independently of mind than could culture itself. All products of human praxis, or labour, are mind-dependent in the sense I am now giving to that expression, for all such products of labour imply, as Marx says, the existence of purpose human activity. In that sense the social realm is a realm of mind-dependence. Without human activity, no social creations—the state, the economy, the family, science—would exist. Indeed, to think otherwise, to 'naturalise' them, to treat them as natural objects rather than as *social* relations, is precisely what Marx meant by 'fetishism'.[8] We shall, henceforward, use 'materialism' and 'realism' as interchangeable names for that philosophy which holds that there is a natural realm, i.e. *some* objects essentially independent of all human activity, whether that activity is thinking, any other variety of mental activity, or the activity of producing use-values for meeting human needs.

As I shall make abundantly clear in what follows, I do not in the least assert that the 'matter' or 'stuff' from which paintings are created is equally mind-dependent. Paintings, or science, or the state, are always materialised things, practices, or institutions. What they are 'materialised in' is not mind-dependent. It is a peculiarity of my terminology that science and the state are not conceived as 'realistic' or 'material', because their existence is essentially connected with the existence of man. We can, if we wish, avoid this peculiarity by including as 'real' or 'material' anything whose existence does not imply the existence of man (like the natural world) or anything which is materialised in something whose existence does not imply man's existence. But nothing, I think, rests on this decision. Feuerbach himself accepts this usage, which implies that realism is not true of the social world. He argues that: '. . . However, this object, *viz;* man, is the only object in which, according to the statement of the idealists themselves, the requirement of the 'identity of object and subject is realised . . .' (*Werke,* p. 518), but this point is, as I have said, only a matter of terminological choice. The important point is that social things, or things under social descriptions, are essentially dependent on man and human activity.

Lenin, in the definition of materialism which we approvingly quoted in the Introduction, does go on to say that: 'Historical materialism recognises that social being is independent of the social consciousness of man'. In the sense of 'independent' we have been employing, this would be a mistake. Like Lenin, we uphold the essential independence of the natural order. But that which is *not* essentially independent of man is precisely social being. Now, it may well be that, when Lenin speaks of social things being independent of mind, he means to deny that they are *in* the mind in what I called 'the narrow sense', the sense in which a phenomenalist could say that they were mentalistic, constructs out of the data of sense. Lenin's attacks are directed at Hume and Berkeley, among others, and it is this sense of 'independence' he may have had in mind when he claimed that social things are independent of man's consciousness. The only point I wish to make is that such things are not independent of man's consciousness in the 'wider sense' of independence I have been using, for their existence *implies* the existence of man.

There is, then, for the realist, no essential dependency of the natural world on that which is human. Unlike paintings and other 'social' or 'cultural' objects, there are for realism natural objects which do not evince the same mind-dependency that the former do. Not everything is mind-independent in this wide sense, but realism asserts that at least something is, and we can usefully refer to whatever is mind-independent as 'nature' or 'natural objects'. In the next two chapters I hope to develop, explain and defend the materialist position, the assertion of the existence of natural, mind-independent objects. In this chapter my task will be to try and show that Marx was a materialist in the sense that I have indicated.

Was Marx a materialist in this sense? It is within the framework of this question that we can begin to come to terms with a view about Marx that one often finds in the literature. First, a distinction is drawn between historical materialism and philosophical materialism. Plekhanov, in *Fundamental Problems of Marxism,* drew a useful distinction between historical materialism, a theory about the explanation of historical change by reference to social forces rather than ideas, God, or whatever, and philosophical materialism, a philosophical and ontological thesis about the nature and constituency of reality. But, whereas Plekhanov treats these two aspects of Marx's thought as inseparable, others have wanted to separate them. Marx himself, it is said, was a historical materialist. It was left to others, namely Engels and Lenin, to foist upon Marxism the philosophical theses of materialism, with which, it is said, Marx's own thought is inconsistent. Indeed, this view continues, far from being inseparably linked as Plekhanov thought, historical and philosophical materialism are actually inconsistent. If Marx's historical materialism holds that 'the premisses from which we begin are not . . . dogmas . . . but real premisses from which abstraction can only be made in the imagination. They are the real individuals, their activity and the material conditions under which they live', then to take as basic to one's understanding of the world matter, or even nature, which treat reality at a different level of abstraction than the level of real individuals' and their activity, seems methodologically inconsistent with historical materialism as Marx understands it. It is Engels, rather than Marx, who provides us with the full statement of philosophical materialism. Engels claims that he read the whole of *Anti-Dühring* to Marx before publishing it. Perhaps Marx was unaware of the inconsistency of his and Engels' views, the argument may run, or although he was aware of the inconsistency between a philosophy that took man as basic and a philosophy that took matter or nature as basic, he was too sick, too busy, or too tactful to mention it. In the course of this chapter we shall want to see what sort of plausibility such a view has, if any, and if it has none, on what sort of mistaken assumptions it rests.

In our discussion of Kant and Hegel, we have already distinguished the essential dependency (of the object on thought) claim and the creation (of the object by thought) claim. It is Hegel, in a way characteristic of much of post-Kantian German philosophy, who espouses a creation claim, and it was this which lead Feuerbach and Marx to see in the Hegelian philosophy a cloak for theology, and especially for the myth of divine creation. The creation claim is obviously the stronger of the two, for an object could be essentially dependent on thought without being itself created by thought, as we saw in the case of Kant's 'matter' of experience. On the other hand, in the Hegelian sense of creation, to which we have already alluded, creation implies essential dependence of the created on the creator, because in creation something creates further developments of itself. Hence, because the latter stages in the development of something *presuppose* the former stages, creation implies dependence. Marx himself marks the fact that creation presupposes dependence: 'A being only considers himself independent when he stands on his own feet, and he only stands on his own feet when he owes his existence to himself. A man who lives by the grace of another regards himself as a dependent being. But I live completely by the grace of another if I owe him not only the sustenance of my life, but if he has, moreover, *created* my life—if he is the *source* of my life; and if it is not of my own creation, my life has necessarily a source of this kind outside it'.[9] Thus as Hegel and Marx would understand it, creation implies dependence but, presumably, not conversely. It is for that reason I have said that creation is the stronger notion of the two.

Marx denies both the creation of anything by thought, and the essential dependence of natural objects on thought. It is important to see which passages in Marx deny which claim. Let us take the stronger, creation claim first: Marx's denial of the creation of anything by thought comes, primarily, in his *Critique of Hegel's 'Philosophy of Right'*.[10] Marx's method in *The Critique,* borrowed from Feuerbach, is itself evidence for the denial of the creation claim. Essential to the transformative method, whether used by Feuerbach or Marx, is the idea that Hegelianism inverted the relation between thought and object, between conception and reality. The transformative method was itself a critique of this inversion, a transformation of Hegelian Subject to predicate and Hegelian Predicate to subject. For Marx, Hegelian Philosophy had erred, for 'the Idea is given the status of subject . . . the real subjects—civil society, family, circumstances, caprice, etc.—become unreal, and take on a different meaning of objective moments of the Idea' (p. 8). For Hegel, they merely acquire 'the meaning of a determination of the Idea, result and product of the Idea'. Family and civil society 'according to Hegel, (are) made by the actual Idea . . . they are precisely the finiteness of this Idea; they owe their existence to a mind other than their own; they are determinations established by a third . . . for that very reason they are also determined as . . . the proper finiteness of the "actual Idea". . .' (p. 9). According to Idealism reality is a creation of thought: 'Speculative philosophy expresses this fact [viz, the state issuing from family and civil society] as an achievement of the Idea . . . the deed of an Idea—Subject . . .' Marx takes this creation in its explicitly theological sense: 'The soul of objects, in this case that of the state, is complete and predestined before its body, which is, properly speaking mere appearance. The concept is the Son within the

"Idea", within God the Father, the *Agens*, the determining, differentiating principle. Here "Idea" and "Concept" are abstractions rendered independent' (p. 15). Finally, and perhaps most unambiguously:

In truth, Hegel has done nothing but resolve the constitution of the state into the universal, abstract idea of the organism; but in appearance and in his own opinion he has developed the determinate reality out of the Universal Idea. He has made the subject of the idea into a product and predicate of the Idea. He does not develop his thought out of what is objective, but what is objective in accordance with a ready-made thought which has its origin in the abstract sphere of logic (p. 14).

In these passages, which are representative of the tone and theme of his *Critique of Hegel's 'Philosophy of Right'*, Marx denies the Hegelian creation claim. Objects are not 'result' or 'product' or 'issues' of Idea; nor is Idea a 'subject' with creative powers, the powers of praxis. Indeed just the opposite is the case, and that is the core of the transformative method's message.

The materialist theme is taken up again and repeated in *The Holy Family* in an amusing passage which occurs in the section entitled 'Das Geheimnis der spekulativen Konstruktion' and which parodies the Hegelian philosophy:

If from real apples, pears, strawberries, almonds I form the general notion fruit, and if I go further and *imagine* that my abstract notion, *the* fruit . . . exists as an independent essence of the pear, the apple etc., I declare therewith—speculatively expressed—*the* fruit to be the 'substance' of the pear, the apple, the almond, etc . . . I then, pronounce the apple, pear and almond to be merely existing modes of the fruit . . .

The speculation which out of different real fruits has produced as the fruit of its abstraction *the* fruit, must consequently . . . attempt to get back again . . . to the actual multiform, profane fruit, the pear, apple, almond, etc . . .

It arises, answers the speculative philosopher, because the fruit is not dead, undifferentiated, static essence but a living, self-differentiating dynamic essence . . . the different profane fruits are different life-forms of *one* fruit: they are crystallisations which the fruit itself builds. For example in the apple, *the* fruit give itself an 'appley', in the pear, a 'peary' existence . . . The fruit posits itself as apple, posits itself as pear, posits itself as almond . . .

The ordinary man feels that he is saying nothing extraordinary when he says that apples and pears exist. But the philosopher, when he expressed this existence in speculative fashion, feels that he has said something *extraordinary*. He has accomplished *a miracle*, he has produced from the unreal *conceptual* notion, the fruit, real, natural entities, apples, pears, etc . . . he has *created* these fruits out of his own abstract understanding . . . In recognising any existent thing, he imagines that he is completing a creative act.[11]

These passages show what never has, to the best of my knowledge, been disputed in any case, viz., that Marx denied the Hegelian doctrine which involved ascribing to thought the ability to create all of nature, every object, or even any object, out of itself. But what of the weaker, dependence claim? These passages do not seem to show that Marx rejected the essential dependency of nature on what is human. For that we must look elsewhere. In particular, the examples Marx uses in his denial of creation will not support a denial of dependence. This is because some of the examples are of 'cultural' or 'social' objects—the state, family, and private property. Even if thought does not *create* the state, or the family, it is clear that they, for their existence, are essentially dependent on human, purposeful activity. The state is not independent of the activity of real men. So Marx's examples, from *The Critique*, may deny the creation claim but do not themselves support the essential independence claim for natural objects.

Many, although not by any means all, of Marx's denials of the essential dependence of Nature on what is human, can be found in *The Economic and Philosophical Manuscripts of 1844*. This may be thought surprising since the *Manuscripts* have been used for 'proving' precisely the opposite point, as we shall see later in the chapter when we come to discuss Kolakowski. The lesson in this is, I think, that it is particularly important to interpret Marx's often aphoristic way of saying something by looking at the overall purpose of the passage from which the aphorism is taken. This is true of Feuerbach as well. We noted before how Feuerbach spoke of the identity of subject and object, which appears to contradict our interpretation of Feuerbach as a realist about objects, but remarked how this seemed to mean for him only 'the sensory contemplation of man by man', an innocuous claim for our interpretation. One can see the same retention of Hegelian jargon, but given new meaning, at work in *The Economic and Philosophical Manuscripts*. It is important not to be taken in by it, and above all else, not to base one's interpretation on the occurrence of the Hegelian jargon alone. For example, in *The Manuscripts* Marx says: 'Thinking and being are thus no doubt *distinct,* but at the same time they are in unity with each other'.[12] What does this do to our claim that Marx denied the dependence of natural being on thought? Absolutely nothing, as one can see when one looks carefully at the whole passage and sees that *all* Marx means by this bit of misleading Hegelian jargon is that through his self-consciousness man is aware of himself as social (hence, the 'being' side of the dichotomy) as well as individual (the 'thinking' aspect of the distinction). The Hegelianesque aphorism seems to serve only as a rather strange summary for the preceding paragraph: 'Man, much as he may therefore by a *particular* individual . . . is just as much the totality . . . the subjective existence of thought and experienced society present for itself . . .' The sort of point I am making here is, I believe, a general point which it is important to bear in mind in dealing with *The Economic and Philosophical Manuscripts*. We shall return to more of these sorts of passages when we come to discuss some of the influential misinterpretations of Marx later in this chapter.

The denial of the essential dependence of natural objects on thought occurs scattered throughout *The Manuscripts* and occasionally elsewhere, but primarily in the third 'manuscript', in the section which deals with Hegel's philosophy. The denials of dependence come either by way of explicit assertion of the essential independence of nature, or more often, by way of criticism of the Hegelian view of the essential dependence of nature on thought. I wish to quote and to remark on ten such passages. My own feeling is that a careful reading of *The Manuscripts* could not leave the reader in any doubt that Marx believed, *at least* very much more often than not, that nature existed essentially independently of all that is human. What is more likely is that the reader of *The Manuscripts* may feel that these passages contradict other things which Marx also occasionally says there which suggest essential dependence between Nature and society, or the human. My task will be now only to cite those passages which show Marx holding an independence claim, as he must do if he is to be counted a materialist. I reserve for my later discussion of Kolakowski the task of showing Marx's basic consistency, of showing how passages in Marx appear to argue for a dependency of nature on the human only when taken out of context. In context these passages in no way contradict an independence claim in the way they are often thought to do. Let us first, then, look at ten passages in which Marx says or implies that natural objects are essentially independent of the human:

(1) Man is directly a natural being. As a natural being and as a living natural being he is on the one hand furnished with natural powers of life—he is an *active* natural being. These forces exist in him as tendencies and abilities—as *impulses*. On the other hand, as a natural corporeal, sensuous, objective being he is a *suffering,* conditioned and limited creature, like animals and plants, That is to say, the *objects* of his impulses exist outside him, as *objects* independent of him; yet these objects are objects of his need . . .[13]

(2) To be objective, natural and sensuous, and at the same time to have object, nature and sense for a third party, is one and the same thing. Hunger is a natural need; it therefore needs a *nature* outside itself, an *object* outside itself, in order to satisfy itself . . .'[14]

'The objects of his impulse exist outside him', and 'Hunger . . . needs a *nature* outside itself'. Later we will see how the essential independence of nature is in no way compromised by the perfectly obvious point that natural objects can come to stand in contingent relations to the human, can become objects of man's hunger, objects of his impulses. If man ceased to exist, the natural world would not necessarily follow suit, and that surely is part of what Marx has in mind when he talks about natural objects being 'outside' man. Indeed, Marx says:

(3) . . . a being which does not have its nature outside itself is not a natural being and does not share in the being of nature.[15]

Not only are natural objects independent of what is human, but in (3) Marx tells us, in Hegelian jargon, that it is necessarily the case that men are in nature. Any being whose nature or *essence* isn't in things 'outside' itself couldn't be; the human is *essentially* dependent on nature.

(4) [In criticism of Hegel's dialectic] On the one hand this act of superseding is a transcending of the thought entity . . . and because thought imagines itself to be directly the other of itself, to be *sensuous reality* . . . this superceding in thought, which leaves its object standing in the real world, believes that it has really overcome it. On the other hand, because the object has now become for it a moment of thought, thought takes it in its reality to be self-confirmation of itself . . .[16]

In (4) Marx makes the same point by way of criticism of Hegelian philosophy. Hegel demotes the 'other' of thought into a moment of thought. In denying that reality is a 'moment' of thought I presume that Marx is saying that it is not in any essential way a thought-dependency. Whatever 'thought' may believe, it 'leaves its object standing in the real world'.

(5) The real subject still remains outside the mind, leading an independent existence.[17]

Marx, in this well-known passage, is speaking of 'the subject' in the sense of the subject of a scientific investigation. His point is that we should not confuse the *reality* of the subject with the methodological 'appropriation' of the subject which is accomplished by reproducing it conceptually from abstractions. The real subject leads an existence independently of the mind which appropriates it. Finally:

(6) The creation of the earth has received a mighty blow from *geogeny*—i. e. from the science which presents the formation of the earth, the coming-to-be of the earth, as a process, as self-generation. *Generatio aequivoca* is the only practical refutation of the theory of creation.[18]

What this shows is, I think, that Marx took creation to be *refuted* by science. Whether this is right or not Marx took this to be the case. Marx in general makes no sharp distinction between philosophy (or theology) and science. The tone set by Marx's insistence on the relevance of geology to the validity of the creation story would be difficult to reconcile with a denial of the independence of the natural world from the human. Marx understood that geogeny, as he called it, taught of a world which had long pre-existed the human, and since he considered the results of the sciences philosophically decisive ('the only practical refutation'), he cannot have thought that any essential dependency existed between nature and man. This impression is, I think, confirmed by a remark in *The German Ideology*:

(7) Of course, in all of this the priority of external nature remains unassailed . . . For that matter, nature, the nature that preceded human history, is not by any means the nature in which Feuerbach lives, it is nature which today no longer exists anywhere (except perhaps on a few Australian coral-islands of recent origin) and which, therefore, does not exist for Feuerbach.[19]

Thus, there is a 'nature that preceded human history', and it then follows that, however much man may transform nature ('it is nature which today no longer exists anywhere'), nature cannot be essentially dependent on the human. There is no doubt that for Marx there is no philosophy which deals in only 'conceptual truths' and which is thereby isolated from factual inquiry. Thus, for Marx, science could be *decisive* in refuting such things as idealism or theism. For him, geology would simply have refuted any denial of the independence of nature, just as 'geogeny' refuted the myth of creation.

In addition to the above quotation from *The German Ideology* there are at least three other places outside *The Economic and Philosophical Manuscripts* in which Marx makes the same point about the independence of nature. All three are concerned with the relationship between material nature and the work process:

(8) The material of nature alone, insofar as *no* human labour is embodied in it, insofar as it is mere material and exists independently of human labour, has no value, since value is only embodied labour . . .[20]

(9) Man has not created matter itself. And he cannot even create any productive capacity if the matter does not exist beforehand.[21]

In *Capital* Marx extends the remarks made in various writings, two of which I have just quoted, into the central feature of his analysis of value and the labour process. The function of human labour is to transform the form matter has, a matter which is itself not reducible to labour, praxis, human creation or transformation. There is both form and matter in any use-value, and the matter is a 'given':

(10) The use-values coat, linen, etc., in short the bodies of commodities, are combinations of two elements, material and labour. If we subtract the total sum of useful labour embodied in the coat, linen, etc., a material substratum is always left, which is furnished without the help of man.[22]

Both in *The Manuscripts*, and elsewhere, the theme of the essential independence of nature, or matter, is one that recurs often enough to be unmistakeable. In a moment, then, we will want to look at some misinterpretations of Marx which are mistaken on just this point, and try to see, if we can, where they have gone wrong. Before we go on to examine these misinterpretations I want to make three specific remarks about the essential independence of Nature from man. I will say more about this in Chapter IV, but I wish now to deal with three points which constantly surface in Marxist discussions of materialism.

If natural things can exist independently of thought, or Nature independently of man, does that commit us (or Marx) to accepting that thought (or society) can also exist independently of nature? We are obviously not committed to this by the independence claim, although sometimes Marxists have wrongly rejected the essential independence of nature from thought on the presumed grounds that such a 'dualism' would commit them to the converse essential independence of thought from nature. One would be committed to this if the 'dualism' of thought and object took the classical form that it does, for example, in Descartes' philosophy. Mind, whose essence is thought, and body, whose essence is extension, are essentially independent one from the other, according to the Cartesian philosophy. Thus it is perfectly possible for mind to exist without body, just as it is possible for body to exist without mind. Marx's materialism does not commit us to anything like this Cartesian dualism. Acceptance of the essential independence of Nature from the human, or of natural things from thought, simply does not imply the acceptance of the converse essential independence of thought or society from Nature, or natural things. It is perfectly consistent to hold that nature can exist independently of thought, or Nature independently of all which is human, and to deny on the other hand that thought can exist independently of all objects, or the subject independently of Nature. In quote (3) above, taken from *The Economic and Philosophical Manuscripts,* we saw how Marx claimed that a being had to have its nature (essence) in the natural world; that is, men had to be essentially dependent on nature. So clearly, for Marx, the essential independence runs in one direction only.

It may well be that this position should be called something other than 'dualist', in order to distinguish it from a classical ontological dualism like that of Descartes. But, by whatever name, this is certainly Marx's position: '. . . the young Hegelians consider conception, thoughts, ideas, in fact all the products of consciousness to which they attribute an independent existence . . .';[23] 'Consciousness can never be anything else than conscious existence';[24] 'The phantoms formed in the human brain are also necessarily sublimates of their material life-process . . . (Ideology and their corresponding forms of consciousness) no longer retain the semblance of independence';[25] and finally, in Capital, Volume I, 'For Hegel the process of thinking, which under the name of Idea, he even transforms into an independent subject, is the demiurgos of the real world, while the real world is only its external appearance. With me, on the other hand, the ideal is nothing else than the material world reflected by the human mind, and translated into forms of thought.'[26] What we find then, in Marx, is a perfectly consistent assertion of the essential dependence of thought, the Subject, on Nature. In short, for Marx, as we all know, there can be a nature without consciousness but no consciousness without Nature. 'Form', says Marx, 'has no validity except as the form of its content'. As there can be no form without content for it to be the form of, so there can be no thought in general without a material world in which it is embodied. The essential independence of nature from thought, the human, does not imply the converse essential independence of thought in general from nature.

Finally, it is worthwhile noting, which is anyway obvious, that we must distinguish between the general fact that there is thought, or recognisable human activity of *any* sort, and particular thoughts. If we follow Marx and hold that thought in general is not essentially independent of nature, we still allow that any particular thought is essentially independent of that of which it is the thought. Between a particular thought and its object the essential independence is two way. There could be stones and stars with no sentient creatures to form the concepts 'stone' and 'star', and there can be concepts like 'witch' and 'unicorn' with no objects or instances. Indeed, this is obviously something any correspondence theory must hold, for correspondence is a contingent relation. If concepts and objects or statements and states of affairs match, if our beliefs do successfully reflect reality, this must be so contingently. It could have been otherwise. Marx's position, then, is this: nature is essentially independent of thought, but thought is not essentially independent of nature. Particular thoughts are essentially independent of any paticular part of nature, and conversely.

The second point I wish now to mention concerning the notion of essential independence is this. Sometimes, when one advances the idea that nature or natural things can exist independently of thought, or the human, the question is raised whether or not thought, or human praxis, isn't also part of nature. Do we deny that it is? And if thought isn't part of nature, to what sort of supernatural existence do we wish to consign it? Of course, we are not denying that the human, that thought or praxis, are also part of the natural order. When Marx says that thought essentially depends on nature, he is asserting that thought is part of the overall system of nature. We might put our point this way. What materialism asserts is that there could be, indeed that there was in fact, a system of nature long before it came to have a particular feature or part, thought or human existence, a part which it does now in fact have.

Karl Korsch seems, in his *Marxism and Philosophy,* to raise just this sort of accusation against what he calls 'vulgar socialism', those who 'separate' thought and being. He criticises any form of Marxism which attempts to 'draw a sharp line of division between consciousness and its object' and to 'treat consciousness as something given, something fundamentally contrasted to Being and Nature'. Korsch says that such views contain 'a primitive, predialectical and even pre-transcendental conception of the relation between consciousness and being'.[27] But to what sort of 'sharp line of division' or 'fundamental contrast' are we committed? We are certainly not, *pace* Korsch, committed to the thesis that thought and nature are somehow ontologically different, that the difference between them is one of a Cartesian-like irreducible ontological difference. Ontologically, thought too is a part of nature, and this is why we said that thought too is part of the overall system of nature. All any reflection theory need assume, against which Korsch argues,[28] is that the relation between particular thoughts and that which they are about is a contingent relation in both directions, but this certainly does not commit us to a 'sharp line of division' between thought and nature in some ontological sense. To think otherwise would be to conflate the epistemological requirement of two-way contingency between a particular thought and its object with an ontological distinction between thought (in general) and nature. Indeed, if one makes an *ontological* distinction between thought and being, then each of the pair would have to be essentially independent of the other, as Descartes for example would claim. The essence of thought and being would be different. But Marx argues for a contingent relation in one direction, between being and thought, but an essential relation in the other. Thus, although the 'essence' of being does not include thought, the essence of 'thought' includes being. The distinction between them cannot be ontological—they cannot constitute *two* separate kinds of things, since thought is *not* essentially independent of being. Because, in classical philosophy, the criterion for something's being *a thing* is its logical independence of everything else, for us the essential dependence of mind or consciousness on nature prevents them from constituting an ontological duality. This is why the whole-part metaphor seems to us more accurate, in the sense that parts cannot *be* what they are apart from the totality in which they are situated. Our epistemological distinction between thought and reality does not commit us, then, to an ontological dualism.

The third point I wish to raise concerns the meaning of 'can exist independently of' or 'is in essential relation to'. I have said little about this except to say, in the chapter on Kant, that it is essential and not causal independence in which we are interested. There is obviously a causal relationship between nature and society, and the essential independence of nature claim never for a moment was intended to deny something so obvious as that. The independence of nature was, we said, its *essential* independence only, in the sense that it could exist even if society or thought or concept or knower or the human did not. Korsch speaks of 'the coincidence of consciousness and reality'[29] without giving any explanation of what he understands by that expression. If this means only that nature and thought, or reality and consciousness, mutually interact, effect one another, it is unobjectionable. If, on the other hand, it means that nature is not even essentially independent of consciousness, then we reject any such absurd conception.

Now, nothing could just exist indeterminately, with no specific properties or features whatever. Thus, what the essential independence of nature must claim is that the existence of nature and *some* of its properties are independent of praxis. I call such properties which, along with existence, are essentially independent of all that is human, natural properties. Many features in nature are introduced by men's activity, which transforms changes, refashions nature. To use Hegelian jargon, nature is not 'unmediated'. It comes to have cultivated cherry trees growing in places where they did not grow before, and that this is so is praxis-dependent. But nature also has natural properties which are praxis-independent. That water has a particular molecular structure, that an atom of gold has a certain subatomic structure, that there is a particular genetic code involved in biological reproduction, that light travels at particular speeds in certain particular circumstances, these are praxis-independent facts about water, gold, organisms and light. Even some natural properties can sometimes be changed by praxis, but whether they can or cannot be subsequently altered, there are at least initially some natural properties of things which are independent of what man does. Of course, he must usually *do* something in order to learn that such things do have the natural properties they in fact possess, but that they have such natural properties is entirely unrelated to his doings. Marx, in the *Grundrisse,* marks the distinction between natural and praxis-dependent properties by speaking of intrinsic and accidental form. He distinguishes wood having the form of a tree and having the form of a table in the following way:

No immanent law of reproduction maintains this form in the way in which the tree, for example, maintains its form as a tree (wood maintains itself in the specific form of the tree because this form is the form of the wood; while the form of the table is accidental for wood, and not the intrinsic form of its substance).[30]

Thus, some of nature's properties, the non-natural ones, like that bit of wood having been worked up into a chair, are praxis-dependent, or 'accidental' to the wood, as Marx says; others which Marx calls 'intrinsic' to the wood, will not be dependent on praxis. One cannot insist upon this too strongly, because Marxists have often assumed that if the essential independence of nature be admitted, one will encounter difficulty in explaining how human praxis can come to change nature. Just this appears to be Korsch's mistaken worry, for he asserts that 'those Marxist theoreticians for whom Marxism was no longer essentially a theory of social revolution could see no need for the dialectical conception of the coincidence of consciousness and reality'. For them, 'a critique of political economy could never have become the major component of a theory of social revolution'.[31] What Korsch apparently assumes is that the essential independence of nature and its natural properties from man leads to the incomprehension of change. But this is clearly an illusion. That some of the properties of things have not been introduced by human praxis does not imply that none have. Moreover, many of the natural properties of nature are themselves susceptible of being changed. Barren soil can become fruitful through irrigation, mountain roads can be built by cutting into the existing rock. So there really seems not the slightest difficulty whatever in giving the notion of change (and revolution) a place just because the 'coincidence' of nature and human activity is denied.

Indeed, to understand precisely why the essential independence (of nature from praxis) claim *is* compatible with the idea that many of the features of reality are dependent on the formative, shaping activities of man is precisely to understand Marx's critique of Feuerbach. I do not propose to describe the shifts and changes in Marx's materialism, and in his attitude to Feuerbach, which there undoubtedly were, or to explain why, from being a hostile critic of a doctrine that he calls 'materialism' (in *The Critique of Hegel's Philosophy of Right*) and an exponent of naturalism and humanism (in *The Economic and Philosophical Manuscripts of 1844*), Marx becomes an exponent of what he himself calls a *materialist* conception of history. But I do wish, however, to say something about the nature of Marx's criticisms of Feuerbach, especially in the famous eleven theses, the 'Theses on Feuerbach', which he wrote in 1845.

The themes of activity and contemplation in one way or another run through all eleven theses. The first is perhaps the fullest expression of Marx's point, and is worth reproducing in full:

The chief defect of all hitherto existing materialism (that of Feuerbach included) is that the thing, reality, sensuousness, is conceived only in the form of the *object or of contemplation,* but not as *sensuous human activity, practice,* nor subjectively. Hence, in contradistinction to materialism, the *active* side was developed abstractly by idealism—which of course, does not know real sensuous activity as such. Feuerbach wants sensuous objects, really distinct from the thought objects, but he does not conceive human activity itself as *objective* activity. Hence, in *Das Wesen des Christenthums,* he regards the theoretical attitude as the only genuinely human attitude, while practice is conceived and fixed only in its dirty—judaical manifestation. Hence, he does not grasp the significance of 'revolutionary', or 'practical-critical' activity.

This thesis is compatible with my interpretation of Marx, and hence tends to confirm the ascription of materialism, the essential independence of nature from thought, to Marx. Marx says that hitherto reality was conceived by materialists only as *the object,* to be contemplated. Marx is critical of this not because it is untrue, but because it is only half of the truth. Indeed, it seems clear that in this thesis Marx sees himself as supplementing Feuerbach rather than emending or altering him. Marx says: '. . . Feuerbach wants sensuous objects, really distinct from the thought of objects . . .' There is no suggestion in this, or anywhere else in Marx's writings that I know of, that Marx rejected Feuerbach's idea of 'sensuous objects really distinct from the thought of objects'. Indeed, notwithstanding the directly contrary interpretation which they have often been given, the 'Theses' seem to me to provide further evidence of Marx's adherence to a version of philosophical materialism. What is the other half of the truth which Marx's materialism wants to preserve? That '. . . human activity itself as objective activity . . .' is activity which can transform, change the character of the natural realm. 'The philosophers have only interpreted the world in various ways; the point is to change it.' A materialism which recognises that there is a natural realm, with a given structure, essentially independent of human thought, a given structure which circumscribes and places limits on the ways in which men can transform objects, can introduce new properties or forms, is a materialism that can embrace both the moments of object and objective activity. Marx's stress on '*objective* activity' itself reinforces what I have been claiming. What is *objective* activity, if not a human praxis that recognises the nature and constraints of an objectively given natural order, which seeks to impress new forms on such a natural order?

Labour is not only consumed but also at the same time fixed, converted from the form of activity into the form of the object; materialised; as a modification of the object, it modifies its own form and changes from activity to being. The end of the process is the product.[32]

This is only the materialism for which we have been arguing throughout.

I think that Plekhanov was right to have suggested that 'If Marx began to elaborate his materialist explanation of history, by criticising Hegel's philosophy of Right, he could do so only because Feuerbach had completed his criticism of Hegel's speculative philosophy.'[33] That is, Marx took Feuerbach's rejection of Hegelian philosophical idealism as given, and was more concerned to build on what Feuerbach had already done, more concerned with doing what Feuerbach had not himself done—to add to Feuerbach's materialism those insights about activity which all materialism previously to Marx had (as Marx claimed) omitted. But to do that was in no way to compromise those real insights of Feuerbach about the existence of nature independently of thought. Marx *adds* the insight that those natural objects, whose existence is not essentially related to what is human, become, or can become, mediated by human activity. In such cases the forms that such objects assume are related to what is human. To say, 'the existence of natural objects essentially independent of praxis' is not to imply that such objects must, somehow, always remain untouched by human minds and hands. Even when they are so touched their existence is still not essentially dependent on their being so touched. We do not bring the natural world into being, as if we were so many gods. It is in the spirit of this interpretation that we can understand many of Marx's remarks. For example, Marx says in the Introduction to *The Grundrisse*,

The concrete subject remains outside the intellect and independent of it, that is, so long as the intellect adopts a purely speculative, purely theoretical attitude.[34]

As long as man does nothing to the natural order it is *only* an order which stands in essential independence of him. None of its properties are yet praxis-dependent. When man adopts a practical attitude to the world, when he does something, the world comes to have shapes, forms which are not independent of 'the intellect', even if the natural world remains itself essentially independent of him.

It is obvious, then, what I think we should say about the charge of incompatibility between historical and philosophical materialism. All turns on what one means by 'philosophical materialism'. But if we do not mean any sort of reductive materialism, in which the whole of the social realm is reducible in principle to matter in motion, then I cannot see that any question of incompatibility could arise. Philosophical materialism asserts the real existence of nature essentially independent of human activity. It certainly need not deny that, in any social-historical accounts, 'the premises from which we begin are ... the real individuals, their activity, and the material conditions under which they live ...' We can refer to the ways in which the natural order constrains and limits men's activity, and this is licensed by Marx's inclusion of 'the material conditions under which they live'. But we would have to do far more than that to produce a 'materialism' incompatible with Marx's historical method. If, in some reductive spirit, we were to replace 'the real individuals' and 'their activity' with other premises concerning the physical composition of the matter which composes them, and then try to infer all of their individual and historical doings from those replacement premises, much as Hobbes imagined we might be able to do, then that reductive materialism would be incompatible with Marx's historical materialism, which insists that we *begin* with *real individuals* in any historical account. It is, however, no such reductive materialism which we are espousing and once this is understood, I think the charge of incompatibility between historical and philosophical materialism, as I understand that latter doctrine, will lose whatever plausibility it may once have had.

Marx's position seems so clearly enunciated, and so obviously true, the reader may wonder why I have taken so much care, and gone to such lengths, to set it out. What I have said so far may seem so evident as to be uncontroversial. Amazingly, this is not so. I will look at three of Marx's interpreters, Georg Lukacs, Alfred Schmidt and Leszek Kolakowski, and show how they misinterpret Marx, or say things which suggest a misunderstanding of precisely this point. Many other interpretations could have been chosen, with equal justification, to make exactly the same point. I think the explanation for this is a failure on the part of these interpreters to free their thought entirely from idealist modes of thinking. However much they would reject the ascription, all I think remain to some degree trapped within an idealist framework, either in the actual content of their ideas, or in the terminology they use, into the straightjacket of which their ideas are then pushed.

It is especially worth noting Lukacs' evasions on the problem of Marx's materialism, for he was certainly one of the ablest and most sensitive interpreters of Marx's thought. Critical discussions of Lukacs have often alluded to idealist tendencies within his *History and Class Consciousness,* and such discussion has dealt with Lukacs' conception of praxis in particular in some detail. Lukacs himself says in the 1967 Preface to the English edition, 'that *History and Class Consciousness* was based on mistaken assumptions'.[35] We can see, I think, that these mistaken assumptions are more basic than his conception of praxis; indeed, these mistaken assumptions are concerned with the very nature of Marx's ontology and epistemology.

Lukacs, as is well known, set out to discuss the various forms that reification assumes in a society whose dominant mode of production is commodity production. The first part of 'Reification and the Consciousness of the Proletariat' discusses the philosophical history of the antinomies of bourgeois thought. Lukacs' discussion centres around the same group of problems that we have been discussing—how to reconcile thought and object, form and content, system and fact—for these are, for him, the antinomies of bourgeois thought, intellectual expressions of reification.

For Lukacs the inability of classical philosophy to accomplish this reconciliation is to be traced to its uncomprisingly theoretical, contemplative stance toward such problems. 'Classical philosophy did, it is true, take all the antinomies of its life—basis to the furthest extreme it was capable of *in thought* [my emphasis]; it conferred on them the highest possible intellectual expression. But even for this philosophy they remained unsolved and insoluble'.[36] Lukacs characterises the central antinomy of bourgeois thought in several ways: thought and object, subject and object, form and content or matter, system and fact. For Lukacs, these antinomies are the by-product of a contemplative, wholly theoretical attitude, and it is for that reason that they remained unsoluble for classical philosophy. It was left for Marx, and the 'philosophy' of praxis that is itself a praxis, to transcend these dualities, these antinomies: '. . . it is not enough that the attempt should be made to transcend the contemplative attutide. When the question is formulated more concretely it turns out that the essence of praxis consists in annulling *that indifference of form towards content* that we found in the problem of the thing-in-itself.'[37] '. . . we can now understand the connection between the two attitudes and see how, with the aid of the principle of praxis the attempt could be made to resolve the antinomies of contemplation.'[38]

Much of what Lukacs says in the essay seems eminently right. But agreement with some of the things Lukacs says about some of the antinomies certainly need not commit us to agreeing with what he says about all the antinomies. Lukacs' stress on totality, as against the atomicity or facticity of an empiricist approach, his description of reality as process and tendency rather than a world of rigid and frozen objects (although why a reflection theory should find the view of reality as process uncongenial is never explained: 'But if there are no things, what is "reflected" in thought?' (p. 200) The right answer to this rhetorical question should be: process and tendency!), all of this is certainly to be welcomed by any Marxist.

Similarly valuable is much of what Lukacs says about the subject-object antinomy. Lukacs often makes clear that he is restricting his discussion to the social world and that, therefore, the objects he is discussing are social objects, or cultural objects as we have called them. 'Thus man has become the measure of all (societal) things.'[39] In the social world, Lukacs is certainly right, there is no rigid separation of subject and object. The social world is, by definition, the world of social objects or cultural objects, as I have earlier called them. If we limit, for whatever reasons, our philosophical ken to them, then it follows immediately that the antinomy of subject and object has been overcome, for cultural objects are just those objects which, as the result of human labour, or of praxis, bear the indellible stamp of subject. Without the subject there could be no cultural or social objects, no social world whatever. All of this is an important legacy of Marx about which Lukacs reminded Marxists following the intellectually (and politically) dark night of the Second International.

But it is also clear from the structure of the article itself that in 'Reification and the Consciousness of the Prolitariat', Lukacs takes himself to be answering, or dissolving, the same problem with which classical German philosophy had struggled, the relationship between thought and object, where 'object' is not necessarily confined to social objects, human creations. In the concluding pages of the essay, Lukacs returns then to the antinomy as expressed not between subject and social object but as expressed between thought and object, as it was in classical philosophy. 'Hence only by overcoming the-theoretical-duality of philosophy and special discipline, of methodology and factual knowledge can the way be found by which to annul the duality of thought and existence'.[40] Or again, 'Thus thought and existence are not identical in the sense that they "correspond" to each other, or "reflect" each other . . . (all expressions that conceal a rigid duality). Their identity is that they are aspects of one and the same real historical and dialectical process.'[41]

If Lukacs means to annul the dualism not just of thought and social existence, but of thought and object or existence *tout court,* then his position is straightforwardly idealist. That such a position is not Marx's, and hence could not possibly constitute a legitimate interpretation of Marx, we have already seen. It is true that within the realm of social objects, in society, thought or subject and existence are not independent, for there could be no social objects without subjects, and no subjects without thought (for part of what being a subject is involves being an individual who can think, plan, decide, etc, etc.). But from that it does not follow that there could be no objects whatever without subjects, or without thought, a position which is a denial of Marx's materialism as I understand it. If what Lukacs is doing is *only* annulling the dualism of thought and social existence, that seems trivially easy even at the theoretical level, let along the practical level.

Sometimes, to be sure, one feels that behind Lukacs' idealist verbiage, his real intentions are not idealist. If 'overcoming the rigid duality of thought and existence' means merely 'that they are aspects of one and the same real historical process', and if *that* simply means that, in the course of history, natural objects, *all* objects, can *in principle* become mediated by man, then perhaps what Lukacs is saying is beyond objection, although even here we would have to explain carefully 'in principle', for there are certainly distant parts of the universe which, on one sense of 'in principle', can *never* be mediated by man. But still, if this were all Lukacs is saying, we could withdraw our objections to it. All we should then like to point out is that the husk of idealist jargon of 'mediation', 'overcoming duality', etc., would have remained long after the kernel of idealist philosophy, which gives life to those expressions and phrases, would have been discarded. Their continued retention could only be misleading, for it tends to obfuscate rather than elucidate what is being said.

Given that Lukacs' position is idealist, or perhaps more fairly, has intimations of a very deep-rooted idealism in it, it will come as no surprise to find that he rejects any sort of reflection theory. Lukacs is absolutely correct in believing that 'In the theory of "reflection" we find the theoretical embodiment of the duality of thought and existence consciousness and reality . . .' and, once having rejected the essential independence of object from thought, he then consistently rejects the epistemological theory which supports and underpins it. Again, Lukacs says that distinguishing between thought and object 'raises the problem of whether thought corresponds to the object'.[42] Finally, 'as long as thought and existence persist in their old, rigid opposition, as long as their own structure and the structure of their interconnections remain unchanged, then the view that thought is a product of the brain and hence such a mythology . . .'[43] Lukacs is right, then, to connect up materialism, the essential independence of some objects from thought, with a reflection theory, and consistent then to say things which tend to suggest the rejection of both. Our criticism of Lukacs, then, is that if we take his idealist jargon seriously, his view is not Marx's view, nor could it be, for what he has produced is an idealist ontology, and theory of knowledge, and that the idealism that has often been attributed to the essay then goes much deeper than even the category of praxis. It goes to the very basic ontology which informs the whole essay.

The second example I wish to look at is Alfred Schmidt, whose book *The Concept of Nature in Marx* is, as he himself describes, 'impregnated with the influence of "critical theory" as developed by the Frankfurt School since the early 1930s'.[44] Schmidt does not seem to me to misinterpret Marx as much as to vacillate in his interpretation. Most of the time his description of Marx's concept of nature seems to me correct. But that description is frequently punctuated with remarks, explanations, glosses which are not only wrong, but at variance with what Schmidt has said elsewhere in the book. I think that the explanation of this is much the same as the explanation I offered for Lukacs' lapses. Schmidt's thought is trapped, to some degree, in idealist jargon, aphorisms, catch phrases, which lack the full-blooded idealism behind them to give them sense and meaning. The jargon is an atavistic remainder, which detracts from a clear exposition of Marx's ideas. It is true, as I have already said, that Marx, particularly in *The Economic and Philosophical Manuscripts,* uses that jargon too, but always in such a way that the context provides a new filling, a new content, for the jargon. Schmidt uses, on some occasions, that jargon without Marx's change of meaning.

Schmidt reminds us that although Marx was concerned almost wholly with the development of historical materialism, he also referred to its 'relation to naturalistic materialism'. Schmidt also agrees that philosophical materialism, in the sense in which I have been using it, is something that Marx's social theory *presupposes.* Thus, 'Marx defined nature (the material of human activity) as that which is not particular to the Subject, not incorporated in the modes of human appropriation and not identical with men in general'.[45] Schmidt goes on to deny that Marx's materialism was to be understood 'ontologically in the sense of an unmediated objectivism', but I take this qualification to have nothing really at all to do with ontology. Marx's materialism *is* an ontological position. Schmidt's qualification seems only to be a Hegelianesque, and misleading, way of saying, that although nature is essentially independent of thought or human mediation, it does not follow that human mediation cannot change or transform that part of nature with which it may come into contact. With that, as I have already indicated many times, I, of course, agree, although I cannot see why Schmidt should make his point in terms of a rejection of ontology: 'Here we meet with a general characterisation of the Hegelian system which shows that Marx's materialism is not to be understood ontologically'.[46]

Again, compatibly with what we have been arguing: 'In fact for Marx the immediacy of Nature, in so far as . . . he regarded it as socially stamped, does not prove to be a vanishing appearance but retains its genetic priority over men and consciousness'; 'Marx described extra-human reality which is both independent of men and mediated, or at least, capable of being mediated by them . . .';[47] '. . . this socially mediated world remained at the same time a natural world, historically anterior to all human societies';[48] and 'Marx . . . insisted nevertheless that the social mediation of nature confirms its "priority" rather than abolishes it. Matter exists independently of men. Men create the "productive capacity of matter only if matter is presupposed"'.[49] Schmidt correctly castigates Jean-Yves Calvez for attaching undue importance to certain aphorisms in *The Economic and Philosophical Manuscripts,* in which Marx 'is concerned to emphasise the moment of social mediation, as against materialists who have ignored human practice', and the result in Calvez, as Schmidt succinctly puts it, is 'a curious idealism of procreation cloaked in sociology'.[49] Schmidt quotes an example of Calvez's 'curious idealism': 'Nature without man has no sense, no movement. It is chaos, undifferentiated and indifferent matter, hence ultimately nothing'.[50] Even chaos is not nothing, but in any case nature without man is not chaos. It has natural properties, a form of its own, and Schmidt elsewhere makes just this point.

If we can agree with all of this, whence comes our disagreement with Schmidt? Unfortunately, what we have quoted so far is not the only side to Schmidt's thesis, for he also says things like the following:[51] 'Hence in a form of materialism [Marx's], the essential content of which consists in the critique of political economy, matter must appear as a social category in the broadest sense' (p. 32); 'Only by recognising, as Marx does, that material reality is from the beginning socially mediated . . .' (p. 35); 'Questions directed to the pre-human and pre-social existence of nature . . . presuppose a definite stage of the theoretical and practical appropriation of Nature', 'all putatively primeval substrates are always already involved with what is supposed to emerge from their activity, and are for precisely that reason by no means absolutely primeval' (p. 38); '. . . pure historically unmodified nature does not exist as an object of natural-scientific knowledge' (p. 50); '. . . as far as the world of experience as a whole is concerned, the material provided by nature cannot be distinguished from the practico-social modes of its transformation' (p. 66); 'The whole of nature is socially mediated . . .' (p. 79). I have listed these passages without succumbing to the temptation to reply to each in its turn. Perhaps, though, a few remarks are in order. How could 'matter' be a social category? Not, I presume, just in that broad and obvious sense in which any category is social, which is true but not very interesting in this context. If that is all that is meant by saying that 'matter must appear as a social category in the broadest sense', the claim is true but rather a dull one. In any case, Schmidt later actually criticises Lukacs for making the same claim: 'But in Marx nature is not *merely* a social category. It cannot be totally dissolved into the historical processes of its appropriation . . .' (p. 70); so it really is not at all clear what Schmidt intends by his own claim. How could anyone say that historically unmodified nature does not exist as an object of natural science, when there exists a science of geology which studies the earth as it was long before the advent of man? And of course the material provided by nature can be distinguished from the practico-social modes of its transformation, as anyone could explain whose job it was to extract crude ore or petroleum from the earth. Schmidt's reference to Marx to justify his claim that Marx tolerates no 'abstract' questions about pre-human and pre-social existence entirely misses the mark, for the passage from *The Economic and Philosophical Manuscripts* which Schmidt cites is about the question of the origin or creation of nature (and man), and not about questions concerning nature prior to man.

Perhaps even more so than the quotations presented thus far, the most damning in Schmidt is this:

It is only possible to speak of natural history when one presupposes human history made by conscious subjects. Natural history is human history's extension backwards and is comprehended by men, as *no longer* accessible nature, with the same socially imprinted categories as they are compelled to apply to *as yet* unappropriated areas of nature. (p. 46)

In one, trivial, sense, it is impossible to *speak* of natural history unless one presupposes human history, for without human beings there could be no speaking about anything. But it simply is not the case that natural history is human history's extension backwards. The claim is phenomenalist in the extreme. Just as the phenomenalists *reduced* material objects, which of course may in fact be unperceived at some time, to a set of permanent possibilities of perception ('would have been perceived if there had been a sentient creature there'), so too Schmidt speaks as if one could reduce all of natural history to permanent possibilities for human history. To all these vacillations, with their inescapably idealist implications, one must say 'No! It is difficult to see why remarks such as these do not damn Schmidt in the same way in which he damned Calvez: 'a curious idealism of procreation cloaked in sociology'.

What we find, then, in Schmidt, is a peculiar blend of valuable and perceptive exposition of Marx's concept of nature on the one hand, and on the other, a set of remarks which, if taken at face-value, seem to take back what has just been claimed in that exposition. Again, the feeling one gets is that some, if not all, of the difficulty arises from the retention of a terminology which is essentially idealist, and into which a materialist message is being made to fit. Schmidt's aim, which is wholly applaudable, is to prevent the materialism which he is describing from degenerating into a materialism which fails to allow for human beings and the ways in which they can change, transform, the reality in which they live. This was, as I have tried to describe, Marx's central aim in the 'Theses on Feuerbach'. But whatever his intention, Schmidt has done more than that. The book is full of lapses into a form of idealism, in which 'the whole of nature is socially mediated . . .' and 'nature cannot be separated from man'. Does this mean that if man had never existed, which is certainly conceivable, nature would never have existed either? And if it doesn't mean that, what does it mean? Is it misleading jargon for something plain and obvious, for example for the fact that after man enters the historical stage, much, but not all, of nature bears the imprint of his handiwork?

Finally, we come to Kolakowski. The idealism of Kolakowski, unlike Schmidt, goes much deeper than terminology, or than blemishing an otherwise valuable exposition. In his 'Karl Marx and the Classical Definition of Truth'[52] Kolakowski presents what I think is a consistent, coherent, and thoroughly idealist interpretation of Marx. I will try to justify my accusation in what follows.

Kolakowski begins by rejecting the Engels-Lenin 'Marxism of a positivist orientation'. Marxism of a positivist orientation turns out to be the view that 'human cognition, though incapable of absolute and ultimate mastery of its object, approaches mastery by constant and progressive evolution. Its limitless striving for perfection is intended to make it more similar to reality, to make it imitate better the external world's properties and relations, which in themselves are independent of this effort and exist beyond the realm of human knowledge'.[53] This reflection or correspondence theory of knowledge and truth is rejected on the grounds that it presupposes an objective world which knowledge has the duty of approaching. No such objective realm exists independently of the knower which he could make his beliefs 'imitate': 'It is true that one of Kant's basic ideas has been retained, the belief that the object cannot be conceived without the subject that constructs it';[54] 'active contact with the opposition of nature creates at one and the same time conceptive man and nature as his object'.[55]

There is, for Kolakowski, no 'world' independent of us. All *things* are socially subjective, for their attributes

. . . are subjective . . . as long as they bear the imprint of the organisational power of man, who sees the world in such terms and from such points of view as are necessary for him to make this observation. It is easy to see that the question of a picture of an absolutely independent reality is incorrectly posed . . .

. . . the picture of reality sketched by everyday perception and by scientific thinking is a kind of human creation (not imitation) . . . In this sense the world's products must be considered artificial. In this world the sun and stars exist because man is able to make them *his* objects . . .[56]

Why has Kolakowski been driven to this position? Because he, like Kant, holds the interpretation claim, the belief that all thought is interpretive, and that its interpretive activity is responsible for *all* our knowledge of the world. Now, however, the *a priori* derives not just from a synthesis of the understanding, but from a 'material' synthesising too. All this is presumably to be included within the 'organisational powers of man'. Thus, any sort of Aristotelian realism, with its doctrine of natural kinds, is rejected, and so too is classical correspondence theory, which would provide it with epistemological support. What we get in its place is a Kantian theory of knowledge, and it is that which leads Kolakowski to reject the independence of nature from thought:

Human consciousness, the practical mind . . . produces existence as composed of individuals divided into species and genera. From the moment man . . . begins to dominate the world of things . . . he finds that world already constructed and differentiated, not according to some alleged natural classification, but according to a classification imposed by the practical need for orientation. The categories into which this world is divided . . . are created by a spontaneous effort . . . to subdue the chaos of reality . . . The cleavages of the world into species, and into individuals endowed with particular traits of being perceived separately, are the product of the practical mind . . .[57]

All categories of thought are interpretive; '"Humanised nature" knows no substantial forms inherent to itself or preceding human . . . consciousness. This means that the former appear as a result of man's intellectual organisation of material . . .';[58] and, in a passage not dissimilar in tone to Hegel's discussion of thought developing its determinations out of itself, '. . . it is even more accurate to summarise his [Marx's] thought by saying that things are consciousness made concrete'.[59]

Like Kant, Kolakowski does not reject the independence claim; he maintains that something exists independent of thought—although, as we have seen, it cannot be the world, the objective realm, things or kinds. In the quotation beginning 'Human consciousness . . .', Kolakowski says that the practical mind, 'although it does not produce existence, produces existence as composed of individuals divided into species and genera'. So Kolakowski inherits 'Kant's problem', for he asserts both (IC) and (IpC). What is it that exists independently of thought? 'Practical activity defines man's consciousness . . . as a tool with which man can introduce into matter a definite system of intellectual organisation'.[59] 'If for Marx, man replaces God - the Creator, still he . . . reminds us of the God of the Averroists who organises the world out of previously existing material'.[60] It is matter, formless, structureless, propertyless, which predates man's conceptual organisation of reality by means of his practical mind.

What if we ask Kolakowski, as we asked Kant, what it is which exists independently of thought, subject, knower? Do we find out by looking at the most recent theory of sub-atomic physics? Not for Kolakowski, for that would be to use interpretive concepts which we 'happen' to impose. Presumably even the concept of chaos, which he also uses, is interpretive. The materiality of the world consists only, he finally says, in its opposition to us:

Thus Marx's world could not be other than material since it poses an opposition to human endeavour. (Moreover, this explanation is tautological, for it is precisely this opposition that defines materiality as we understand it.)[58]

'Nature appears as the opposition encountered by human drives.'[61] Thus, the 'materialism' compatible with such an idealist epistemology is merely the assertion that 'something opposes itself to human endeavour', and this seems to exhaust the content that Kolakowski is willing to give to his claim of an independent reality. A strange materialism; even Bishop Berkeley would be a materialist on such a definition! Kolakowski presents, I think, an excellent example of how an idealist epistemology leads to a rejection of philosophical materialism, with which it is simply epistemologically incompatible. No tendentious redefinition of materialism can really obscure that incompatibility. Perhaps opposition to human endeavour gets us clear of thought, although even Hegel had no difficulty in accounting for a world which wasn't always the way which we would choose it to be. No form of idealism, whether subjective or absolute, *has* to be saddled with voluntarism, such that the world that confronts us can never cross our desires and wishes. But, in any case, opposition to human endeavour will not get us clear of mind, as any common-or-garden variety phenomenalist could show us.

It is comforting in all this to see how little this has to do with Marx. In support of this being the epistemological thought of Marx, Kolakowski cites precisely six references, all of them from *The Economic and Philosophical Manuscripts*. One reference, which he quotes in his second footnote, talks about 'the objects of his [man's] impulses exist outside him, independently . . .'; not only does this *not* support the point that Kolakowski uses it to support, ('the world of things exists for man only as a totality of possible satisfaction of his needs'), but it actually contradicts Kolakowski's point, as I have already argued. A second reference from Marx is a *gloss on Hegel;* '. . . it is *objectivity* which is to be annulled, because it is not the *determinate* character of the object, but rather its objective character that is offensive and constitutes estrangement for self-consciousness'.[62] From this quotation Kolakowski concludes that Marx reproaches Hegel for treating objectivity as consciousness-created, but that Marx criticises Hegel for this on the grounds that it is *only* the determinate character of the object which is so created.[63] In other words, Kolakowski argues that Marx's reproach against Hegel is that Hegel confuses the determinate character of an object with the 'objectivity' of the object as such, and that whereas Marx rejects the Hegelian thesis that objectivity as such is consciousness-created, he accepts that the determinate character of the object is created by consciousness. But it does not seem reasonable to ascribe such a view to Marx solely on the evidence of the clause 'because it is not the *determinate* character of the object'. Marx may have used the clause as a way of emphasis—to bring out the fact that for Hegel it is not *just* the determinate character of the object but rather the object itself which is consciousness created—rather than to contrast Hegel's view with his own, as Kolakowski merely assumes.

A third quote—'The dispute about the reality or nonreality of thinking isolated from practice is purely scholastic'[64]—does not seem to bear on the issues I have delineated in Kolakowski's account of Marx. Materialism and reflection theory could still be Marx's considered views, even if it would be 'purely scholastic' to discuss such views in a way wholly isolated from practice. A fourth quotation is a good example of how not to read the *Manuscripts,* which were, we should always remember, unpublished notes, and hence quotation from which must always be done with extreme care and attention to precise context. Kolakowski examines the passage which *he says* means that 'the reality of any beings whatsoever is defined by the fact that they are both objects for others and have others as their objects'.[65] He

then uses this interpretation of Marx's text to support the point that man
can never know some allegedly given 'existence in itself', a reality
essentially independent of man. This is not what the lengthy passage says.
Marx begins by remarking that the objects of man's impulses are both
'independent of him' and, as objects of his need, objects on which he is
essentially dependent, his 'essential objects'. The essential dependency is
one-way; man is essentially dependent on having material objects, but not
conversely. Marx stresses this by reminding the reader: 'To say that man is
a *corporeal,* living, real, sensuous, objective being full of natural vigour is
to say that he has real, sensuous, objects as the objects of his being . . .' At
least in the opening paragraph the subject that Marx is discussing is man,
or 'animals and plants', and *not* just 'beings' in general, including natural
objects. Thus, so far Marx says nothing which would allow us to conclude
the impossibility of a natural world essentially independent of man.

Now, Marx does go on to speak of 'being(s)', where that is intended to
include any kind of object whatsoever, whether natural or human. In this
connection, Marx makes the following sorts of remarks:

A being which does not have its nature outside itself is not a *natural* being, and plays no part in
the system of nature.

A being which has no object outside itself is not an objective being.

A being which is not itself an object for some third being has no being for its object i. e. it is not
objectively related. Its be-ing is not objective.

An unobjective being is a *nullity* —an *un-being*.

Suppose a being which is neither an object [of another being] itself, nor has an
object . . . Thus, to suppose a being which is not the object of another being is to presuppose
that *no* objective being exists.

There cannot be, Marx seems to be saying, a single 'thing', except perhaps
the Totality of reality, which is not essentially related to something else.
What, then, seems to follow on this view, is that there cannot be in nature
an objective or real being which stands in no essential relation to something
else, but of course Marx does not say to what every such natural object
would have to be essentially related. In particular, Marx is certainly not
asserting that every real natural object must stand in essential relation to
man, or to a human need, and yet it is only if Marx were interpreted in this
preposterous way that Kolakowski's claim about the impossibility of an
'existence in itself', unrelated essentially to what is human, would have *any*
plausibility whatever. There is no suggestion in Marx that, of any pair of
objects which stand in an essential relation and are thereby 'objective', one
of the pair must be living. Therefore, there is no reason why a system of
necessarily inter-related objects could not exist in nature without there
being men or sentient creatures of any sort to whom they were related.

A fifth reference concerns the historical development of the senses: 'The
eye has become a human eye, just as its object has become a *social,* human
object . . .'[66] Kolakowski uses this to argue that the mind is responsible for

'dividing the world in a definite way'. I think a careful attempt to situate the passage in Marx's overall argument will show that Marx has no epistemological theme whatever in mind. He is trying to describe the changes in human beings that will come with the advent of communism. Indeed, the paragraph in question begins: 'The transcendence of private property is therefore the complete *emancipation* of all human senses and attributes . . .' It is disingenuous to try to put this to epistemological purposes. Indeed, the 'seeing' of things differently under communism, isn't literally 'seeing' in the perceptual sense at all, but more like 'regarding'. Under communism, men will *consider* or *regard* things in a different way. They will not regard things 'individualistically' but 'socially': 'need or enjoyment have consequently lost their egotistical nature'. This is not the epistemological point which Kolakowski wishes to make it.

Finally, a sixth reference by Kolakowski is to this sentence in the *Manuscripts:* '. . . and nature, conceived abstractly, in and of itself, perpetuated in its separation from man, is nothing to him'.[67] In one sense, the remark could almost be regarded as a tautology—unmediated nature is a nature man has nothing to do with. Such a tautology certainly won't bear Kolakowski's epistemological burden. But, more importantly, from the structure of the argument here, it is clear that Marx is assigning this view 'nature . . . taken abstractly . . .' to Hegel, and not to the reflection-theory materialist, as one might otherwise have thought. The passage is a difficult one, but his argument seems to be this. Hegel always revolves 'solely within the orbit of thought'. Thoughts are for Hegel, 'fixed, mental shapes or ghosts dwelling outside nature and man'. Thoughts conceived in this abstract way are almost non-human; 'neither could thought be grasped as an expression of man' by Hegel. Such an abstract approach to thought produces an 'infinite weariness' and so Hegel resolves 'to recognise nature as the essential being and to go over to intuition, the abandonment of abstract thought . . .'

The next paragraph begins with the sentence which Kolakowski quotes: 'But *nature* too, taken abstractly for itself—nature fixed in isolation from man—is *nothing* for man'. The quote continues:

It goes without saying that the abstract thinker who has committed himself to intuiting intuits nature abstractly. Just as nature lay enclosed in the thinker in the form of the absolute idea, in the form of a thought entity . . . so what he has let go forth from himself in truth is only this abstract nature, only nature as a thought-entity.

The quotation plainly cannot be made to bear evidence against the reflection theory materialist. 'Nature taken abstractly' or 'in isolation from man' refers to the reified *concept* of nature, one of the thought-forms from which Marx claims Hegel cannot escape, and *not* to a nature essentially independent of human praxis. 'Nature too . . . is nothing for man' is nothing but a comment on Hegel's de-humanisation of all thought, and in particular the idea of nature. Wrenched from context, Kolakowski tries to force the quotation to argue against the materialist conception of a nature 'in isolation from man'. In fact, in context, it is clear that the quotation argues against the idealist, against Hegel, who isolates the idea or thought of nature from man by his abstract treatment of thought. All this is a far cry from the interpretation that Kolakowski attempts to give it.

I have spent so much time discussing Kolakowski's misuse of the *Manuscripts* because I think it is symptomatic of the ideological misuse to which they are often put. As I said before, they are full of Hegelian terminology, but given changed meaning and import by their use and the context in which they are situated. If one is not careful to see this, quoting them out of context can become a way of making them say what they were never intended to say. They certainly become, in Kolakowski's hands, a way in which to saddle Marx with an idealist epistemology that he never seriously held. Perhaps Kolakowski was half aware of this: 'We know, of course, that we are spinning out suppositions based on unfinished and not unequivocal texts. An overdetailed interpretation of aphorisms runs the risk of letting us ascribe to their Author statements that might well surprise him'[68]. I don't believe that one could fairly accuse Kolakowski of overdetailed interpretation of the passages from the *Manuscripts* that he cites.

Finally, I do not wish to argue that there are *no* remarks in the *Manuscripts of 1844,* or elsewhere in the so-called 'early' writings of Marx, which suggest or imply a position incompatible with the materialism that I ascribe to Marx. I do not want to be understood as arguing that *nothing* in the whole of Marx's writings, and especially in the chronologically earlier portion of them, suggests anything at variance with the idea of a natural realm which is essentially independent of man. I do not know what to make of Marx's statement that 'man is the immediate object of natural science'.[69] He also says, more understandably, that 'nature is the immediate object of the science of man', but these do not appear to be for him, the same thing. Elsewhere in *The Manuscripts,* and occasionally elsewhere, there are remarks which do indeed stand in need of explanation. Each passage must be treated carefully within context, and often any apparent inconsistency with the materialism I have ascribed to Marx then vanishes. But I should not like to rest my case on the claim that every such remark loses its inconsistency with materialism when looked at with precise and close scrutiny. What I would claim, however, is that such remarks are numerically few or occur in unpublished manuscripts as jottings or occasional thoughts, and thus, taken as a whole, are entirely insufficient for either building a coherent interpretation of Marx's materialism, or for refuting an alternative interpretation otherwise well grounded in the texts, and on so much of what Marx does say in a considered way elsewhere.

In this chapter, I have tried to limit myself to discussing misascriptions of a non-materialist ontology to Marx, or non-materialist misdescriptions of Marx's ontology, although in discussing Kolakowski I also touched on various epistemological misascriptions as well. I have deliberately refrained from dealing with any of those discussions of the nature of truth which abound in the literature on Marxism and which ascribe to Marx a theory of truth drawn from his remarks on praxis and which claim that such a theory is incompatible with, and constitutes Marx's rejection of, a correspondence theory of truth. It will be recalled that I have not claimed that one finds in Marx a well-worked out correspondence account of truth. Rather, what I have said is that one does find in Marx a clear account of philosophical materialism, and such an account 'needs' a correspondence theory of truth. It would be embarrassing to my thesis if we found Marx rejecting a correspondence theory of truth. It is true that this would not necessarily refute my claim, for we could hold that Marx simply was not aware of the epistemological demands his materialism placed upon him. Happily, we do not need to argue in this way, for there is no inconsistency whatever between a classical correspondence theory and Marx's remarks on truth and praxis. It is Kolakowski who perhaps more than anyone else is responsible for this confusion, at least in the recent discussion of a Marxist theory of truth. Correspondence theory does not assume that somehow change is impossible, that the world is given, fixed in some frozen form, and that thought is consigned to reflecting eternally the unmoving way the world is. Indeed, it is not clear who, other than Zeno and Parmenides, ever thought such an absurd thing, but what is clear is that praxis and correspondence co-exist as easily as any two ideas can. In whatever ways man revolutionises his material circumstances, his thought can come to correspond to, or reflect, that set of changes. The reality which corresponds to thought at one time need not be the same reality which corresponded to thought at some earlier time. As reality develops or is transformed, so should our thought or beliefs about it. Thus, it is unnecessary to *contrast* Marx's theory of praxis with 'the classical definition of truth', since they are eminently compatible.[70]

Notes: Chapter III

[1] Dupre, Louis, *The Philosophical Foundations of Marxism*, New York, Harcourt, Brace & World Inc., 1966, p. 223.

[2] Ollman, Bertell, *Alienation,* Cambridge, Cambridge University Press, 1971, p. 53.

[3] Marx, Karl, *Capital* Vol. I, Progress Publishers, Moscow, 1965. 'Afterword to the Second German Edition', p. 19.

[4] Marx, Karl and Frederick Engels, *Collected Works,* Volume I, Lawrence and Wishart, London, 1975, 'Difference Between the Democritean and Epicurean Philosophy of Nature', pp. 34-76.

[5] Marx, Karl and Frederick Engels, *The German Ideology,* Progress Publishers, Moscow, 1965, p. 37 and p. 31.

[6] Marx, Karl, *Economic and Philosophic Manuscripts of 1844,* Progress Publishers, Moscow, 1967, p. 155, Marx's footnote.

[7] Marx, Karl, *Capital* Vol. I, p. 178.

[8] See the section of *Capital* Vol. I entitled 'The Fetishism of Commodities and the Secret thereof', pp. 71-83 and Norman Geras, 'Essence and Appearance: Aspects of Fetishism in Marx's *Capital*', *New Left Review,* 65, pp. 69-85. In what follows, I use 'objects' and 'objective' to refer to *natural* objects and the *natural* world. When I wish to refer to social

objects or the social realm, I explicitly use the qualification 'social' or 'cultural'. In this usage I am following Marx's own use of 'object' and 'objective'. When I refer to social *objects* as 'objects' I do not mean to deny that they are relational, in Marx's sense, or have a relational aspect.

9   *Economic and Philosophic Manuscripts* (hereafter abbreviated *EPM*), p. 104.

10 For following page references see Karl Marx, *Critique of Hegel's 'Philosophy of Right'*, edited by Joseph O'Malley, Cambridge, Cambridge University Press, 1970.

11 From Karl Marx and Frederick Engels, *The Holy Family*, in *Collected Works*, Vol. 4, pp. 57-61.

12 *EPM*, p. 98.

13 *Ibid*, pp. 144-145.

14 *Ibid*, p. 145.

15 *Ibid*, p. 145.

16 *Ibid*, p. 150-151.

17 Marx, Karl, *Introduction To The Grundrisse* in *A Contribution to the Critique of Political Economy*, introduction by Maurice Dobb, Lawrence & Wishart, London, 1971, p. 207.

18 Marx, Karl, *EPM*, pp. 104-105.

19 Marx, Karl and Frederick Engels, *The German Ideology*, p. 59.

20 Marx, Karl, *The Grundrisse*, quoted in Alfred Schmidt, *The Concept of Nature in Marx*, New Left Books, London, 1971, p. 30.

21 Marx, Karl and Frederick Engels, *The Holy Family*, quoted in Alfred Schmidt, *op. cit.*, p. 64.

22 Marx, Karl, *Capital*, Vol. I, p. 43.

23 Marx, Karl and Frederick Engels, *The German Ideology*, p. 30.

24 *Ibid*, p. 37. Note the force of 'can never', which suggests essential dependence of consciousness on existence.

25 *Ibid*, p. 38. Again, note the force of 'necessarily'.

26 Marx, Karl, *Capital*, Vol. I, p. 19.

27 Korsch, Karl, *Marxism and Philosophy*, New Left Books, London, 1972, pp. 108-109.

28 *Ibid*, footnote on p. 109.

29 *Ibid*, pp. 77-78, where Korsch adds that such a coincidence must 'characterise every dialectic . . .'

30 Marx, Karl, *The Grundrisse*, translated by Martin Nicolaus, Penguin Books, Harmondsworth, Middx., 1973, p. 360.

31 Korsch, Karl, *op. cit.*, p. 78.

32 Marx, Karl, *The Grundrisse*, p. 300.

33 Plekhanov, G. V., *Fundamental Problems of Marxism*, Lawrence & Wishart, London, 1969, p. 31 and ff.

34 Marx, Karl, *Introduction to the Grundrisse*, in *A Contribution to the Critique of Political Economy*, p. 207.

35 Lukacs, Georg, *History and Class Consciousness*, Merlin Press, London, 1971. Preface to the New Edition.

36 *Ibid*, p. 148.

37 *Ibid*, pp. 125-126.

38 *Ibid*, p. 126.

39 *Ibid*, p. 185.

40 *Ibid*, p. 203.

41 *Ibid*, p. 204.

42 *Ibid*, p. 200.

43 *Ibid*, p. 202.

44 Schmidt, Alfred, *The Concept of Nature In Marx*, New Left Books, London, 1971, p. 9.

45 *Ibid*, p. 27.

46 *Ibid*, p. 30. For some reason the word 'epistemology' is considered an acceptable word on the Left, but 'ontology' is not. I cannot understand the poor repute into which 'ontology' has fallen. Marxism, indeed any scientific theory, must make existential commitments of

one sort or another, the only question being which ones to make. Those Marxists who object most to ontology seem to end up (unconsciously?) committed to an idealist one.

47   *Ibid*, p. 29.
48   *Ibid*, p. 33.
49   *Ibid*, p. 96.
50   *Ibid*, p. 97.
51   Schmidt, Alfred, *The Concept of Nature in Marx,* for this and subsequent page references given in the text.
52   Kolakowski, Leszek, 'Karl Marx and the Classical Definition of Truth', pp. 58-86 in *Marxism and Beyond,* translated by J. Z. Peel, Pall Mall Press, London, 1969.
53   *Ibid*, pp. 59-60.
54   *Ibid*, p. 69.
55   *Ibid*, p. 74.
56   *Ibid*, p. 67-68.
57   *Ibid*, p. 66.
58   *Ibid*, pp. 69-70.
59   *Ibid*, p. 75.
60   *Ibid*, p. 77.
61   *Ibid*, p. 64.
62   Marx, Karl, *EPM*, p. 147.
63   Kolakowski, L., *op. cit.*, p. 65 and p. 63.
64   Marx, Karl, '*Theses on Feuerbach*', second thesis, in *The German Ideology*, p. 659.
65   Marx, Karl, *EPM*, p. 145. Discussed by Kolakowski on p. 64. The five quoted 'remarks' are from this section of the *EPM*.
66   *Ibid*, pp. 99-100.
67   *Ibid*, p. 156.
68   Kolakowski, *op. cit.*, p. 75.
69   Marx, Karl, *EPM*, pp. 103-104.
70   See Peter Binns, 'The Marxist Theory of Truth', *Radical Philosophy*, No. 4, 1973, for a survey of some of the alternative Marxist views on truth. Binns' position provides a 'pragmatist' contrast to my own. I certainly agree with Binns that 'an idea is [not] material . . . because it is about atoms and physicality' (p. 7), and the non-reductive materialism which I attribute to Marx does not commit us to such a thesis. But I do not agree with Binns when he procedes to conclude that an idea is material 'because it becomes a material force in a really existing society'. An idea is material only in the sense that it is necessarily 'embodied' in material reality, as I tried to make clear earlier in this chapter. But the idea does not need to be 'about' the reality in which it is embodied or concretised. The failure to note this point may be partly responsible for the conflation of Marxism and reductive materialism by many writers. Naturally, we do not dispute Binns' claim that ideas can be a force in society, but this is not the same thing as their materiality. An idea with no force or social efficacy is no less material, or materialised, than a forceful one.

CHAPTER IV

TOWARDS A MARXIST THEORY OF KNOWLEDGE

> 'You are metaphysicians. You can prove anything by
> metaphysics; and having done so, every metaphysician
> can prove every other metaphysician wrong—to his own
> satisfaction. You are anarchists in the realm of thought.
> And you are mad cosmos-makers. Each of you dwells in a
> cosmos of his own making, created out of his own fancies
> and desires. You do not know the real world in which you
> live, and your thinking has no place in the real world
> except in so far as it is phenomena of mental aberration.'
>
> Ernest Everhard, in Jack London's
> *The Iron Heel*

In this and the next chapter I wish to accomplish two tasks. First, I want to discuss in a quite general way some of the characteristics which, I think, any *acceptable* theory of knowledge must possess, or which any theory of knowledge must have in order to be judged *adequate*. In order to assess the adequacy of any particular theory of knowledge, or even any particular kind of theory of knowledge, one needs some general criteria of adequacy, some grasp of what some of the features are, possession of which is a necessary condition of adequacy or acceptability. Second, using these features as touchstones, I will discuss, again in a quite general way, how and why a reflection theory of knowledge suitably stated can pass the tests of adequacy which I have set. It will be convenient to raise this general question about reflection theories through a discussion of some of the recent work of Lucio Colletti. In the sixth and final chapter I will turn my attention specifically to a discussion of Lenin's *Materialism and Empirio-Criticism* in which Lenin espouses one particular variety of a reflection theory. Reflection theories, *suitably stated,* may pass the tests of adequacy, but some versions of reflection theory may not do so. In that chapter, then, I shall raise the specific question of whether, or to what extent, Lenin's version of reflection theory is adequate.

My discussion of the six features or characteristics which I want to focus on will be uneven. Some receive only brief treatment; others will receive a somewhat more thorough discussion. I want to stress at the beginning that my purpose in this chapter is not to 'prove' to professional philosophers that any adequate theory of knowledge must do or allow for the things I require. Rather, I think that the six features are ones which Marx himself would have insisted upon, or are broadly 'Marxist' in their perspective. Thus, it is my intention to argue with Marxists that reflection theory, suitably stated, passes the test of adequacy by possessing features which they will agree are necessary.

Naturally, I think that such features are not only 'Marxist', but also correct, and thus I think that it is sensible from any view point to require that a theory of knowledge have those features. I hope, therefore, that many others will agree to such features or constraints as well. But I repeat that I do not intend my discussion to convince an entrenched opponent whose outlook inclines him to doubt quite systematically almost everything which I will be saying. To an entrenched opponent much of what follows may appear as *obiter dicta;* to someone generally sympathetic to the epistemological position I adopt, I hope my discussion moves beyond the standard recitation of these points, which abound in the Marxist literature, by pointing to the existence of genuine problems and difficulties which must be dealt with. I try to go beyond the mere repetition of well-worn slogans. Finally, I should add that I do not intend my list of features or criteria to be exhaustive, or sufficient, for the adequacy of a theory of knowledge. To mention just one example, I do not discuss holism versus atomism, the idea of system, an issue which has provided Marxists with one important criticism of the standard approach of the empiricist tradition. Rather, I have chosen the six items which I do discuss because they are the very ones which it is often said that no reflection theory can possess. For instance, the Marxist literature abounds with the accusation that reflection theory is undialectical, individualistic, and accepts the world just as it is given, thereby discounting change. My choice of items for inclusion has been dictated by that fact alone, and not out of a belief that these items are all, or even the most important, criteria for assessing the adequacy of a theory of knowledge.

What are these features or characteristics which we can reasonably demand that any adequate theory of knowledge must have? They are, I submit, (1) that is respects the irreducibility or reality of the external world, (2) that it be consistent with science, (3) that it have a *social* conception of knowledge, (4) that it can account for human activity as central to an understanding of knowledge, (5) that it be, in a sense to be explained, a dialectical theory, and (6) that it does not necessarily accept the world as it appears, but permits access to the way the world essentially is. I would now like to explain and expand upon each of these points in turn although, since some of the points are internally related to others, what I say under one heading will often be related to other points as well.

1. A theory of knowledge must be *adequate* to the real cognitive suitation in which men find themselves. This is something which empiricist epistemology has generally failed to do. Given what we *know* about human beings, and their material environment, empiricist epistemology proves to be literally incredible. The very titles of some of the recent 'classics' substantiate this incredibility: *Der Logische Aufbau der Welt, The Structure of Appearance, Our Knowledge of The External World.* Any

credible theory of knowledge must *begin* with the knowability of an essentially mind-independent world, a world which would exist (and not just counterfactually!) even if every kind of sentient being in the universe were to be eliminated tomorrow, or indeed had never even come into existence. All reductionist doctrines—idealism, in both its subjective and absolute disguises, phenomenalism, classical empiricism, Machian positivism, Platonism, the Kantian thesis that limits knowledge to the world as it appears and never as it is—all of these doctrines are to be rejected. The physical world is not a construct out of experiences, ideas, Ideas, impressions, or sense data, whether actual or hypothetical, nor is our knowledge restricted to a realm which is so constituted. Any credible theory of knowledge must be realist in the sense in which I have been using that term.

There is a sense in which even Hume or Berkeley might accept the statement that there are tables, chairs, physical objects in general. The point is that acceptance of such statements has, for them, to be accompanied by an analysis of what such statements mean. What their analyses purport to show is that such 'physical objects' do not have a mind-independent status, since statements about them can be understood as, reduced to, sets of statements which are only 'about' the contents of the mind. Thus, to be a realist, it is not sufficient just to accept the statement that physical objects exist, and then couple that statement with an 'analysis' which dispenses with the claim of mind-independence. Realism takes physical objects seriously, not merely paying lip-service to their existence, and 'seriously' here means 'understood as essentially independent of mind'. Finally, this last statement or claim, 'physical objects are essentially independent of mind', does not itself seem to be something which a Hume or Berkeley could formally accept, while giving it an analysis on which the commitment to essential independence of mind had been expelled!

I began by saying: 'Given what we *know* about human beings and their material environment, empiricist epistemology proves to be literally incredible.' Someone might reply to this: 'You claim to *know* these things. But how can you justify these cognitive claims about men and their environment? Certainly if we could *know* that men did exist in a world which was essentially independent of mind, then we agree that this would be something reasonable to demand of a theory of knowledge. But this is patently question-begging, for we can ask of you how you are entitled to *that* bit of knowledge. Surely an adequate theory of knowledge must be able to provide an answer to that question, and not merely begin with it as an assumption.' How can we, then, justify the claim that I think every man naturally accepts when he has no philosophical axe to grind, that physical objects are essentially independent of mind?

What such an imaginary reply shows, I think, is that the whole epistemological programme of systematic justification of our knowledge must be rejected, along with the impeachment of the mind-independence of the material world. It is not possible, even as a mildly amusing analytical exercise, to show how our knowledge of a mind-independent world can be reconstituted, like Florida orange juice, on some pre-selected basis, which is conceived as having some epistemological advantage because it does not itself assume mind-independence. It is this impossibility which, throughout the history of modern philosophy, tended to drive the systematic justificationists toward scepticism, because there always seemed to be something in our knowledge which could not be justified on each pre-selected basis. Thus, modern philosophy's standard diet of attempting to account for, and finding problematic, various entities or procedures. If one begins with sense data or impressions, the justification of belief in mind-independent objects becomes problematic. If one starts with observable behaviour, other minds constitute a difficulty. If one is limited to the experiences one can introspect in oneself, then the Self seems to vanish. If observable entities are the only permissible basis for justification, theoretical entities pose a problem. If deduction is the only criterion for rational thought, induction may appear unjustified. Similarly, too, for deduction itself, the past, values, or causality. On some pre-selected basis, nearly everything can be made to appear problematic, since the basis will be too weak to license justification for what one had hoped to justify. Mind-independence, in the same way, has appeared problematic, because no basis seemed strong enough to bear its justification.

The point I am making against the possibility of foundationalist attempts at justification is hardly an original one. In W. V. O. Quine's use of Otto Neurath's marvellous metaphor: 'Neurath has likened science to a boat which, if we are to rebuild it, we must rebuild plank by plank while staying afloat in it. The philosopher and the scientist are in the same boat. If we improve our understanding of ordinary talk of physical things, it will not be by reducing talk to a more familiar idiom; there is none.'[1] But the point I am trying to make is directed not just against foundationalist attempts at justification, but against any non-circular attempts whatever. Consider, for example, a coherentist account of justification, which might argue that belief in a mind-independent world of physical objects is justified because it yields the overall simplest system of beliefs possible. Material objects are 'posits', on such an account, ways of simplifying, organising, the infinite variety of human experience into manageable proportions. Introduction of such physical objects provides us with the 'smoothest and most adequate overall account of the world'.[2]

We reject all such attempts at justification, whether foundationalist, coherentist, transcendental, or whatever. What these attempts have in common is that they seek to justify the belief in a realm essentially independent of mind by reference to something else, whether sense experience or coherentist considerations of simplicity, where the 'something else' does not itself presuppose the existence of the mind-independent reality for which the justification is being sought. In particular, we also reject the idea that mind-independent reality has the status of a 'posit', a theoretical entity introduced for the sake of producing a maximally coherent system of beliefs, which can be used to account for and simplify observation reports and on whose basis such reports can themselves be corrected, in order to preserve overall smoothness and simplicity, in order to maximise coherence in the tissue of our beliefs.

Someone might now argue that what we have done is to have made belief in a material reality an *a priori* belief or principle, an *a priori* assumption. But this is not so. To say of a belief that it is '*a priori*' is to provide it with a sort of justification. Rather, what we claim is that this belief has *no* justification, in the sense in which the truth of what does the justifying does not itself depend on the truth of what is being justified. In short, there are no non-circular justifications for the belief in a material world. Thus, in answer to the earlier imaginary reply which I sketched previously, we can say that we agree that we can ask *how* we know that there are material objects (essentially independent of mind) but that the *only* answer to this is a scientific answer, which includes reference to retinas, optic nerves, and pressure receptors in our limbs, things which are themselves material things. The only answer is the scientific answer. Beyond that way of answering the question there is no   more basic, philosophical answer, and it is mere illusion to believe otherwise. The goal of systematic philosophical justification for physical object beliefs is not a reasonable task for any theory of knowledge to engage in. We can explain naturalistically how we can come to have such knowledge, but only by using a natural science which presupposes that there is a material world. Such a 'justification' by science is circular, for the purposes of the philosopher, but this shows only that the philosophical task of justification is not one we ought to pursue.

It is in this spirit that I interpret Marx's cryptic eighth thesis in his *Theses on Feuerbach:* 'All mysteries which lead theory to mysticism find their rational solution in human practice and in the comprehension of this practice.'[3] It is wrong to read this as a statement of pragmatism, which is foreign to Marx's overall outlook in any case. Marx is not saying that belief in a material world is justified because it works in practice. The thesis is not an attempted *solution* to the problem of the justification of our belief in the material world, through practice or through anything else. Rather, the thesis signifies an abandonment of the need to look for a philosophical solution, for it is an abandonment of the very question of philosophical justification for our belief in a reality essentially independent of mind. Once we engage in, and comprehend practice, from that vantage point the philosophical puzzle of justification for such knowledge simply dissolves. We do not answer the philosophical question, but forget it. 'The real premisses from which we begin . . . are the real individuals, their activity, and the material conditions under which they live.'[4]

Thus, as naturalists we eschew all attempts to justify, by non-question-begging arguments, our belief in mind-independent objects; we merely begin with them. It is the original sin of most modern philosophers that they tailored their theories of knowledge so as to ward off that demon, scepticism, by trying to answer the philosophical questions of justification. From Descartes to Hegel, and beyond, the question that occupies centre-stage epistemologically in bourgeois thought is: with what premisses can we begin in order to justify our knowledge? This is as true of Hegel, who discusses the question in 'With What Must the Science Begin?',[5] as it was of Descartes in *The Meditations*. These philosophers have paid far too much attention to the sceptic or immaterialist. We do not seek a more refined answer to Hegel's or Descartes' question, to use in reply to the sceptic. We ignore the sceptic philosophically, and the challenge he threatens. We ignore the sceptic at the intellectual level because we think the solution to his difficulties are not philosophical, but of another order entirely. These sceptical doubts arise *within* the traditions of bourgeois thought, on whose presuppositions and assumptions about man, the world, and the nature of cognition these doubts depend for their very formulation.

Roy Bhaskar, in his recent book *A Realist Theory of Science,*[6] attempts to construct a transcendental argument which moves from the premiss that there is science to the conclusion that the objects of science are intransitive (real or mind-independent) and structured (do not necessarily appear or manifest themselves). For example, one of his several arguments for the mind-independence of the objects of science runs as follows:

For Kepler to see the rim of the earth drop away, while Tycho Brahe watches the sun rise, we must suppose that there is something that they both see (in different ways). Similarly, when modern sailors refer to what ancient mariners called a sea-serpent as a school of porpoises, we must suppose that there is something which they are describing in different ways. The intelligibility of scientific change (and criticism) and scientific education thus presupposes the ontological independence of objects of experience from the objects of which they are the experiences.[7]

Now, I think that it can be shown that, in fact, all of Bhaskar's transcendental arguments are either invalid, or ineffectual against the target, or question-begging. For example, concerning the above argument for the reality of objects, the following comment is in order. Bhaskar *assumes* in his argument that scientific change amounts to changing theories about that which does not itself change, which is precisely what Bhaskar needs to prove. Given that alternative (neo-idealist) interpretations of scientific change exist, according to which there is no neutral world 'shared' by different theories or paradigms, Bhaskar needs to argue for this assumption about the nature of scientific change, which he does not do. So his conclusion about the existence of mind-independent objects does not follow from the premiss of scientific change, unless that premiss is given a 'realistic' interpretation. It is not then surprising that the conclusion follows.

Much more importantly than any particular criticism which one could make against his transcendental arguments, we can question his transcendental method of argument. In his arguments both for the reality and structured nature of the objects of science, Bhaskar uses this transcendental method: assuming the admittedly contingent fact that science exists, he attempts to show that science is possible only on the assumption that its objects are real and structured. The conclusions of transcendental arguments comprise what Bhaskar terms 'a philosophical ontology': 'The status of propositions in ontology may thus be described by the following formula: It is not necessary that science occurs. But given that it does, it is necessary that the world is a certain way . . . given that science does or could occur, the world *must* be a certain way. Thus . . . that the world is structured and differentiated can be established by philosophical argument . . .'[8] Philosophy, for Bhaskar, can tell us what the world *must* be like.

My criticisms of Bhaskar's transcendental arguments for the existence of a mind-independent order concern two related points. First, I dispute the legitimacy of producing any arguments of *any* kind which purport to justify philosophically (i.e. non-circularly) our belief in the essential independence of the world from mind. We do not argue *to* the extra-mental existence of tables and chairs, as Bhaskar does. On a naturalist perspective, we begin with them. It concedes far too much to those who wish to impeach the mind-independence of the external world, of material reality, to think that we could take as premiss that science exists and argue from that to the conclusion that its objects are real. If we begin with science, then we begin with a particular human institution, and human beings *are* a special sort of physical object. To use Hegelian jargon, Bhaskar takes as immediate that science exists and as mediated by it that real objects exist. In fact, to take science as immediate is to take real objects as immediate as well. No argument is necessary, as I have already claimed.

Second, I dispute with Bhaskar the legitimacy of the notion of transcendental arguments, the conclusions of which are meant to comprise a philosophical ontology. The correct slogan here is, I think, this: mind-independent existence can never appear in the conclusion of a deductively valid argument unless mind-independent existence is assumed in a premiss. This seems to be an application of the rule that in a deductively valid argument nothing can appear in a conclusion which wasn't already, at least covertly, in the premisses. Thus, 'there is a chair' can appear as the conclusion in a deductively valid argument, whose premiss is 'There is a red chair'. But no deductive or transcendental argument can conclude to mind-independent existence unless its premisses assume mind-independent existence. What shall we say, then, about Bhaskar's 'transcendental arguments', the conclusions of which comprise his philosophical ontology? Bhaskar attempts to argue from 'Science exists' to 'There are real, mind-independent objects'. If 'Science exists' is not itself taken realistically, as a claim about a material human practice, then the argument must be invalid. One cannot pass from a premiss which makes no assertion of real existence to a conclusion which does. On the other hand, if 'Science exists' is taken in a realist sense, then Bhaskar's argument is trivial. On this interpretation of his premiss, Bhaskar is arguing from the premiss that mind-independent reality exists (for it is in such a reality that science is 'materialised') to the conclusion that mind-independent reality exists, hardly a surprising feat.[9] For all arguments with contingently true premisses, such arguments can have conclusions about mind-independent existences, but all such arguments need premisses about mind-independence in order to be deductively valid. Indeed the point is, I think, generalisable as a criticism of all such transcendental arguments for the existence of mind-independent reality. Either the premisses are 'weak' (i.e. do not assume mind-independence), in which case the argument cannot be valid, or the premisses are 'strong' (i.e. assume mind-independence), in which case the valid argument becomes uninteresting.

2. Any adequate theory of knowledge must be consistent with science. It is inimical to the spirit of any adequate philosophical theory to try to set *a priori* bounds and limits to the path of science, because our conception of philosophy is one that makes it *continuous* with science, and hence *a posteriori* in character, although more abstract than any of the particular sciences. Its abstraction differentiates it from the sciences in degree but not in kind.

This conception of philosophy, on which it is the most abstract of the *a posteriori* sciences, arises out of a scepticism about the very possibility of semantically based, non-trivial conceptual or analytic knowledge.[10] Whatever exception we may wish to make for 'formal' disciplines such as logic and mathematics—and I am not sure whether they should constitute exceptions—the point is that we simply are not in possession of a semantic theory powerful enough to substantiate the claim that there are non-trivial, interesting, *a priori* truths which depend for their truth merely on the meanings of the words or expressions involved in their formulation. We may find that 'all bachelors are unmarried' is analytic, but we are not going to obtain any likely candidates of the sort which have traditionally interested philosophers. Since there are, we claim, no such things as non-trivial, purely conceptual truths based on the meanings of words alone, which could constitute a legitimate field for study by the philosopher, no such truths on which the analytic philosopher could happily exercise his skill at *a priori* unpacking, then either philosophy is illegitimate because it has no field of study, or its field has the same kind of *a posteriori* character that the fields of every other discipline have. We hold that what philosophy studies, what constitutes its field, *is* the other sciences. This explains why philosophy is, like the other sciences, empirical in character and at the same time more abstract. It is empirical because the sciences it studies are themselves *a posteriori;* it studies their *a posteriori* truths. But it studies the most general truths of the special sciences, and so has an altogether more abstract character than they have. This seems to be Marx's own conception of philosophy: 'When reality is depicted, philosophy as an independent branch of knowledge loses its medium of existence. At the best its place can only be taken by a summing-up of the most general results, abstractions which arise from the observation of the historical development of men'.[11]

This conception of philosophy is, and always has been, available as an alternative to the orthodox conceptual analysis paradigm which has permeated contemporary British philosophy to such a suffocating extent. I think a Marxist conception of philosophy, which I have been trying to describe, comes close to what has sometimes been called 'naturalism'[12] or 'naturalistic realism':

According to naturalistic realism . . . there are no philosophical doctrines which are either epistemologically prior to, or independent of, all other statements in the admissible, structure of human knowledge . . . Although there may be logical priority among sets of doctrines in the sense in which philosophical doctrines are in some sense both more general assertions than those of science, include the doctrines of science in their subject matter, and even in some sense constitute a framework for the expression of scientific knowledge, they are in no sense immune from criticism emanating from the development of science. Indeed, philosophical doctrines are held explicitly to evolve in dynamic interplay with the evolving scientific world view itself.[13]

Perhaps it is this broadly empirical conception of philosophy which Lukacs had in mind in the following remark, which is at one and the same time critical and constructive: analytic philosophy reserves for itself the job of 'uncovering and justifying the validity of the concepts formed' instead of 'breaking through the barriers of this formalism which has fallen into isolated pieces, by means of a radically different orientation of the problematic, an orientation towards the concrete, material totality of what can and should be known. Philosophy in this case would be adopting the same position towards the individual sciences as the latter in fact adopt towards empirical reality.'[14] Nor is it surprising that such a conception of philosophy should be inimical to Bhaskar who, after all, conceives of a philosophical ontology, composed of the conclusions of transcendental arguments. For Bhaskar, philosophy is not broadly empirical: 'It seems to me to be always a mistake in philosophy to argue from the current state of a science (and especially physics).'[15] This is not Marx's conception of philosophy, which is supposed to be 'a summing-up of the most general results' of any of the special sciences, physics included. Bhaskar's philosophy purports, rather, to tell the sciences the way the world *must* be. On our conception of *a posteriori* philosophy, this is not a legitimate enterprise.

To say that philosophy is itself, broadly speaking, 'scientific' in character has the ring to it of what Putnam once called 'nineteenth century materialism, or to be blunt about it, village atheism'.[16] We realise, though, that uncritical adulation of science can all too easily be overdone. No critical person ought to have a wholly uncritical attitude about anything, and *a fortiori* not about science either. We recognise that what may pass as science at any particular time may itself be influenced by the ideological perspectives of those who pass as scientists. Science, like anything else, is a human institution, with a history, and located within the domain of class struggle. Therefore, what is regarded as 'scientific' in the natural sciences is in principle no more free of being susceptible to ideology and the effects of class struggle than is what is regarded as 'scientific' in the human sciences.

Whether or not this is so is at least in principle detectable by using scientific methodology, and this presupposes the reasonableness of the conception of a science of ideology. We can use, then, part of science to correct other parts. It is perfectly possible to use science or scientific methodology to question the credentials of some particular piece of science, or indeed to question the credentials of some extensive part of science, or its method. But what, for us, can make no sense is to ask whether all science and its methodology may be suspect, for there is no Archimedean point lying outside science altogether which would provide any purchase for making such a question intelligible to us. Criticism of science from within science does not support the idea of the possibility of a philosophical criticism of all science. There is no philosophical criticism from a 'conceptualist point of view', in the way in which, for example, much of the literature in philosophical psychology attempted to criticise psychology and ended by telling us such things as that there were no such things as dreams, only dream reports.[17] If logic is *a priori,* then there are certain *a priori* formal standards of criticism like consistency which can be brought to the special sciences. But apart from this possibility, we do not accept the 'conceptual confusions', 'category mistakes', and 'semantic infelicities' which it was said by philosophers that many of their unsuspecting scientific colleagues had unwittingly made. The jokes told in philosophical circles about analytic or ordinary language philosophers claiming that something was conceptually impossible one day, only to find on the next that science had discovered that what was thought to have been conceptually impossible had actually happened, have their point. The spectacle of philosophy attempting to instruct science using 'purely conceptual' standards is a just object of derision. The difficulty in telling science what the world *must* be like is that the world may not turn out to be that way.

So far, it is true, the concept of 'a general summing-up' remains a mere cipher. One strand in the notion is certainly the idea of generalising from the results of the special sciences in providing answers to what have been recognised as the traditional philosophical problems. However, it should not be thought that there is no 'linguistic' element to a 'general summing-up'. Drawing distinctions, refining concepts, choosing the better of alternative, possible descriptions of something—this 'linguistic' activity can be part and parcel of science and the critique of science, for none of this need be done from an *a priori* point of view. Thus, when Marx criticised classical political economy for failing to develop the notion of labour-power, or for failing to distinguish price and value, or for conflating the value of labour and the value created by labour, we can understand this 'linguistic' criticism as legitimately scientific criticism of political economy. Decisions about how to talk about the facts can also be governed by *a posteriori* considerations, rather than allegedly *a priori* considerations of meaning and conceptual truth. Summing-up is always a linguistic phenomenon, and it must therefore be a matter of concern as to *how* that summing-up is to be done. Equally, it can always be legitimate to criticise how someone else has performed his summing-up. But that does not render such summing-up, or criticism of it, *a priori,* or undertaken from an *a priori* perspective.

Our general rejection of *a priori* method in philosophy means that no philosophical position can be insulated from the relevance of science, with which philosophy is continuous. Thus, it is reasonable to demand that a theory of knowledge be consistent with science. It must be consistent with special sciences, such as perceptual psychology, learning theory, cognition studies, and so on. This is both a strength and weakness of classical empiricism, which intended to generalise and build on the scientific theory of information or concept acquisition as it existed in its infancy in the eighteenth century. Hume, for example, is sometimes criticised by analytic philosophers for not drawing a distinction between the analytical or conceptual contributions and the empirical, psychological elements which are combined in his philosophy. For us, it is a strength of Hume, *vis-à-vis* his contemporary critics, that he did not try to separate the continuous and ultimately inseparable theory of knowledge and psychology. Hume's weakness is that the science he uses is simply outdated (and arguably ideological in any event). What is to be criticised is the methodology not of Hume, but of those pieces of epistemology artificially disguised as conceptual analysis, to which science is supposed not to be relevant and which often unintentionally embody the outdated science of an earlier epoch, despite their empirical disclaimers. Similarly, we noted in Chapter I Strawson's criticism of Kant, on the grounds that Kant had admixed (what he intended to be) an *a priori* theory of knowledge with what were merely empirical results. We do not criticise Kant on these methodological grounds, although we certainly acknowledge that the science from which he draws has progressed far beyond the state it was in during his lifetime.

But, it may be asked, does not our theory of knowledge attempt to instruct science in just this *a priori* fashion? First, what is the status of materialism itself, the claim that something exists essentially independently of human activity? Is this knowable *a priori,* or a regulative rule of reason? It does not seem to be *a posteriori,* and yet seems to be a philosophical result. Second, does such a materialism commit us *a priori* to the existence of matter, belief in which is as outdated as phlogiston or the aether? How can philosophy saddle science with a dogma drawn from the nineteenth century? Suppose science tells us (as indeed it does tell us) that, ultimately, the world is composed of various forms of energy, fields of forces, or whatever. As materialists, do we tell science to behave itself? Is Bhaskar's claim that it is always a mistake in philosophy to argue from the *current* state of science justified after all? For example, Susan Stebbing, in her *Philosophy and The Physicists* (Pelican Books, 1944), assumes that dialectical materialism is engaged in precisely just this sort of *a priori* imposition on science:

Lenin and other dialectical materialists have as much an axe to grind as any Gifford Lecturer. The 'materialists'—to give them the name which they so ardently admire—seek at all costs to establish some form of metaphysical materialism. Scientific results must somehow or other be forced into an interpretation which will yield the special philosophical views upon which their political philosophy is professedly based. There is as much bad metaphysics and immature philosophising among the upholders of dialectical materialism . . . as among those who support the philosophical idealism of the pulpit. (p.7)

We shall have to inquire to what extent, if any, Lenin can justly be accused with the sort of charges Stebbing brings against him, and this we shall undertake in Chapter VI. Meanwhile, it is worthwhile noting that Stebbing almost certainly means by 'materialism' the kind of reductive materialism we have eschewed. Stebbing says that 'If I have succeeded in showing that the present state of physical theories does not warrant any form of idealism, it must not thereby be concluded that I suppose it to warrant any form of materialism'. However, the form of materialism we have defended is simply equivalent to the denial of idealism, so that the materialism Stebbing has in mind must be the more specific, reductive materialism, which is not simply equivalent to the denial of idealism.

This accusation of *a priori* imposition on science grossly misunderstands what it is to which Marx's materialism commits us. Materialism, as I have described it, asserts the existence of something essentially independent of thought, mind, or human praxis. I have often called that something an 'object', even when I discussed Kant, although for Kant the fact that our experience is one of *objects* itself arises through the activity of thought. Talking about *objects* as that which materialism commits us to may itself be wholly misleading. It may well be—and Engels himself insists that this is so—that the division of reality into discontinuous discrete objects is something essentially related to the activities of human thought. Engels' own view is that reality is process, divisions and distinctions in which are made by our mind in its effort to grasp, comprehend, understand, the reality which lies before it.

The great basic thought that the world is not to be comprehended as a complex of ready-made *things,* but as a complex of processes . . . is now scarcely ever contradicted. The old metaphysics, which accepted things as finished objects, arose from a natural science which investigated dead and living things as finished objects . . .[18]

My own point here is not that Engels' view is necessarily the correct one. The point, rather, is that Engels was quite right to regard the question of what is the nature and structure of that which exists essentially independently of us as a question for scientific investigation. Our beliefs about its nature or structure have changed as the natural sciences have themselves changed, and it is important not to tie materialism down to outdated beliefs about the nature of mind-independent reality which are taken from a particular stage in the development of the natural sciences, a mistake which many materialists have certainly too often made. Our ordinary modes of understanding reality, which divides it into *things* of familiar *kinds,* has no specially sacrosanct status. Reality could be essentially as it was described as being by Greek atomists, eighteenth, nineteenth, or twentieth century chemistry and physics, or as is more likely, not exactly like any of the theoretical descriptions natural science has yet produced. The question is not one philosophers have anything to dictate about in *a priori* fashion to natural scientists. All materialism does commit us to is the belief that something exists essentially independently of human thought or activity; for its proper description one relies on natural science.

But what of materialism itself? Is that an *a priori* truth that philosophers can foist upon natural scientists who unwittingly may be lead to an 'idealist' interpretation of their results? Does the commitment to materialism as we have explained it at least attempt to instruct science *a priori* in the minimal commitment to there being something or other which is essentially independent of mind?

I have already argued that materialism is not itself *a priori* true. Moreover, I claimed, against Bhaskar, that there are no deductively valid, non-question-begging arguments which are able to establish the conclusion that materialism is true. If materialism were either an *a priori* truth, or there were such interesting, valid transcendental arguments, we could thereby provide a justification for our belief in the mind-independence of the natural world, and this is precisely what I have denied.

I spoke earlier of the vision of philosophy, shared by Marxism and others, as broadly *a posteriori,* continuous with the development of natural science. I also quoted Marx's remarks about philosophy having as its legitimate task only 'a summing-up of the most general results' of science. But what shall we say about materialism? If materialism is not an *a priori* truth, is it one that at least *in principle* could be established by science? Is it *a posteriori?* Does science give materialism any inductive support?

At first sight it might be thought that materialism is straight-forwardly *a posteriori.* For example, is the denial of materialism, which holds that world is essentially dependent on mind, really consistent with the findings of science? Geology informs us that there was a time at which a natural world existed, but no human mind or thought to grasp it. Does this geological fact 'confirm' the essential independence of the natural world? If so, could this then count as a scientific *a posteriori* justification of materialism? Does science establish materialism inductively?

Unfortunately, the relationship between materialism and science is not so straightforward. Idealism, as the denial of materialism, can always be made consistent with science in the following way.[19] It is clear that there has existed a world unrelated to human mind. But idealism may then appeal to Infinite or Absolute Mind to which the natural order would have always stood in relation (and necessarily, rather than contingently so). Indeed, this attempt to make science and idealism formally consistent will always force idealism into a form of theology. There may have been a natural world unrelated to finite minds, but Infinite Mind, or Absolute Spirit offers itself as a first-class candidate to the idealist as that to which the natural world has always stood in essential relation. The denial of essential independence must then collapse into a version of Hegelian absolute idealism. This verdict reinforces, I think, the point that Hegelian jargon taken seriously cannot be detached from the general idealist framework in which it is situated.[20] What better argument can we offer to those Marxists who use the jargon of the inseparability of nature and mind (or thought, or man) than the argument that such jargon must ultimately be understood as theology? Since everyone knows that there has been a natural order without human minds, insistence on the jargon can only lead to the inseparability of the natural order and mind itself, or of the natural order and the cosmic Man.

Thus, materialism is one form of atheism, and idealism a form of theism. I accept that both materialism and idealism are inductively consistent with the results of science. In this way, science neither 'disconfirms' idealism nor, therefore, 'confirms' materialism; no straightforward empirical, a posteriori inductive justification of materialism is possible. Theology has always been able to guard itself against empirical refutation; there is no evidence which could disprove the contention made by Hegel that nature is necessarily related to Absolute Mind. Indeed, even a careful, circumspect statement of divine creation is possible which makes it compatible with science. Since empirical evidence cannot refute idealism, that evidence does not provide a justification for the denial of idealism.

Although a posteriori justification of materialism is not possible, there is still a sense, I think, in which materialism is continuous with the sciences, is an 'a posteriori' philosophy, whereas idealism is not. It is difficult to specify precisely in what this continuity consists, but it has to do ultimately with unity of approach or outlook. To look at the world materialistically is to look at it in the same sort of way as one looks at it as a scientist. It is a 'diurnal philosophy'[21] which asks us to accept science at its face value, not to move beyond the reality our science attempts to describe for us. It is the philosophy of the a posteriori, literally the philosophy for science. Idealism, as a theology, demands a break with scientific modes of thought and reasoning. It bifurcates methodology, demands a dualism in our understanding. It is in that sense discontinuous with science. It is not a philosophy of the a posteriori in approach or method, although it is not inconsistent or incompatible with science. Idealism is the 'nocturnal philosophy'.

I have steadfastly maintained the impossibility of providing a non-circular justification of materialism. Earlier I argued that it had no deductive justification, and now I have been arguing that it has no a posteriori, inductive justification, since both materialism and its denial are consistent with scientific evidence. In keeping with the earlier vision of philosophy I sketched, I still claimed that there was a sense in which materialism remains continuous with science, a philosophy of the a posteriori if not quite an a posteriori philosophy.[22] It, and not idealism, is a general summing-up of science. Even if this last claim be accepted, I do not claim that it provides a justification for materialism. No non-circular justification is possible. The idealist could retort that, for him, continuity with science does not itself constitute a reason in favour of a philosophy, rather discontinuity with science ought to be the *sine qua non* for acceptance of the claims of a philosophy. Thus, I cannot see that the fact that materialism expresses the 'spirit' of science, if it be a fact as I have claimed, can constitute a non-circular justification of materialism to a determined opponent.

This is, I think, as it should be. I said earlier about the sceptic, who refused to accept the extra-mental existence of objects, that we ignore him at the intellectual level, that no rational justification for the denial of scepticism is necessary because we think that the solution to his difficulties are not really philosophical at all, but of another order entirely. Similar comments are in order about the idealist, who denies the essential independence of the existence of the natural order from the existence of thought or mind. Ultimately, the choice between materialism and idealism is the choice between two competing ideologies. The choice is not an 'epistemological' choice to be made on grounds of stronger evidence or more forceful argument, but is a 'political' choice to be made on class allegiance. Although materialism, as we have discussed it, is not *all* there is to Marxism—since it is a doctrine far less controversial than Marxism is—there is certainly no Marxism without it. As an idealist, one cannot, objectively, be on the side of the proletariat in class struggle; its interests and ultimate role in history cannot be advanced following the political practice that tends to flow from an idealist or theological perspective. The history of the workers' movement after Marx and Engels has, I believe, born out the truth of this claim time and time again. If it is true, then this should be what determines the final, political choice between idealism and materialism, and not a futile, continuing search for deductive or inductive arguments in favour of one or the other.

3. Knowledge is irreducibly *social*. This claim has been made many times before, and I do not now wish to rehearse all the various things which this rather ambiguous claim has been, or could be, taken to mean. It is certainly true that Descartes, the classical empiricists, and Kant had, in different ways, a very asocial conception of knowledge. 'What can *I* know?' rather than 'what can *we* know?' is for them the logically prior point of departure. One of the genuine insights of Hegel and the Hegelian movement, including philosophers like Bradley and Bosanquet, is the re-location of epistemological (and moral) questions back into the community. This Hegelian insight is one that Marx made his own. This is true also for much of the Wittgensteinian tradition, with its emphasis on the oft repeated but little understood notion of 'a form of life', with its insistence on the priority of a public language to any form of private language or discourse.[23]

There is one point about the social nature of knowledge which I should like to touch upon. In the practice of acquiring knowledge (or values, since precisely parallel remarks to the tension between community and individual knowledge can be made about the tension between community and individual values), whether as a scientist or simply at the level of ordinary experience, each man receives a social transmit, a portion of the collected wisdom (or values) of the society in which he finds himself. He receives such knowledge through his learning contacts with others, either before he is able to reflect critically on what he is learning or often simply as a matter of fact without critical reflection, even if he is capable of it.

Although each man receives such a social transmit, no man is *bound* to it, for he can come to critically reflect on anything which he is taught. That is, he can come to critically reflect, *if* the transmission mechanism has operated on him by respecting him as a rational agent, for people who are brainwashed, indoctrinated, etc., often are not *capable* of coming to critical reflection. Thus, in certain conditions which it is not now important to specify more precisely, not only can a man add to what he learns, but he can come to reject or revise that which he has been taught. Within certain constraints, the knowledge which an individual acquires for himself after receiving the social transmit can be corrective as well as additive.

This is a commonplace, but it is one well worth restating, for the following reason. On the individualist conception of knowledge, so common to philosophy as it is shaped by the bourgeois mode of production, a man appeared to be able to reject everything which he had been taught. This is an absurdity, and Descartes' individual quest for certainty was absurd for this reason. Descartes was genuinely worried that he may have accepted as true, false beliefs, opinions, prejudices which he may have acquired by learning in an uncritical way. His worry was genuine insofar as it grew out of a sense of the influence of the church, its dogma and its use of ancient school philosophy, over the minds of his contemporaries. Hence, Descartes undertook to reject everything which he had been taught, in order to rebuild knowledge on the firm individual certainties which could not possibly be false.

Had Descartes really been able to dispossess himself of all that had been socially transmitted to him, would he have been able to proceed in his quest for firm and secure knowledge? It does not seem so. We do not deny that, in addition to a social transmit, a man receives a biological transmit.[24] On the contrary, Marxist materialism must be especially alive to the ways in which the natural world continues to exercise its influence, its constraining and limiting influence as well as the possibilities it provides, over social man. The extent of the importance of the biological transmit is an empirical, *a posteriori* question,[25] and the role of philosophy is to sum up, rather than dictate, these scientific results. But it does, as a matter of 'deep' fact, seem to be true of men that with the biological transmit alone, they are capable of almost nothing in the way of knowledge acquisition, beyond that which we might attribute to some of the higher animals. Thus, we can say that if Descartes had really been able to dispossess himself of all that had been socially transmitted to him, he would not have known how to proceed. He would not have known and could not have acquired the technique for acquiring secure knowledge, for knowing that there is a *technique* for the acquisition of knowledge is itself a piece of socially transmitted knowledge that one acquires from others. If Descartes could have emptied himself of all previously acquired knowledge, and the techniques which are part of that knowledge, he would also have had to dispossess himself of the twenty-one rules which he sets out in his *Rules For the Direction of the Mind*. Men learn from others that 'If we are to understand a problem perfectly, we must free it from any superfluous conceptions, reduce it to the simplest terms, and by a process of enumeration, split it up into the smallest possible parts' (Rule XIII). This is not an innate truth with a biological basis; it is one we learn, for there is nothing inconceivable in the idea that the best way to understand a problem is by drawing as many links as we can between it and superfluous conceptions. Thus, to dispossess oneself of *all* that one has been taught is to dispossess oneself of the rules which one could use to acquire new knowledge for oneself. In such a case, Descartes literally would not have known what to do next. Replacement or correction of socially transmitted knowledge by the individual presupposes the existence of socially transmitted goals and techniques which give correction and replacement their intelligibility. No justificationist programme which is to begin with individually acquired certainties only, independent of all other knowledge which is to be based upon it, can account for the need for the ineradicable presence of some social transmit in all knowledge acquisition or replacement. Everything can be replaced, but piecemeal only, while one preserves something of the social transmit that provides the anchor for the lever of replacement.

If the idea of rejecting all that one has received by way of social transmit is the Scylla of individualist conceptions of knowledge, there is a related Charybdis which lurks within some idealist and neo-idealist theories of knowledge. Their social conception of knowledge (or values) becomes far too strong, so that an individual can reject nothing of what he has been taught, can obtain no critical distance from any of the beliefs he has acquired from his social environment. He has become trapped inside a form of life. Much of what Hegel says suggests this difficulty, for example his remarks on the fate of a man who tries to be better than the ethical level reached by his society. So too, this difficulty is suggested by some of the things Kuhn says about those poor unfortunates locked within a period of normal science, or is suggested by the fate of the linguistic innovator according to a strict ordinary language philosophy.

It is thus important to get the social and individual mix right in a theory of knowledge. A man *must* as a matter of fact receive a social transmit: 'The solitary and isolated hunter or fisherman who serves Adam Smith and Ricardo as a starting point, is one of the unimaginative fantasies of eighteenth century romances *à la* Robinson Crusoe . . . This is an illusion and nothing but the aesthetic illusion of the small and big Robinsonades'.[26] The biological transmit is insufficient. Robinson Crusoe, supposing he had never had *any* human contact, would never have developed very far epistemologically, regardless of how fine a specimen he may have been biologically. But, although a social transmit is necessary in order to initiate the process of learning and knowledge acquisition, once the process is in working order the transmit can be jettisoned. A man can usually correct what he believes to be in need of correction or modification in what he has been taught.

This commonplace, as I have called it, has a special relevance to the development of a theory of ideology. Ideologies are tissues of beliefs, especially about man and society, which individuals acquire in various ways, either 'naturally', because reality appears to be as the ideology says it is, or 'artificially', through the propagation and reinforcement of such beliefs by various social mechanisms. However, having received those ideological perspectives, individuals are not incapable of correcting and changing them. In all societies (except full communism) we expect men to be the recipients of ideologies in some measure or other. The class nature of all societies, the division of labour, and the remnants of these even in a society in transition to full communism, insure that in some measure truth will be distorted in the social transmit. But men are not necessarily trapped within these distortions.

Sometimes, theories of ideology can be stated in ways which neglect this truth. For example, Franz Jakubowski claims that 'a false consciousness *must* therefore correspond to a particular social situation, to a position in society from which correct knowledge is *impossible*' [my emphasis].[27] Jakubowski quotes Max Weber, who seemed to have the same sort of 'bondage to a point of view' in mind, but applied it equally to Marxism as well as other class outlooks: 'The materialist conception of history is not some kind of taxi, which one can get into or out of at will; once inside, even the revolutionaries themselves are not free to leave it'. Finally, Jakubowski says again: 'Ideology as false, partial consciousness corresponds to a particular position in society from which a correct, total understanding is impossible.'[28]

It is true that Marx's own formulations often suggest the view that, given that a man occupies a certain place or position in society, he *must* hold a certain ideological position. How else, it might be asked, are we to comprehend Marx's well-known dictum in the Preface to *The Critique of Political Economy,* that 'it is not the consciousness of men that determines their being but, on the contrary, their social being that *determines* their consciousness' [my emphasis]? 'Determines' seems to carry the implication that a man *could* not have had any alternative consciousness.

Marx's other expressions for this relationship between social or class position and ideology or consciousness tend to be highly metaphorical, and 'weaker' in the sense that they do not have the strong, determinist flavour generally associated with a verb like 'determines'. Elsewhere in the Preface for example, Marx speaks of consciousness *reflecting* or *being appropriate to* the mode of production. Such formulations do not carry the same suggestion that men are trapped within the views which are transmitted to them. Indeed, it is not really clear at all that Marx's use of 'determines' carries this suggestion. One writer has reminded us that Marx's concept of determination may not be the same as ours.[29] Marx's concept has a specific location within the philosophical tradition of Spinoza and Hegel, and carries essentially the idea of a limitation. To determine is to make determinate, to give something determinations, properties, and thereby to delimit more specifically what kind of thing it is. If we take Marx's use of 'determines' in this sense, we can interpret Marx as saying that mode of production or social and class position tends to limit or constrain the range of beliefs which individuals are likely to find plausible and hence to adopt. In this sense a mode of production, or a specific position in it, acts as a 'blinker' which tends to close off from view various alternative beliefs. On this 'limitation' reading of the way in which being *determines* consciousness, which I think is a perfectly natural one given Marx's intellectual formation, any trace of the suggestion that a man is *trapped* inside an ideology vanishes. Marx provides us with a social conception of knowledge, but one which avoids trapping individuals inside the social knowledge (or ideology) which they receive, by allowing for the possibility that they may be able to extricate themselves from it. As we shall see when we come to discuss the essence and appearance distinction, what Marx does think necessary is that social being, under specific conditions, does *appear* in a certain way. But it is not necessary that men take those appearances for reality, although it is natural that they should tend to do so, and hence it is not necessary that they hold ideological beliefs about themselves and the society in which they find themselves. They can come to know that such appearances are not indicative of what their situation essentially is, and however naturally tempting such appearances may be to men, there is no *necessity* that they succumb to them in forming their beliefs, however likely it may be that they will do so.

4. Marxists often remark, and rightly so, that the fundamental difference between Marxism and many (but not *all*) other philosophies is that Marxism makes absolutely central to its outlook the social practice of man. But what does this claim amount to and precisely which are the 'many other' philosophies which do differ from Marxism in this respect?

It is probably not necessary today, as it sometimes has been in the past, to point out that whatever the centrality of praxis means for Marxists, it cannot be identified with pragmatism, the doctrine which *identifies* truth and usefulness. In whatever other ways Kolakowski misinterprets Marx in the article of his which we have been discussing, he certainly gets right the distinction between pragmatism and Marxism: 'we are . . . entitled to consider the first pragmatists advocates of the philosophy of individual success that for so long nourished the mind of the New World in its rapid economic development. One can find some of James' [the pragmatist philosopher] formulas duplicated almost literally in the writings of Henry Ford.'[30] Similarly, we agree with Ludovico Geymonat's insistence that the praxis that is central to both Marx and Lenin's theory of knowledge does not constitute a variety of pragmatism:

It is often maintained that an explicitly or implicitly pragmatist orientation is to be found in many of Marx's writings and even in some pages of Lenin. According to this point of view, the realism ascribed to Lenin represents nothing more than a dogmatic residue inherited from Engels . . .

We of course have no intention of denying that Lenin often makes reference to practice as the criterion for distinguishing what is true and what is false. The crux of the matter, however, is whether practice is taken simply as a *confirmation* of the objectivity of certain 'relative truths', or whether the use of practice as a criterion is taken to be a denial of the existence of any purely theoretical source of truth.[31]

Geymonat distinguishes, then, between the view that practice is a *criterion* of truth, a way of telling the true from the false (or the meaningful from the meaningless), and the view that practice is a *definition* of truth (or meaningfulness), only the latter of which is pragmatism. Geymonat argues that only the former, but not the latter, can be attributed to Lenin, and his conclusion should be extended to deny the attribution of pragmatism to Marx as well. There are remarks in Marx's writings which suggest that the former view, that practice is a criterion of distinguishing between the true and the false, which Geymonat ascribes to Lenin, was Marx's position too. The second of Marx's 'Theses on Feuerbach' claims that 'in practice, man must prove the truth . . .' But whether or not these remarks justify the ascription of this position to Marx, by itself this would seem to fall far short of making the notion of practice central to one's philosophy. Surely the centrality of praxis means something more than this.

The way in which practice is central to Marxism is that it makes the social practice of men its central object of study. Marxism is literally the study of praxis, because praxis is its object. 'The chief defect of all hitherto existing materialism . . . is that the thing, reality, sensuousness, is conceived only in the form of the object . . . but not as human sensuous activity, not practice'. Human sensuous activity is the object of Marxism. The study of such activity, of human labour, and especially (but not only) the 'concrete' study of it as it is shaped and formed within specific modes of production, is its main concern. We said earlier that philosophy differed from the special sciences in being not *a priori* but rather more abstract. Moreover, we said that the object of philosophy, its field of study, was the sciences and their results, for which philosophy served as a 'general summing-up'. Human praxis, and the material conditions in which it occurs, is the object of Marxism; Marxism is the object of study of Marxist philosophy. The purpose of a Marxist philosophy is to 'sum up' the general results of the study of man and his material environment, and it is this purpose which explains the abstract character that Marxist philosophy, like any philosophy, is bound to assume. Marxist philosophy makes the study of praxis its object of study.

There is, then, room for an abstract Marxist philosophy of praxis and scientific studies of particular concrete forms of praxis. From this perspective, I think we can argue that there is nothing intrinsically ideological or non-scientific about studying praxis from an abstract point of view, so long as it is tempered and formed by the results of concrete study. There is nothing intrinsically ideological or 'unscientific' about Marx's early philosophical writings, simply because they *are* philosophical. In *The Economic and Philosophical Manuscripts,* for example, Marx is not doing science but philosophy, and there is nothing *ipso facto* wrong in that. Philosophy may not *be* science, since it is rather a 'general summing-up' of science, but the fact that it is strictly non-science does not make it *un*scientific. Indeed, we argued earlier that materialism, which is a philosophy and not strictly a science, was itself a 'scientific' philosophy, in the sense of being a philosophy which was continuous with the sciences and 'summed up' the methodology and outlook of the sciences. The interesting question about the philosophy of Marx's 'early' works can only be whether or not such studies *are* rooted in the scientific studies of concrete forms of praxis. If there were to be any epistemological 'break' in Marx's work, it could only be that Marx leaves off doing *a priori* philosophy for *a posteriori* philosophy. [32]

It is true that Marxist philosophy makes practice central in another way. In addition to the study of practice being its (abstract) object, it is a practical philosophy, a philosophy of action as well as a philosophy about action. 'The philosophers have only *interpreted* the world, in various ways; the point, however, is to *change* it.' But the aspect on which I wish to focus here is the way that Marxist philosophy makes practice central in the sense that it studies practice, rather than in the sense in which it is itself a practice.

Which philosophies can and which cannot study practice? Marx makes it clear that there is a sense in which Hegelian idealism also can study activity, for he says in the first thesis concerning Feuerbach that 'the *active* side, in contradistinction to materialism, was developed by idealism.' Marx, however, goes on to criticise this study of activity by idealism, since it was a study developed '*only* abstractly since, of course, idealism does not know real, sensuous activity as such [my emphasis]'. Hegel's study of activity was only abstract, *unrooted* in concrete elaborations of activity. Thus, the activity Hegelian idealism studied could never be the social activity of men, but only the activity of Man as such. The underpinning for such an abstract study could never come from 'below' but only from 'above'—the activity of Man could only be underpinned by a study of the activity of Absolute Spirit, Idea, or whatever. 'To begin with, they [the followers of Hegel] extracted pure unfalsified Hegelian categories such as "substance" and "self-consciousness", later they desecrated these categories with more secular names such as "species" "the Unique", "Man", etc.' [33]

Marx makes it clear that 'the chief defect of all hitherto existing materialism . . .' is that it could study objects but not practice at all, whether concretely or abstractly. This, let us suppose, was true of Feuerbach. But why does Marx extend these remarks to all 'hitherto existing' forms of materialism? Why should this be a plausible criticism of non-Marxist materialism in general?

It is clear that Marx uses 'materialism' very widely. It may be that my interpretation will not cover all those theories which Marx labels 'materialist' in that well-known section of *The Holy Family* entitled 'Critical Battle Against French Materialism'. But I think that, when Marx criticises 'all hitherto existing' materialist doctrines, he is thinking primarily of reductive materialism. He cites Gassendi, Hobbes, Bacon, Holbach, La Mettrie, as well as others, and he does seem to have principally in mind those forms of materialism which would deny the irreducibility of human activity. The world and everything in it is, at bottom, matter in motion, and then human activity can be reduced to, understood as, a particular sort of motion of a special sort of matter.

But why then couldn't reductive materialism take human practice as its object of study? There is no reason why one should require that the object of study be an *irreducible* object. Suppose, as a reductive materialist would insist, human practice could be reduced to matter in motion. Thus, suppose 'I made a chair' could be reduced to a set of statements about the physical motion of certain bits of matter. Can't reductive materialism still derivately study human practice? Sometimes reduction is confused with elimination. The reductive materialist does not eliminate human practice, but only shows that it can be reduced to, understood as, a form of matter in motion. Human practice is not eliminated, but only seen to be a *derivative* phenomenon. Reductionist analyses explicate, rather than extrude what is analysed from the world. Why should Marx, or anyone who wishes to study human practice, object to this?

I think Marx's objection could be phrased in the following way. What are the criteria for a successful reduction? It is generally recognised that truth-value equivalence between reducing and reduced statements must hold; statements about human practice would be true if and only if the replacing sentences about matter in motion were. But another, somewhat vaguer requirements is often mentioned: 'We fix on the particular functions of the unclear expression . . . and then devise a substitute, clear and couched in terms to our liking, that fills those functions. Beyond those conditions of partial agreement, dictated by our interests and purposes', preservation of other features or functions is not necessary.[34] Thus, we demand not only sameness of truth-value between reducing and reduced statements, but also that we can and do use the reducing statement for the same essential purposes as we used the reduced one. We can perhaps bring out this requirement with an example. Suppose we try to reduce moral statements to descriptive statements, as for example any form of naturalism would attempt. It is not sufficient for reduction that truth-value equivalence be established. We should also be able to use the descriptive, reducing statements to *commend* certain courses of action, a function which moral statements clearly perform. Whether these functions do carry over, or can be carried over, is a matter of empirical fact. It does, as a matter of fact, seem to be the case that we can commend action to people by saying, naturalistically, that such action will make people happy, or create opportunities for human development, or whatever naturalistic 'replacement' for moral statements we may prefer. Indeed, given the bad reputation morality and moral words have earned, it is arguably easier to commend with the replacement than with the original moral assertions. This, I think, is an important step in arguing that the alleged fact-value dichotomy can be bridged by naturalistic reductions, since such reductions can preserve the essential functions of moral discourse by transferring them to naturalistic discourse. That this transfer of functions is possible is a *fact*. Thus, whether or not reductions are acceptable or successful is very much an *a posteriori* affair.

We can understand Marx as saying that this transfer of function is *not*, in fact, accomplished in the case of reduction of human practice to matter in motion. We cannot do, or get done, with the reducing talk all that we could do, or get done, with the reduced talk. In the *Theses on Feuerbach,* Marx describes two different attitudes, the theoretical and the practical. His claim is that studying objects and studying human praxis gives rise to these two *different* attitudes. Because Feuerbach does not make human practice the object of his study 'he regards the theoretical attitude as the only genuinely human attitude, while practice is conceived and fixed only in its dirty-Judaical form of appearance. Hence he does not grasp the significance of "revolutionary", of "practical-critical" activity.'

Let us, for the sake of argument, grant Marx his factual claims. Suppose, as a matter of psychological fact, that the study of objects (matter, for instance) tended to give rise to a contemplative attitude, which tended to translate itself generally into political attitudes of passivity and quiescence. Suppose, on the other hand, that the study of human practice was far less likely to do so, that more commonly such a study gave rise to a practical, 'revolutionary', attitude which lead people to try to change, transform, their material environment. Would this not by itself be a considerable argument against the possible success of any such reduction? If the attitudes one adopted were, as a matter of fact, unbridgeably different toward activity and things, action and matter, this could explain why Marx does not allow a reductive materialism to be a philosophy of (derived) practice. No such reduction would be acceptable, since sameness of essential attitudes would fail. If this were so, one could see the point of saying that *only* a non-reductive materialism could be a philosophy of praxis, and hence to see what was the inadequacy in 'all hitherto existing' versions of materialism. Their 'reductions' could not have explained or analysed activity, but in the end only gotten rid of it altogether by replacing it with something about which we have very different attitudes. Their reductions could not be successful, because any such reduction to 'matter-in-motion' terms could not be a reduction *of* practical human activity at all. Only a non-reductive materialism can constitute a study of praxis, whether it be an abstract philosophical study of praxis in general, or a special scientific study of particular, concrete forms of praxis.

5. It is not uncommon for Marxists to mark this stress on human activity which we have just been describing by speaking of a dialectic of activity and nature, or of praxis and the natural world, in order to underline the requirement that a theory of knowledge must be able to account for activity and change as well as the objectivity of a natural order as it is given to us. In this sense, an adequate theory of knowledge, which recognises the reciprocal relations which hold between nature and praxis, must be dialectical. Man does not just learn mechanically about natural (and social) reality; he can change them too.

This too is not a novel point. But I think that this dialectic of praxis and nature must be understood in a special way, which permits them *not* to constitute a dialectic of 'equals'. This raises for us the question of just what a dialectical relation is, and it is to answering that question that I now turn as a way of explaining how and why praxis and nature cannot be a dialectic of 'equals', as indeed many other pairs cannot be either.

It is strange that Marxists use the concept of dialectics, or dialectical relations, so often, and yet have spent so little time in explaining what is meant when speaking in that way. Furthermore, in those few instances in which some have dealt with the problem of dialectics, in the end they have been content with old slogans to cover over, rather than solve, real problems.

An essential strand in the notion of a dialectical relation is that the relation is reciprocal, or two-way. If two events (occurrences, states of affairs, or processes), *a* and *b,* are reciprocally interconnected, then *a* stands in the relation of cause to *b,* and *b* stands in the relation of cause to *a.* This is not the only strand in the complex notion of a dialectical relation. I do not offer causal reciprocity as an adequate explication of all that is meant by calling a relation 'dialectical'. Perhaps it is not even the most important constituent of that idea. It does not capture the ideas of necessary opposition or real contradiction, which are essential ingredients of the idea of dialectics. However, reciprocity does represent, I think, *one* of the features of that relation which is often in the minds of those who speak of dialectical relations. Engels, for example, in *The Dialectics of Nature,* calls dialectics 'the science of interconnections', and this vision of the reciprocal inter-connectedness of things is an oft repeated theme in any discussion of dialetics. Again, in *Anti-Dühring,* Engels says:

We find that cause and effect are conceptions which only hold good in their application to individual cases; but as soon as we consider the individual cases in *their general connection with the universe as a whole,* they run into each other, and they become confounded when we contemplate that universal action and reaction in which causes and effects are eternally changing places, so that what is effect here and now will be cause there and then, and *vice versa* [my emphasis].[35]

The stress that one finds on reciprocity, or action and reaction, in Hegel as well as in Marx and Engels, is derived from what they all seemed to have considered an unduly asymmetric conception of causality which needed supplementation. The Humeian account of causality, for example, portrays causal relations (between *particular* events or states of affairs) as unidirectional, with the causal 'arrow' moving in a single direction only. If *a* and *b* refer to particular events, or whatever, then if *a* causes *b, b* cannot also cause *a*. This asymmetry is insured by the Humeian temporal requirement that a cause must precede its effect. If *a* causes *b*, then on the Humeian account *a* must temporally precede *b*. But *b* cannot then cause *a*, since nothing can temporally precede itself. So, on this account of causality, if *a* causes *b* (where '*a*' and '*b*' refer to particulars), then we can infer that *b* does not stand in the relation of cause to *a*. Causality is not, on this account, a reciprocal or dialectical relation.

Following the lead of Kant's Third Analogy, Hegel wanted to stress the extent to which causality is a reciprocal relation. On what I believe is the most plausible interpretation of what Hegel is doing in those sections of *The Lesser Logic* and *The Science of Logic* in which he deals with causality and reciprocity, Hegel is not contradicting the 'standard' account, concerning the asymmetry of particular causal relations. Rather, Hegel is reminding us of the prevelance, in society and in organic nature, of what we might call 'feedback' mechanisms where, in a sense compatible with the standard account of causality, two things are cause and effect of one another. Thus, Hegel claims that there is a sort of conceptual 'inadequacy' that arises if we stick at the level of asymmetric causality, for it involves us, he argues, in always chasing an infinite chain in both directions, always looking for a further cause of the cause, and a later effect of the effect. From the point of view of reciprocity, asymmetric causality is inadequate. Hegel grants that the 'standard' notion of causality makes it asymmetric:

> While cause and effect are in their notion identical, the two forms present themselves so that, though the cause is also an effect, and the effect is also a cause the cause is not an effect in the same connexion as it is a cause, nor the effect a cause in the same connexion as it is an effect.[36]

Every cause is an effect, and every effect a cause, but not 'in the same connexion'. *Each* particular causal relation is one-way, and hence causality, thus far, is not a reciprocal relation.

Hegel continues in the subsequent paragraph of the *Logic* to advance to reciprocity proper, which immediately takes up and transcends the truth of causality, for as Hegel says, 'Reciprocal action realises the causal relation in its complete development'. He explicates *his* notion of reciprocity in this way:

> It is this relation . . . in which reflection usually takes shelter when the conviction grows that things can no longer be studied satisfactorily from a causal point of view . . . Thus in historical research the question may be raised in a first form, whether the character and manners of a nation are the cause of its constitution and its laws, or if they are not rather the effect. Then, as the second step the character and manners on the one side and the constitution and laws on the other are conceived on the principle of reciprocity: and in that case the cause *in the same connexion as it is a cause* [my emphasis] will at the same time be an effect, and *vice versa*. The same thing is done in the study of nature, and especially of living organisms. There the several organs and functions are similarly seen to stand to each other in the relation of reciprocity. Reciprocity is undoubtedly the proximate truth of the relation of cause and effect.[37]

Reciprocity, then, is a development and elaboration of causality. It transcends the inadequacy of causality, simply because it permits an escape from infinite regress (and progress) by turning the causal arrow back upon itself:

In reciprocity . . . the rectilinear movement out from causes to effects, and from effects to causes, is bent round and back into itself, and thus the progress *ad infinitum* of causes and effects is, as a progress, really and truly suspended.[38]

I do not think that there is any real inconsistency whatever between a standard, asymmetric account of causal relations and the social or organic 'feedback' mechanisms about which Hegel reminds us. It is true that Hegel emphasises the importance of a sort of causal phenomenon which Hume does not consider, but the asymmetric and reciprocal accounts are clearly operating at different levels. Asymmetric causality holds between *particular* events (occurrences, states of affairs, processes); symmetric or reciprocal causality operates when it does at the level of event-types, or kinds of occurrences. Hegel does not himself mark the distinction in this way, but it seems clear from the examples he mentioned—historical research and the study of natural organisms—that this is what he intends. He does not, I think, mean to claim that *particular* causal relations are symmetric or reciprocal.

A case will make this distinction clear. We make reciprocal causal claims like the following: the fall in the value of the pound leads to increases in the rate of inflation and increases in the inflation rate lead to a fall in the value of the pound. Imagine the following, rather simple example. A heating and a cooling element are wired to one another in such a way that increases of temperature of the heating element bring about decreases of temperature of the cooling element, and decreases of temperature of the cooling element cause increases of temperature of the heating element. Here we can make a simple, reciprocal causal claim about the relation between two particular things, the heating and the cooling elements. But such reciprocal causal claims are never about particular occurrences or events, but about kinds of events or types of happenings. Falls in the value of the pound lead to increases in inflation, and inflationary increases lead to falls in the pound. Temperature increases in the one element lead to decreases in the other and conversely. We can always reintroduce asymmetry at the level of particular causal claims, claims about causal relations between particular events rather than kinds of events. For instance, it may be that the heating element increasing its temperature from $5°C$ to $6°C$ (a particular event) causes the cooling element to decrease its temperature from $9°C$ to $8°C$ (a particular event). That causal relation is asymmetric, because it is not true that the cooling element decreasing its temperature from $9°C$ to $8°C$ *also* caused the heating element to increase its temperature from $5°$ to $6°C$. It may have brought about a *further* particular occurrence, perhaps the rise in the temperature of the heating element from $6°$ to $7°C$, which is itself another asymmetric causal claim about particular events. At the level of particular events, causal asymmetry is preserved. Reciprocity manifests itself only at the level of kinds.

Sometimes the reference to the particular events of the relevant kind can only be accomplished by using a time reference. If, for example, we had a blue and red light bulb wired to one another so that the blue's lighting lead to the red's lighting, which in turn lead to a (further) instance of the blue's lighting, it may be that the difference between any two occurrences of the blue's lighting can be distinguished only by a reference to time, or place in a sequential ordering. Perhaps the seventh lighting of the blue bulb causes the seventh lighting of the red and in turn the seventh red lighting brings about the eighth blue lighting. The point is that by whatever method of referring to particulars we can manage, we can always produce causal claims about the relations between those particulars, relations which are asymmetric or unidirectional. I do not say that it is an easy task to establish these claims. In ongoing 'feedback' mechanisms we may readily see how to produce very general, reciprocal causal claims about the two-way causal relations holding between kinds of events. But it may be exceedingly difficult to see how to establish the right asymmetric, particular causal claims. As the pound falls, inflation spirals, and as inflation spirals, the pound falls. It may be far from obvious which bit of the pound's fall causes which percentage increment in the inflation rate, and which bit of the fall is caused by inflationary increases. But we do think that there are such particular events which are asymmetrically related, and we would not claim to have fully understood such 'feedback' mechanisms unless we could see how, *at least in principle,* to individuate instances of the fall and increments of the inflation rate so that such asymmetric claims can at least be formulated. Indeed, to say that two kinds of happenings are reciprocally related simply means that some instances or particulars of the first kind of event asymmetrically cause some instances or particulars of the second kind and other instances or particulars of the second kind asymmetrically cause other instances or particulars of the first kind, so we must know how at least to individuate instances or particulars of the two kinds.

These general remarks set the stage for a related set of problems which have bedeviled historical materialism almost from its inception. There are various pairs which, according to Marxism, *are* reciprocally related, and it is often said that only a 'mechanical' version of Marxism could deny this two-way causality.

This is the mechanical materialist conception, not the dialectical materialist conception. True, the productive forces, practice, and the economic base generally play the principal and decisive role; whoever denies this is not a materialist. But it must also be admitted that in certain conditions such aspects as the relations of production, theory, and the superstructure in turn manifest themselves in the principal and decisive role . . . This does not go against materialism and firmly upholds dialectical materialism.[39]

Thus, base and superstructure, forces and relations of production, being and consciousness, production and consumption, exchange value and market price, nature and praxis, are all said to constitute reciprocally related pairs. But, as Mao's remarks make clear, such reciprocity is supposed to be *in addition to* some kind of asymmetry, not at its expense. In every example, the first of the reciprocally related pairs is held to be, in some way, primary, or basic, or ultimately decisive, or determinate in the last instance. All of these qualifications are asymmetric qualifications, for if, for example, base determines superstructure in the last instance, it is not meant to be equally true that superstructure determines base in the last instance. Thus, historical materialism is committed to finding ultimate causal asymmetries between causally reciprocal things, and it has never really been clear how this is to be done. Naturally, particular causal relations are asymmetric. If something's happening in the base leads to something else's occurring in the superstructure, then that is an asymmetric causal relation. But, with reciprocally related pairs, such asymmetric particular causal relations hold *in both directions* between the pairs. Clearly, what Marxism needs is a way to establish some sort of priority or causal asymmetry at the general level, the level of kinds, and it is this which has never been clarified by historical materialists.

In particular, if praxis and nature were *only* reciprocally related, each would be 'equally' a function of, or dependent on, the other. There could be no grounds for selecting nature (or praxis) as in some sense primary or basic, for these would be asymmetric qualifications. Both 'basic to' and 'primary in relation to' name asymmetric relations. If nature is primary in relation to praxis, then praxis cannot be primary (in the same sense) in relation to nature. But the primacy of nature over praxis (or over thought or mind) is what any realist position demands. How then shall we account for this asymmetric primacy while at the same time preserving a dialectical or reciprocal perspective?

It is worthwhile pausing at this point, if only to show why one candidate for introducing the desired asymmetry at the level of *particular occurrences* will not work. Suppose someone tries to interpret 'ultimately decisive' in a *temporal sense.* Although now, it might be said, individual occurrences at the level of the forces of production cause happenings or events at the level of the relations of production, and *vice versa,* the circle of mutual interaction *began at some time* by an individual happening at the level of the forces of production. The circle was begun by one individual event from one side of the pair, and that is sufficient for claiming that, in an asymmetric sense, that member of that pair is ultimately decisive or primary. But it is easy to see why such a simpleminded solution is not going to work. We will, on such a reading, be pushed farther and farther back in history to find our initial moment in the causal series, and such a search begins to look like a search for the 'first cause', a search which Marx accused the political economists of, and against which he warned in the *Economic and Philosophic Manuscripts.* Moreover, such a reading of the primacy of forces over relations of production would still not permit us to say that *present* forces of production determine (ultimately) *present* production relations, and hence would not justify a Marxist analysis of any social formation subsequent to the first cause which concentrated on the forces of production of that society. Similarly for the priority of nature over praxis. Nature and praxis reciprocally interact. The asymmetric priority of nature over praxis cannot be established merely by the claim that there was a nature at a time before there was praxis. Such priority is not very interesting, any more than the 'priority' of the blue bulb over the red would be on the grounds that we began the circuit with an occurrence of the blue's lighting. There is no sense in which the blue is 'ultimately decisive' over the red at later times, and no methodological reason to investigate the bulbs in such a way that made attention on the blue bulb primary for any study of the 'feedback' mechanism. If we want to introduce asymmetries into our pairs, *temporal* priority of an event occurrence of one kind over any event occurrence of the other kind is not what we want.

There is a tendency within historical materialism which, surprisingly, seems to deny any *real* asymmetry at any level between such pairs. There are remarks of Engels which might *just* suggest this:

In order to understand the separate phenomena, we have to tear them out of the general inter-connection and consider them in isolation, and there the changing motions appear one as cause and the other as effect.

But the real culprit here is Ollman, in his recent *Alienation*. Ollman's argument is that Marx, following in the philosophical footsteps of Spinoza and Hegel, assumes that there are necessary, internal relations between each thing and *every* other thing. On this conception an internal relation is certainly a reciprocal relation. If *a* is internally related to *b*, *b* is internally related to *a*. If all relations are internal, how can we establish any asymmetries at all?

. . . to single out any aspect as the determining one can only be a way of emphasizing a particular link in the problem under consideration. Marx is saying that for this factor, in this context, *this* is the influence most worth noting, the relation which will most aid our comprehension of the relevant characteristics.[40]

Ollman seems to argue, then, that there are not *really* any asymmetric relations between things, but that we look at things 'as if' there were such asymmetrics in order to aid our comprehension. But then we want to know if we could have just as well comprehended things from the contrary asymmetric perspective. Could we just as well have studied production so that it appeared ultimately determined by consumption and distribution? Is it just arbitrary that Marx considered the being-determining-thought relation torn loose from the general interconnection of things, so that he might just as well have chosen to consider the thought-determining-being relation as the ultimately decisive one? Of course these choices are not, for Marx, arbitrary. It is true that these choices, choosing these asymmetries over the reverse asymmetries, 'most aid our comprehension of the relevant characteristics'. But is this not so because there do exist these asymmetries in the natural and social world? The reason why it most aids our comprehension to study consumption as determined ultimately by production rather than as ultimately determining production is that—consumption *is* ultimately determined by production! Not all relations between things can be internal relations, because this affords us no opportunity to find real asymmetries in the world, and no opportunity to explain the nature of *science,* whereby such asymmetries are investigated. If all relations are internal, if everything is interconnected to everything else, then that is *all* that can be said. That we want to say more is clear evidence that there are other kinds of relations, namely asymmetric ones, where the reverse is not equally true.

The first thing which must be pointed out is that the pairs we have mentioned make it seem that causality is a relation between particular *things* (in the widest possible sense of 'thing'). Causal relations appear to hold between *the* forces and relations of production, exchange value and prices of production, being and thought. As long as this is not seen to be a misleading way of speaking, the problems of reciprocity and asymmetry will never be solved. Causal relations hold between events, or states of affairs, or happenings, or processes. Engels often speaks of causality between 'motion', and this is, I think, his way of marking the same point that I am getting at. Causality holds between the motions of things, not between things (or moments, or factors, if one prefers more Hegelianesque ways of speaking). Thus, according to Engels, motions 'pass into one another, mutually determine one another, are in one place cause and in another effect'.[41] Sometimes he speaks in the language of substantives: 'overproduction and mass misery—each the cause of the other'.[42] But these substantives can easily be converted into descriptions of types of events or states of affairs—'commodities being overproduced' and 'the working class's being impoverished'. Causality holds always between events or states of affairs, or whatever, but never just between things.

We saw before that in those cases in which reciprocal causal relations held between two kinds of events or states (falls in the value of the pound, increases in the rate of inflation), we could reintroduce asymmetry at the level of particular events. But we also found reason to doubt that this was the asymmetry that historical materialists need. We assumed that the single kind of event which happened to the pound which yielded both causes and effects was its falling, and the single kind of event which occurred to the rate of inflation and which yielded both causes and effects was its rising. I propose to reintroduce at the level of kinds a more interesting sort of asymmetry than the asymmetry which exists at the level of particulars by abandoning this assumption. Let us say that two things (base and superstructure, for example) are reciprocally related when events or states of one cause events or states of another. Now, the kind of events or states of the first which are cause of some events or states in the second may *not* be the same kind of events or states of the first which are the effects of events or states of the second thing. For instance, suppose a blue heating element and a red cooling element are wired together so that the blue element's heating causes the red element to light, and the red element's cooling causes the blue element to light up. This provides us with reciprocity, since the two elements are interconnected, although the kind of connection is different in each direction and is itself asymmetric. The blue's heating and the red's lighting are asymmetrically connected, as is the red's cooling and the blue's lighting. But why would such an asymmetry be of any more interest than the temporal one at the level of particulars, where the features of each of the cause and effect which were causally relevant were the same? Two examples may help us answer the question: base and superstructure; nature and praxis.

Marx and Engels both spoke often of form and content when they discuss these problems of the relations between base and superstructure. In *Capital,* Volume I, Marx speaks of the form and content of law.[43] Engels often uses the distinction, especially in his correspondence. In his well-known letter to Bloch, Engels asserts:

. . . according to the materialist conception of history, the *ultimately* determining element in history is the production and reproduction of real life. More than this, neither Marx nor I have asserted . . . The economic situation is the basis, but the various elements of the superstructure . . . also exercise their influence upon the course of the historical struggles and in many cases preponderate in determining their form. There is an interaction of all these elements in which . . . the economic movement finally asserts itself as necessary . . .

. . . the economic ones are ultimately decisive but the political ones, etc., indeed even the traditions which haunt human minds also play a part, although not the decisive one.[44]

In a letter to Mehring (September 28 1892), Engels criticises Prussian romanticists of the historical school who fail to deduce 'the form of economy from production', and instead deduce 'production and distribution from the form of economy'. Again, in the same letter, Engels praises such romanticists who 'might have seen in the case of feudalism how *here* the form of state evolves from the form of economy'.

I do not say that these remarks constitute a theory. But they suggest that Marx and Engels were thinking that there were different aspects (form and content) of base and superstructure which were involved in the interaction. Sometimes form and content are employed by Marxists to suggest what is relatively inessential (the form) and what is relatively essential (the content). For instance, Jakubowski says that 'the forms of state are as diverse as the forms of capitalist economy to which they correspond. They have only one essential feature in common, which is that they express the domination of the bourgeoisie.'[45] Jakubowski seems to contrast form as inessential with what is essential.

I do not have a more developed theory about how to execute this programme. But surely some such programme is necessary. We want to hold that such a pair as base and superstructure displays causal reciprocity, and yet, unlike the simple examples of light bulbs and heating elements, there is some interesting sense in which base is ultimately the primary partner in the pair. We cannot achieve this unless the asymmetric connections between them in one direction use *different* kinds of events or properties than the connections in the other direction, and unless one set of events, properties, states, or whatever are more 'important' or 'basic' than the other. Perhaps, in setting out this distinction between form and content, one could rely here on some of the work of the Marxist structuralists to explicate the notion of structure or form. It ought to be noted, though, that the impression one gets from the scattered remarks of Marx and Engels is that content is basic and form relatively inessential, whereas structuralists presumably would insist that form is what is essential in understanding a mode of production.

On the question of the *different* features or properties to use in the different directions in which causality connects nature and praxis, there are more obvious candidates. Indeed, as I have already mentioned in Chapter III, we need to distinguish natural and artificial properties. Human praxis is able to impose many new forms or properties on what there is in the world. Men can act on, change, transform, refashion nature. To use Hegelian jargon, the world in this way becomes 'mediated' by praxis. Feuerbach did 'not see how the sensuous world around him is, not a thing given direct from all eternity, remaining ever the same, but the product of industry, and of the state of society . . . Even the objects of the simplest 'sensuous certainty' are only given him through social development, industry and commercial intercourse.' That a cherry tree appears in Germany is the consequence of human activity. Thus, the independence of nature from praxis is its essential independence, the independence of its existence, not the independence of all its many forms and properties from the existence of praxis. Even if there were no human beings, no thought, no mental activity, no praxis, there could still be a world, a nature, for the existence of nature is not dependent on the existence of praxis. Although some of nature's properties e.g. that cherry trees grow in Germany, are dependent on praxis, its existence is not. Such a claim has no necessary temporal requirement. It would be true even if, somehow, nature and praxis were miraculously co-terminous in their origins.

Nothing can just exist with no features or properties at all, in a wholly indeterminate way. Thus, natural things not only exist independently of praxis, but some of their properties must be praxis-independent as well. Not only is the existence of cherry trees praxis-independent (although their property of being cultivated in Germany is *not),* the essential structural properties of cherry trees—whatever it is that makes a tree a *cherry* tree— is praxis-independent too. Thus, for naturally occurring animal kinds, their genetic structure is praxis-independent; for naturally occurring elements, their subatomic structure is praxis-independent. For artificially occurring things, whether paintings or plant hybrids, whatever is used to make them is (ultimately) praxis-independent too. Of course, many of the non-essential properties of naturally occurring things are in fact praxis-independent too.

This, then, provides us with our dialectic of 'unequals', for we have now found our importantly or relevantly asymmetric relation. The existence and essential structural properties of nature, or of naturally occurring things, are independent of praxis, even if the other forms they can be given are not so independent, and this praxis-independence is asymmetric, since neither the existence of praxis nor any of its properties is independent of nature. There could be no praxis without a material world in which it existed. Praxis affects nature and nature affects praxis, and thus our view is dialectical. But praxis does not affect nature in just the symmetrically same way, in just the same connection, in which nature affects it. Our dialectic permits asymmetries, and because essential independence is on one side only, one can see the point of saying that it is nature which is in some way primary or basic. There is an asymmetry. Even under full communism, where man's power over nature has reached its fullest extent, a realm of necessity remains. Nature remains to limit and condition the praxis of man. Praxis and nature constitute a dialectic of 'unequals'. Man depends for his existence on nature, but the favour cannot be reciprocated.

6. The final form of economic relations as seen on their surface, in their real existence and consequently in the ideas by which the bearers and agents of these relations seek to understand them, is very much different from, and indeed quite the reverse of, their inner but concealed essential form and the concept corresponding to it.[46]

An adequate theory of knowledge must not necessarily accept the natural or social world as it appears, but must be able, if necessary, to penetrate or 'go behind' the appearances to the 'concealed essential forms' of the social or natural world. Marx makes this same point about both the natural and the social sciences, whose tasks are to discover those concealed essential forms, although it is social science in which he is primarily interested. In the natural world, the sun appears to move around the earth, but the matter is essentially the reverse, and we need a natural science, astronomy, in order to find this out.[47] Similarly, in certain (but not all) modes of production, social reality appears other than it is. Because of the fetishism for which the circulation of commodities is responsible,[48] Marx says that this gulf between appearance and essence in the social world is one that grows up especially under capitalism, since its mode of production is commodity production. 'Vulgar economy everywhere sticks to appearances in opposition to the law which regulates and explains them';[49] 'Vulgar economy feels particularly at home in the estranged outward appearances of economic relations . . . these relations seem the more self-evident the more their internal relationships are concealed from it.'[50] Marx calls this political economy 'vulgar' precisely because it accepts appearances, does not attempt to penetrate beneath the appearances. It is only a science that does penetrate appearances that can unlock the tightly kept secret of commodity production. Were there no gulf between essence and appearance the need for a science to bridge such a gulf would itself disappear. Under such conditions, science would become otiose. 'All science would be superfluous if the outward appearance and the essence of things directly coincided.'[51] Under capitalism these do not coincide. Science is necessary for the study of social reality, and vulgar political economy constitutes an abandonment of the scientific task rather than its (even partial) execution.

Although it is an anachronism to try and fit Marx's distinction between essence and appearance precisely to any distinction in contemporary philosophy, it is fair to say, I think, that Marx's distinction is closer to the distinction between unobservable entities and observable entities than it is to reality and apperance. Marx does not assume that what is essential is what is real, and what is appearance is unreal. Appearances are not, for him, merely a figment of the imagination; they do not constitute a shadowy phenomenal realm which only half-exists if it exists at all. For example, socially necessary labour-time is essential, but its appearance is exchange—value. But exchange-value is not imaginary, unreal. It is as *real* as labour and labour-time.[52] '. . . the labour of the individual asserts itself as part of the labour of society, only by means of the relations which the act of exchange establishes directly between the products, and indirectly, through them, between the producers. To the latter, therefore, the relations connecting the labour of one individual with that of the next appear, not as direct social relations between individuals at work, but as what *they really are,* material relations between persons and social relations between things'. [my emphasis] [53] The distinction that Marx draws is, then, closer to the distinction between what is observable and what is not. Exchange-value and its magnitudes are observable. But what is necessary for understanding the society is to see how exchange-value and its magnitude depend on abstract labour and socially necessary labour-time, and these two last mentioned things do not directly 'appear'. They are 'unobservables'.

A necessary condition for drawing this distinction between appearance and essence, between what appears and what does not appear, is the acceptance of the existence of unobservable entities, things or states or mechanisms which are unappearing but reference to which must be made in order to explain events or happenings in the world of observables. The empiricist and positivist traditions were prevented from taking this distinction as unproblematic because of their loathing for unobservables, their insistence on verifiability, which accounted for their reductionist programme for theories and theoretical statements. Theories for them became not ways of talking about unobservable entities, but either translatable in principle (either in full or partially) into a set of observation statements about manifest entities, or mere heuristic instruments for prediction or explanation, inference rules for moving from one observation statement to another.[54]

The insistence on the reality of these hidden, unmanifested things or structures, brings us to the second half of Bhaskar's couple: 'intransitivity and structured nature'. This insistence on the real existence of the mechanisms or structures which may not appear is very often called 'realism' too—'scientific realism', in order to distinguish it from the realism of objects or nature in general which we have been discussing hitherto. Scientific realism poses the reality not just of the world independent of praxis, independent of the human, but specifically the reality of unobservables, non-appearing entities. The first position, realism, is what Bhaskar intends by his claim of the 'intransitivity' of objects, the existence of objects independent of our experiences of them; the second, scientific realism, is what he intends by his claim about 'the structured nature' of reality, the existence of unobservable entities which may never be directly experienced or directly observed at all.

Can we produce an *argument* against those empiricists or positivists who deny the (irreducible) existence of unobservables, unobservables which are needed to help set out, in part, Marx's distinction between essence and appearance? Our position on the reality ('intransitivity', for Bhaskar) of objects was a naturalistic one, in that we refused to accept the legitimacy of giving any philosophical-justificationist arguments which purported to show that the material world existed. It is true that we also agreed that the reality of objects could not be evidenced by any empirical findings whatever, but we still held materialism to be a 'naturalist', or scientific, philosophy in the vaguer sense that it was methodologically closer to the sciences than was its denial. But can we give philosophical arguments for the existence of unobservable entities ('structured nature' of the world, for Bhaskar)? Or is there any conceivable empirical evidence for their existence? I wish now to look at Bhaskar and Putnam, the first of whom attempts to offer just such deductive arguments for their existence, and the latter of whom attempts to produce just such relevant empirical evidence for their existence.[55]

Bhaskar attempts to argue, as he did before, from the existence of science as premiss, but now to the conclusion that the world is 'structured', that entities, mechanisms, or structures exist which are unobservable but which explain the actual experiences or observations that we do have or make. Science in this argument is taken by Bhaskar to indicate or comprise *any* investigatory activity in which experimentation is necessary, for he claims that for his argument he needs only two premisses: '(i) that men are causal agents capable of interfering with the course of nature and (ii) that experimental activity, the planned disruption of the course of nature, is a significant feature of science.'[56] Bhaskar's transcendental argument for the structured nature of reality, which he repeats at several points, runs roughly as follows: In experimental activity, the experimenter brings about a sequence of events which would not occur naturally, without his intervention. But although he does bring about the observed sequence of events, he still does *not* bring about or 'produce' the ways of acting of the underlying causal mechanisms or structures which he is thereby able to identify, or the causal laws which describe those ways of acting. Thus, concludes Bhaskar, there must be an ontological distinction between the sequence of observed events which the experimenter has brought about *and* the causal laws, or the ways of acting of the unmanifested causal mechanisms whose activities are described by the laws. If the experimenter produces the one but not the other, then they cannot be the same thing, and hence, at least in this sense, the world must be structured into two levels, an observable level of events and an unobservable level of underlying causal structures or mechanisms. There can be no account of the place of experimentation in science, according to Bhaskar, by anyone who does not accept the structured nature of reality, the existence of essences or unobservables.

I do not dispute the *truth* of Bhaskar's substantive conclusion. Like him, I accept a broadly realist account of causality, which does involve reference to the causal powers of things and their characteristic ways of acting, underlying structures, unmanifested mechanisms. Like him, I think that the empiricist account of causality, which identifies causality with its manifestations, is wholly misguided. My criticisms which follow are meant only to dispute Bhaskar's claim that one can produce interesting, non-circular, deductively valid arguments for the truth of realism or scientific realism, for the intransitive or structured nature of reality. I think that reality is both intransitive and structured, as I have repeatedly made clear, but I do not think that one can demonstate the truth of this by so-called transcendental argument. My purpose, then, is to show why this particular argument for the truth of the structured nature of reality, which I have just outlined, fails. It is not my purpose to suggest that this conclusion is actually false, since indeed I do not think that it is false.

Bhaskar's argument is not an interesting, non-circular, deductively valid argument for the *truth* of the scientific realist thesis because it contains a false premiss. His argument turns on the claim that the experimenter produces a sequence of events, but neither the characteristic ways of acting of the underlying causal mechanism in question nor the causal laws which describe those causal powers. But in what sense does an experimenter bring about the sequence of events? Suppose a world in which match strikings are only rarely followed by match lightings because of the infrequent occurrence of oxygen in the atmosphere. An experimenter then introduces oxygen and notes that, in the presence of oxygen, the striking will be followed by lighting. It is misleading to claim that 'we are a causal agent of the sequence of events, but not of the causal law which the sequence of events, because it has been produced under experimental conditions, enables us to identify.'[57] In what sense has the experimenter *produced* the sequence? He produced the antecedent event, striking the match in the presence of oxygen, which would not occur naturally. He also, indirectly, produced the consequent event, the lighting of the match since that event would not have occurred unless he had introduced oxygen into the atmosphere surrounding the match. But Bhaskar's argument conflates the artificiality of the occurrence of the antecedent, and the (indirect) artificiality of the occurrence of the consequence, with the non-artificiality, the non-produced 'naturalness', of the sequential relation that exists between the two and which the empiricist identifies as the causal relation. That sequential relation is not itself artificial, for given that the antecedent does occur—whether naturally or artificially—the experimenter is not responsible for producing or bringing about (after he has produced the antecedent) what it is to which the antecedent will lead. If the empiricist proposes 'Striking matches in the presence of oxygen is followed by matches lighting' as part of his analysis of 'Striking matches in the presence of oxygen causes them to light', it is no part of his case that the antecedent events which are referred to in his analysis must occur naturally.

What we can say, then, is this. Let a and b be the antecedent and consequent events in the sequence. The experimenter directly produced a. Because he directly produced a, he also, indirectly, produced b. But it does not follow that he produces *that* b follows a (the sequential relation between them), for that may very well not be within his control. We do not necessarily produce or bring it about that those two events stand in whatever sequential relation in which they do stand. We are *not,* as experimenters, responsible for the fact that, when the antecedent does occur, whether naturally or artificially, it is to be followed by the particular consequent in question. Thus, it is not true that the experimenter produces the sequence, and hence there is no obvious contrast between the artificiality of the sequence and the non-artificiality of the powers or laws which describe them, for Bhaskar to use in order to support his ontological distinction between these two things. No foothold remains for driving an ontological wedge between on the one hand allegedly *produced* sequential relations and on the other allegedly *non-produced* causal laws or ways of acting, powers, of mechanisms or underlying structures. Hence, Bhaksar has not offered a valid deductive argument for the truth of the conclusion that the world is structured, because at least one of his premisses is false.

It is worth noting that we are sometimes able to *produce* new sequential relations in nature and that one of the ways in which we can do so is just by *producing* new causal powers in things, by changing, altering, or transforming their old characteristic ways of acting, although we do not typically do this in an experimental situation. For example, suppose that when a certain plant contracts a certain disease, the disease invariably proves fatal to the plant. Contracting the disease is followed by the plant's death. We might produce a new, disease-resistant strain of the plant. For the new strain, contracting the disease would no longer be followed by the plant's demise. Our doing this rests on our ability to transform the powers of the plant by tampering with whatever mechanisms in the plant are involved in the fighting of the diseases which it contracts. Thus, in fact both the sequential relation of events and the ways of acting of the mechanisms involved *can* be either artificial or natural, produced or non-produced, and this ought to increase our conviction that no argument can be correct which attempts to distinguish between events and powers of mechanisms on the grounds that one or the other must be or cannot be produced artificially. And when sequential relations between events are produced, as Bhaskar wrongly claims they always are in experiments, it is typically in such cases that new causal powers are also produced—transformed, altered, changed—as the means of producing such new sequential relations between events.

Marx's own position bears some resemblance to Bhaskar's. 'All science', we quoted Marx as saying, 'would be superfluous if the outward appearance and the essence of things directly coincided'. Presumably, from the premiss that (non-superfluous) science exists, Marx would have us conclude that the world is structured into essences and appearances. Indeed, this is the crux of the Marxist notion of 'the withering away of social science', since in a communist society in which social relations are transparent and do not appear other than they are, no science of those social relations, no political economy, would be necessary. Marx's examples from the natural sciences, in which the disjuncture between essence and appearance occasions the necessity for science, are the elemental appearance of air, which is in fact essentially a mixture, and the apparent motion of the sun relative to a stable earth, when in fact the matter is essentially just the reverse. If essence and appearance were not disjointed in this way, if for example, the nose were so constructed that nitrogen was channelled through one nostril and oxygen through the other, or if we had enormous periscopes attached to our eyes, we might be immediately aware of the way that air and celestial motion essentially are. In that case, science as discovery would seem to be otiose.[58]

But Marx is wrong in treating it as an assumption, without need of further argument, that if there were no essences, no sense could be made of the notion of 'finding something out' about the world, which is the idea common to both Marx's and Bhaskar's positions. It is not surprising that Marx does not deal with this complication, but rather more surprising that Bhaskar does not. Suppose we were to say that the need to find something out about the appearances—to explain or predict or account for them—is marked by the need to have scientific *theory* of some sort. A world in which there was really nothing further to find out about the facts we had already amassed might be a world in which there was no need to go beyond appearances to the level of theory. But even if we accept this, we have not yet got our essences, for to speak of essences is already to assume a particular interpretation about the nature and function of theories in science, and one to which alternatives exist. To rephrase the point in terms of Marx's and Bhaskar's arguments, from the fact that (non-superfluous) science exists, or that experimental activity occurs, we may, perhaps, be able to conclude that there is a need for theoretical modes of explanation. But there still remain alternative accounts of scientific theory, both instrumentalist and descriptivist (or reductionist), which do *not* assign to theories the role of making reference to unobservable entities in the world.[59] These non-realist accounts are certainly wrong, but we need to show this. That there are these alternative, non-realist interpretations of theoretical statements is sufficient to show that no argument from the sole premiss that science or experimental activity exists to the conclusion that the world is structured into essences and appearances can be valid unless the premisses also give us some reason to discount these alternatives. What would be needed is an argument that shows why the realist account of theoretical statements, according to which they *refer* to unobservable entities, is the correct account, rather than any alternative account which does not construe them as playing this referential role. Again, this point is a further application of our earlier argument, that in a valid deductive argument nothing can appear in the conclusion that is not already in the premisses. Unless we simply *stipulate* that science has, as its task, the discovery of unobservables, no premisses about the role of experiment in science *could* validly imply the conclusion that there are unobservables, since that conclusion says more than what the premisses say. That theories exist *may* not say more than is said by the premisses, but that conclusion is, by itself, neutral between realism and its alternatives. Once again, then, I think we have reason to suspect the legitimacy of Bhaskar's mode of transcendental argument, for there *cannot* be any interesting, non-question-begging, valid deductive arguments for the conclusion that there are unobservables, any more than there could be for the reality of the world.

Hilary Putnam offers a different argument for ruling out these non-realist alternatives. On Putnam's argument, realism (of theoretical entities) is not a necessary condition for the very possibility of science. No transcendental arguments are employed. 'Science may exist in a non-structured world' is not *a priori* false, a contradiction in terms, as it would have to be construed as being by Bhaskar. Rather, scientific realism, the assertion of the existence of essences or unobservable theoretical entities as that to which theories make *reference,* is for Putnam an empirical hypothesis and, if true, is contingently or *a posteriori* true. The argument for realism is a species of inductive argument. Thus, Putnam claims: 'That science succeeds in making many true predictions, devising better ways of controlling nature, *etc.* is an undoubted empirical fact. If [scientific] realism is an explanation of this fact, realism must itself be an over-arching scientific hypothesis.'[60]

What is it that realism explains for Putnam? The heart of his argument is given by the notion of convergence. Scientists, as a matter of fact, when devising new theories, attempt to preserve as much as possible of the old theory. They try to devise a new theory from whose standpoint the older theory appears as a limiting case, or a special case. But why should scientists be interested in this convergence? Why should they care about the older theory? Why not simply jettison it as an arcane encumbrance?

Realism can be employed as an explanatory hypothesis to account for this search for scientific convergence. We then assume as realists that typically, at least in the 'mature' sciences, the older theory *refers* to some theoretical entities, but is not completely true, since at least some of what it says about those entities will have been found to be false. Consider now the position of the scientist searching for a successor theory. He wants his new theory about those same entities to be *true*. But if his new theory is to have a chance of being true, then from *its* standpoint, the earlier theory must be seen as an 'approximately true', or true in the limit, description about those same entities concerning which he hopes to give a true description. But this strategy *is* a strategy of seeking theoretical convergence. Thus, a realist interpretation of theories, one which construes them as making reference to entities, provides a rationale for and an explanation of the fact of scientific convergence, and according to Putnam, no alternative position can provide a rationale for this.

Of course, Putnam does not claim that the history of science is nothing but the history of theoretical convergence. In the cases in which convergence does occur, the realist says that both old and successor theories *refer* to the same entities, but the older theory provides only an approximately true account of them: ' . . . we can assign a referent to "gravitational field" in Newtonian theory from the standpoint of Relativity theory . . . a referent to Mendel's "gene" from the standpoint of present-day molecular biology; and a referent to Dalton's "atom" from the standpoint of quantum mechanics.'[61] But, even if always sought, convergence is not always found. There are no theories which succeeded phlogiston theory or the theory of the aether which referred to the same entities as those theories did. Often convergence occurs; sometimes it does not.

Suppose that convergence never did occur. Suppose all theory succession followed the phlogiston-oxydisation pattern (no cross-theory referent) rather than the Daltonian atom pattern (a series of atomic theories referring to the same entity). Rather than convergence, let us imagine that each theory-change constitutes so fundamental a switch that we do not allow sameness of referent across scientific revolutions and the 'paradigms' which they separate. 'What', asks Putnam, 'if *all* the theoretical entities postulated by one generation . . . invariably "don't exist" from the standpoint of the later science?'[62] We might then abandon realism, for in that case there would be no convergence which we could use realism to explain. In this sense, on Putnam's argument, realism is an empirical hypothesis. We could imagine science, interpreted à la Kuhn[63] for example, such that each generation's science denied that the science of its predecessor referred to anything. We could have, in such a case, scientific theories, but there would be no foothold for giving them a realist interpretation. In a Kuhnian scientific world, in which theories would be 'incommensurable', the nature of scientific change does not permit the notion of identity of reference across theories. But such a Kuhnian scientific world is *not* our world, according to Putnam, for ours displays convergence as well as revolution, commensurable theories referring to the same things as well as incommensurable ones. But that the Kuhnian world is at least an imaginable one shows, again, that Bhaskar's argument could not have been correct, for in a Kuhnian world we would have science, and need theories 'to find things out' (in some sense), but need not construe those theories as performing a referential function. In such an imaginary situation, we would be justified in rejecting realism, and yet still be engaged in the normal sorts of scientific activity.

Putnam presents us, then, with empirical evidence for the truth of realism, whereas Bhaskar purported to offer us valid deductive argument. But how good is Putnam's evidence? Before I say something about Putnam's evidence itself, I want to make a comment about how Putnam's position, even if it were acceptable for natural science, would not help us in showing that theories in social science were to be interpreted 'realistically'. Putnam guards himself against this sort of criticism by limiting his claim to 'mature sciences'; perhaps he would not consider any social science a 'mature science'. But for those of us who consider historical materialism as 'mature' as any natural science, perhaps these remarks will carry some weight.

In the social sciences there are many cases in which there is widespread non-convergence, and we might still wish to argue for a realist interpretation of these non-converging theories. What we find in the social sciences is not occasional non-convergence, as one finds in the natural sciences with the example of phlogiston, but rather widespread failure of convergence generally. There is an obvious, but less formal sense of convergence, related perhaps to the more formal one Putnam employs, in which a succession of social theories can converge. Consider, for example, the well-known case of the political economies of Smith, Ricardo and Marx, indeed of the whole tradition of classical political economy which ends with Marx. It is not that Marx's theory contains the theories of his predecessors as 'limiting cases'. Rather, Marx's political economy includes and goes beyond—'transcends', in the Hegelian jargon—the theories of his predecessors by building upon and refining them, drawing distinctions which they were not able to draw, developing them. In this informal but perfectly acceptable sense, one can speak of converging theories in the social sciences. Similarly one can also say that from the perspective of Marx's political economy, the theories of Smith and Ricardo were *approximately* true.

Classical political economy presents us with the happy example of converging theories in social science, informally understood. But, in Marx's terms, classical political economy was to give way to vulgar political economy, in the measure that the possibility of science was undermined by the sharper intrusion of ideology and class struggle into the study of society. Thus, post-Marxian social science is marked by *divergence* rather than convergence. Marxist and non-Marxist political economy, historiography, sociology, anthropology, tend to diverge rather than converge, yet Marxists still wish (or ought to wish) to give Marxist social theories a realist interpretation. How are we to understand this?

I do not consider this point an objection to Putnam's position, but only a reminder of its limitations. One can expect converging theories only in those areas in which the effects of ideology remain weak and indirect. Social science long ago ceased to be such an area; natural science *could* also become more of an ideological battleground than it is, as indeed it has sometimes become at certain crucial moments in history. The limitation in Putnam's hypothesis, then, is that it only works for non-ideologically-infested science. If we were arguing for a realist interpretation of one of a group of diverging theories, and that divergence is due to ideology and its effect, one would have to supplement Putnam's position to cover this sort of case.[64]

Let us return to the assessment of the empirical evidence which Putnam presents, even if we restrict Putnam's evidence and convergence-hypothesis to the natural sciences. What *is* Putnam's evidence? First, Putnam gives content to the realist position by means of two principles, which he labels '(1)' and '(2)': '(1) Terms in a mature science typically *refer*. (2) The laws of a theory belonging to a mature science are typically approximately true.' Realism as an explanatory hypothesis is said, then, to explain the following:

. . . scientists act as they do because they belive (1) and (2) and their strategy works because (1) and (2) are true.[65]

Thus, the hypothesis comes in two parts. First, scientists *try to make* theories converge. That is supposed to be a fact. The empirical hypothesis for explaining this fact is that they believe (1) and (2), that is they believe that realism is true. But of course, that scientists believe that realism is true does not *show* that it is true. I think that if one could, in fact, show *even* that scientists believe, by their scientific behaviour, that realism is true, that by itself would be an interesting result. But it certainly does not show that realism is true. Now, the second part of the hypothesis is this. It is not only a fact that scientists 'act as they do' (viz, try to make theories converge), but it is also a fact that 'their strategy works', that is, that their theories *do* converge. The explanatory hypothesis for why their theories do converge is then that *realism is true,* '(1) and (2) are true'.

But the second part of the hypothesis is not an empirical, explanatory hypothesis of a fact at all. No opponent of realism would ever grant that it *was* a fact that theories converge, for that is precisely what he disputes. Indeed, this can be brought out in the following way. Putnam argues that it is an *a posteriori* explanation of convergence that realism is true. But what does it mean to say that two theories converge? Presumably, two theories converge only if they say true or approximately true things about the same referent. That is, 'convergence' can only be explicated using the realist position. If the theories converge, it *follows* that realism is true, because of what 'converge' means. The relationship between the 'fact' of convergence and realism is not that realism is an empirical, explanatory hypothesis for convergence. Rather, they are tied in a non-empirical way through the meaning that Putnam gives to convergence. Indeed, it is because 'convergence' has loaded into its meaning the truth of realism that no non-realist could ever agree that it *was* a fact that theories converged. A non-realist might be willing to talk of the *apparent convergence* of theories, thereby expelling with that description any assumptions about the truth of realism. But the explanatory hypothesis for apparent-convergence will not be that realism is true. It might only be that scientists believe that realism is true, and thus make it appear that theories converge. Thus, either Putnam's empirical evidence is put in a non-circular way so that its description does not presuppose the truth of realism, in which case it does not support the realist hypothesis, or it does support the realist hypothesis, but only because the truth of realism has been built into the description of the empirical evidence in a way which renders the whole argument circular.

What then shall we say about scientific realism? Can we argue in any sense to the conclusion that there are unobservable entities, Marx's essences, to which science refers in order to explain appearances, or observables? We have seen how at least one deductive argument, Bhaskar's, fails, and how at least one attempt to show that unobservables exist by *a posteriori* or inductive means, Putnam's, fails. Is there any other way to show that there are unobservables?

I think that the right way to do this is as follows. I want to argue that realism, the realism or materialism that commits us to the existence of something essentially independent of thought or mind, itself commits us to scientific realism, the existence of unobservables. As I have said before, I do not think that there are any interesting, non-circular arguments for the truth of realism. But I do think that there is an interesting, non-circular argument that shows that *if* realism is true then scientific realism is true, and so if we accept the former, we are *ipso facto* committed to the latter. The problem of unobservables, I think, can only arise within a phenomenalist, non-materialist framework. Without that framework, the problem cannot arise.

How can we show that this is so? It has been pointed out many times before that none of the unobservables of scientific theory are in principle or logically unobservable (as God, for example, is supposed to be for the believer).[66] Unobservability of scientific entities rests on contingent facts about the nature of the thing in question and the nature of human perceptual mechanisms. We can always imagine the world changing, or being different, in certain ways so that what had previously been unobservable becomes observable. '. . . there are no *a priori* or philosophical criteria for separating the observable from the unobservable. By trying to show that we can talk about the *possibility* of observing electrons without committing logical or conceptual blunders, I have been trying to support the thesis that any (non-logical) term is a *possible* candidate for an observation term.'[67]

The observable-unobservable scale is a continuous one. Where the line is drawn at a time depends on the scientific theories prevalent at that time about the thing in question and about our perceptual apparatus. Things which are at one time unobservable, like molecules or genes, can become observable, as our perceptual powers are artificially extended by means of microscopes, telescopes, etc. We could imagine human mutants being born who could 'directly' perceive x-rays or ultraviolet radiation. The scale is continuous, and where the cut is made tells us about the current state of science. The cut between observables and unobservables cannot be one of ontological significance.

That the scale is continuous is important. What is it, after all, to be committed to the existence of real objects? It is to be committed to something whose existence does not essentially depend on being related to thought or mind. To say that there are real or material objects is to say, in a way which cannot be explicated by counterfactuals, that they exist when no one is, or could be, observing them. Thus, physical objects do not cease existing when there are no experiences of them. Because the observable-unobservable distinction exists on a continuous scale, because there are only *a posteriori* reasons for drawing it where it is drawn at any given time, unobservable entities in science are not different from unobserved doors, chairs, or tables. It is only a contingent fact that an unperceived door is unperceived and it is only a contingent fact that electrons are unperceived. If we accept that the door is a material object, then we are committed to its unperceived, non-counterfactual, existence. Similarly, we are committed to the possibility of there being unobservables which are contingently unobservable because of smallness of size, for example. If we take, for instance, the smallest observable particle and cut it in half, we will then have two contingently unobservable particles. If that original smallest observable particle is conceived realistically, then its two contingently unobservable halves are no more troublesome ontologically than would be its continued existence when we looked away. To conceive of the particle realistically is to conceive of its non-counterfactual continued existence when, *for any contingent reason,* observation is no longer possible.

Thus, rejection of the realist perspective concerning the existence of the unobservable entities of scientific theory goes with the rejection of realism in general. I do not think that the doctrines of instrumentalism and descriptivism, as the alternatives to realism in the philosophy of science are sometimes called, would ever have arisen had phenomenalism not itself been once so prevalent in contemporary philosophy. Once phenomenalism had been rejected, the serious reasons for objecting to the existence of unobservables, or Marx's essences, had been undermined. What I think is surprising in contemporary philosophy is that these debates in the philosophy of science have enjoyed a prolonged life, which has continued long after the realist-phenomenalist controversy is generally considered to have been resolved in favour of the former. These debates in the philosophy of science do not deserve that prolonged life, since the debates should have been settled at the very same moment as was the phenomenalist-realist debate. We do not, then, present empirical evidence for scientific realism, as does Putnam, nor produce a 'transcendental' argument for scientific realism from the possibility of science, as does Bhaskar. We show, rather, that, although we cannot argue for materialism or realism in general, scientific realism is part and parcel of that earlier commitment.

Finally, what I take my argument to have shown is that, *in principle,* there is no problem about the existence of unobservables. If unobservables are contingently unobservable, then their unobservability due to smallness of size, for example, could present no more difficulty than the unobservability of the planets of distant stars, due to their distant spatial location. It does not follow that *each* and *every* scientific theory should be interpreted 'realistically', as making reference to unobservables. Particular cases, like quantum mechanics, may well present special problems which make us wonder if they should be interpreted realistically. But aside from particular problems about the nature of the particular 'unobservable entity' in question, there *is* no general problem of unobservables on a materialist perspective.

Notes: Chapter IV

1 Quine, W. V. O., *Word and Object,* The M. I. T. Press, Cambridge, 1960, p.3.

2 *Ibid,* p.4 and also see p.22.

3 Marx, Karl, *Theses on Feuerbach,* in Karl Marx and Frederick Engels, *The German Ideology,* Progress Publishers, Moscow, 1965, p. 661.

4 *The German Ideology,* p. 31.

5 Hegel, G. W. F., *Science of Logic,* I, transl. by W. H. Johnston and L. G. Struthers, George Allen & Unwin, London, 1966, pp. 79-90.

6 Bhaskar, Roy *A Realist Theory of Science,* Leeds Books, Leeds, 1975.

7 *Ibid,* p. 31.

8 *Ibid,* p. 29.

9 Bhaskar's 'realism' is my 'realism' in the narrow sense—the denial that objects are literally 'in' the mind; that is, the denial of phenomenalism. Realism in the wide sense implies not only that objects are not phenomenal, but that their existence does not *imply* the existence of mind. Thus, science is not phenomenal, but its existence certainly implies the existence of mind. But this difference between Bhaskar's and my use of 'realism' does not affect the present discussion.

10 See for example, W. V. O. Quine, 'Two Dogmas of Empiricism', in *From a Logical Point of View,* Harper Torchbooks, New York, 1963, pp. 20-46; Hilary Putnam, 'The Analytic and the Synthetic', *Minnesota Studies in the Philosophy of Science,* III, University of Minnesota Press, Minneapolis, 1962, pp. 358-397; Morton White, 'Analytic-Synthetic: An Untenable Dualism', in L. Linsky, *Semantics and the Philosophy of Language,* University of Illinois Press, Urbana, 1952. For a discussion of the difficulties of producing analytic truths about natural kind words, see Hilary Putnam, 'Is Semantics Possible?' in *Language, Belief and Metaphysics,* eds. H. E. Kiefer and M. K. Munitz, State University of New York Press, 1970, pp. 50-63.

11 *The German Ideology,* p. 38. Engels also, and especially in *Anti-Dühring,* stresses the impossibility of *a priori* knowledge. For a development of some of Engels' remarks on the nature of language, see Hilary Putnam, 'Explanation and Reference', in Pearce and Maynard, eds., *Conceptual Change,* Reidel, Dordrecht, 1973, pp. 199-221. Compare also Marx's remark later in the *German Ideology* that 'when we conceive things . . . as they really are and happened, every profound philosophical problem is resolved . . . quite simply into an empirical fact' (p. 58).

12 See for example, W. V. O. Quine, 'Epistemology Naturalized', in *Ontological Relativity and Other Essays,* Columbia University Press, New York, 1969; Donald Campbell, 'Evolutionary Epistemology', in *The Philosophy of Karl Popper,* ed. P. A. Schilpp, Open Court, La Salle, Illinois, 1974; Donald Campbell, 'Methodological Suggestions . . .'

Inquiry, Vol. 2, 1959, pp. 152-182 and Stephen Toulmin, *Human Understanding*, Vol. I, Oxford University Press, Oxford, 1972.

13 Hooker, C. A., 'Philosophy and Meta-Philosophy of Science', *Synthese*, Vol. 32, Nos. 1/2, pp. 177-231. Quote is from p. 206. This was essentially Feuerbach's conception of philosophy too. In a letter to Bolin Feuerbach claims that his philosophy 'has nothing in common with traditional philosophical thought, including that of Kant; that its basis is natural science to which alone belongs past, present and future . . .'; *Ludwig Feuerbach in seinem Briefwechsel und Nachlass*, ed., by Karl Grün, Vol. II, Leipzig, 1874, p. 191.

14 Lukacs, Georg, *History & Class Consciousness*, Merlin Press, London, 1971, p. 109.

15 Bhaskar, Roy, *Op. cit.*, p. 109.

16 Putnam, Hilary, 'What is Realism?', *Proceedings of the Aristotelian Society*, N. S. Vol. LXXVI, 1975-1976, p. 178.

17 See Malcolm, Norman, *Dreaming*, Routledge & Kegan Paul, London, 1962, and criticism by Hilary Putnam, 'Dreaming and Depth Grammar', in *Analytical Philosophy*, edited by R. J. Butler, Basil Blackwell, Oxford, 1962.

18 Engels, Frederick, *Ludwig Feuerbach and the End of Classical German Philosophy*, Progress Publishers, Moscow, 1969. p. 39-40.

19 It is interesting to compare idealism (the essential dependence of nature on praxis or mind) with the phenomenalists' attempt to be consistent with science. How could the alleged reduction of physical objects to sense data (the contents of mind) account for the obvious truth of the existence of unobserved objects? The phenomenalists attempted to manage this through the device of *possible* sense data. The claim that an object existed at a certain time unobserved could then be rendered counterfactually by the claim that if there would have been an observer at that time, he would have had sense data (of such an object). Thus, the assertion of the existence of unobserved objects, it was hoped, could be rendered by an assertion about the possible but non-actual existence of observers and sense data. Our ontological commitment to physical objects would be thereby reduced to commitment to actual and possible observers and the contents of their minds. We know that such a reduction in fact fails, that our assumptions about material objects cannot be recaptured by such a reduced talk about observers and sense data alone. But at least sense data and observers provided likely candidates for the attempt to make phenomenalism consistent with such obvious truths about unobserved objects.

But how could the denial of the essential independence of the natural world be made consistent with the geological belief that there was a time at which there were no sentient creatures with minds or thoughts to which the natural world was related? Could 'there was a natural world but no minds' be rendered counterfactually? *Unless* the denial of materialism merely collapses into phenomenalism, there are no *two* likely candidates for the counterfactual reduction. Minds might offer themselves as one candidate: '. . . if there had been minds'. But 'if there had been minds', then what follows? Nothing about the actual world, since that cannot reappear in the reducing counterfactual. There simply is no likely second candidate, in addition to minds, for the reduction to proceed in this case.

Existence assertions about unobserved physical objects might have been thought to go over counterfactually as assertions about possible observers and sense data à la phenomenalism; for the denial of the kind of materialism we have been discussing, there is no second candidate to use in the reduction of actual assertions about a natural world to a counterfactual, which would thereby make the denial of materialism formally consistent with the belief in a world which pre-existed any mind whatever. Hence, the need for this sort of idealism to import the deity.

20 Colletti has argued in a similar vein, that the very notion of dialectics is bound up with the idealist denial of matter, for dialectics in the hands of Hegel leads to the 'annihilation of matter'. Colletti is correct since literally, for Hegel, matter is its other, consciousness. But this is *not* to say that there cannot be a Marxist dialectics, similar in many respects to the Hegelian, but with the Hegelian 'total' denial of the principal of 'abstract identity' replaced with some sensible modification. What in particular must remain in a Marxist dialectics is the notion of real contradiction, which is the element that Colletti singles out for special

abuse. See Lucio Colletti, 'Contradiction and Contrariety', in *New Left Review*, 93, Sept-Oct 1975, pp. 3-29, and the reply to Colletti by Roy Edgley, 'Reply to Colletti', *Critique*, No. 7.

21 'Nocturnal' and 'diurnal,' to characterise anti-scientific and scientific philosophies respectively, are terms used by Gaston Bachelard. See Dominique Lecourt, *Marxism and Epistemology*, New Left Books, London, 1975. Bachelard considered realism to be a (or *the*) nocturnal philosophy, but what is surprising is that Lecourt, who is a Marxist, never criticises Bachelard for this assumption. Bachelard seems to have had the following consideration in mind: What is wrong in empiricist and positivist philosophy of science is its 'continuism', that it does not account for the 'rupture' between earlier and latter sciences, and even more importantly, for the 'rupture' between science and ordinary modes of thought. But Bachelard must have thought that any philosophy which postulates a continuing real world independent of theories is committed to this sort of continuism. Bachelard is certainly wrong about this, since he confuses continuism in epistemology and in ontology. The continuism in empiricist philosophy arises from the epistemological commitment to theory-independent observations. The realist belief in a continuing word, apart from theories about the world, is not at all necessarily committed to this form of epistemological continuism. Radically different theories can be about the *same* world.

22 In this sense, Marxist philosophy would be a scientific philosophy, just as Marxism is itself a science. Unlike idealism, it would restrict itself to 'summing up' scientific results, rather than going beyond them.

23 But I do not subscribe to any form of the private language argument since it is a *transcendental* form of argument. I claim that no deductive argument *could* be valid whose conclusion is that there is a public language and none of whose premises assume that there is a public language. For some examples of the extensive literature on transcendental arguments, both in Kant's philosophy and more generally, see: S. Körner, 'The Impossibility of Transcendental Deductions', *The Monist*, July 1967; Eva Schaper, 'Arguing Transcendentally', *Kant-Studien*, Vol.63, 1972; Jay F. Rosenberg, 'Transcendental Arguments Revisited', *The Journal of Philosophy*, 1975, pp. 611-642.

24 Cf. Timpanaro, Sebastiano, *On Materialism*, New Left Books, London, 1975.

25 See for example, the debate on innate ideas, 'Symposium on Innate Ideas', *Boston Studies In The Philosophy of Science*, Vol. III, Humanities Press, 1968, pp.81-107. Contributors were Noam Chomsky, Hilary Putnam and Nelson Goodman.

26 Marx, Karl, *Introduction To The Grundrisse*, in *A Contribution to the Critique of Political Economy*, ed. Maurice Dobb, pp. 188-189.

27 Jakubowski, Franz, *Ideology and Superstructure*, Allison and Busby, London, 1976, p. 99.

28 *Ibid*, p. 104.

29 See the article by John McMurtry, 'Making Sense of Economic Determinism', *Canadian Journal of Philosophy*, Vol. III, No. 2, December 1973, pp.249-261.

30 Kolakowski, Leszek, 'Karl Marx and the Classical Definition of Truth', in *Marxism and Beyond*, transl. by J. Z. Peel, Pall Mall Press, London, 1969.

31 Geymonat, Ludovico, 'Neopositivist Methodology and Dialectical Materialism', *Science and Society*, Summer, 1973, pp. 178-194.

32 I do not assert that there *was* a break even in this sense. *The Manuscripts* are called 'Economic *and* Philosophical', and it seems clear that the philosophical aspects themselves arise from the economic studies Marx was then pursuing. Whatever weaknesses in the philosophy there are may arise from weakness in the parallel economic study from which they arise. But this would mean that there was no *methodological break*, but only (which is not very surprising) that the economic studies of the latter Marx are more developed and sophisticated than those of the earlier Marx!

33 Marx, Karl, and Frederick Engels, *The German Ideology*, p. 29.

34 Quine, W. V. O., *Word and Object*, pp. 258-259.

35 Engels, Frederick, *Anti-Dühring*, Progress Publishers, Moscow, 1969, p.32. See also in *Dialectics of Nature*, International Publishers, New York, 1973, pp. 170-171: 'causality—The first thing that strikes us in considering matter in motion is the interconnection of the

individual motions of separate bodies, their *being determined* by one another.'

36 Hegel, G. W. F., *The Logic of Hegel*, translated by W. Wallace, Oxford University Press, Oxford, 1972, paragraph 153.
37 *Ibid*, paragraphs 155-156.
38 *Ibid*, paragraph 154. 'This bend which transforms the infinite progression into a self-contained relationship . . .'
39 Mao Tse Tung, 'On Contradiction', in *Four Essays on Philosophy*, Foreign Languages Press, Peking, 1968; see pp. 24-29.
40 Ollman, Bertell, *Alienation*, Cambridge University Press, Cambridge, 1971, pp. 17-18.
41 Engels, Frederick, *Dialectics of Nature*, pp. 170-171.
42 Engels, Frederick, *Ludwig Feuerbach and the End of Classical German Philosophy*, Progress Publishers, Moscow, 1969, p. 47.
43 Marx, Karl, *Capital*, Vol. I, Progress Publishers, Moscow, 1965, p. 84.
44 Marx, Karl, and Frederick Engels, *Selected Correspondence*, Progress Publishers, Moscow, undated, pp. 498-500.
45 Jakubowski, Franz, *op. cit.*, p. 44.
46 Marx, Karl, *Capital*, Vol. III, Progress Publishers, Moscow, 1966, pp. 208-209.
47 Marx, Karl, *Capital*, Vol. I, pp. 316, 280, 74, 41.
48 See Marx's discussion in Chapter I, section 4 of *Capital*, Vol. I, 'The Fetishism of Commodities and the Secret Thereof', pp. 71-83.
49 Marx, Karl, *Capital*, Vol. I, p. 307.
50 Marx, Karl, *Capital*, Vol. III, p. 817.
51 See Geras, Norman, 'Essence and Appearance: Aspects of Fetishism in Marx's *Capital*', *New Left Review*, No. 65, pp. 69-85; and G. A. Cohen, 'Karl Marx and the Withering Away of Social Science', *Philosophy & Public Affairs*, Vol. I, pp. 182-203. For Marx, the motivation for searching for essences was *explanatory*—essences provide the explanation for the structure of appearances, why they are as they are. Thus I agree with Ernest Mandel: 'Marx did not see the task of science solely as the discovery of relations obscured by their superficial appearance, but also as the explanation of these appearances themselves, in other words as the discovery of the intermediate links, or mediations, which enable essence and appearance to be reintegrated in a unity once again'. *Late Capitalism*, New Left Books, London, 1975, p. 15. In the human sciences at least, essences are not *things*, but *relations*, e.g. the relations of production of a society.
52 Geras, Norman, *op. cit.*, pp.74-76.
53 Marx, Karl, *Capital*, Vol. I, p.73.
54 For a discussion of phenomenalism and instrumentalism, see Russell Keat & John Urry, *Social Theory as Science*, Routledge and Kegan Paul, London, 1975, or Leszek Kolakowski. *Postivist Philosophy*, Penguin, Harmondsworth, Middx., 1972.
55 Bhaskar, Roy, *A Realist Theory of Science*, and Hilary Putnam, 'What is Realism?', both already quoted.
56 Bhaskar, Roy, *op. cit.*, p. 54.
57 *Ibid*, p. 33.
58 This example is due to G. A. Cohen, see note 51 above.
59 Again, see Keat and Urry, or Kolakowski, or Ernest Nagel, *The Structure of Science*, Routledge & Kegan Paul, London, 1961, for an account of these positions.
60 Putnam, Hilary, 'What Is Realism?', p. 178. Putnam has apparantly abandoned this position, which he now calls 'metaphysical realism'. See his Presidential Address, delivered to the American Philosophical Association Meeting in Boston, on 29 December, 1976, to be published by the APA in the autumn, 1977.
61 *Ibid*, pp. 180-181.
62 *Ibid*, p. 183.
63 See Kuhn, Thomas, *The Structure of Scientific Revolutions*, 2nd Edition, University of Chicago Press, Chicago, 1970.
64 It is interesting to consider cases of 'converging' theories where we do not wish to explain convergence by a realist hypothesis. Consider, for example, the case of first-order moral theories, theories about the good life, the good for man, virtue, or some similar topic.

Again, in a very informal sense of convergence, such theories can converge. Each may be a development and refinement of its predecessor; each may attempt to include within it the insights of its predecessor, but to 'transcend' whatever limitations there are inherent in those insights. Indeed, such was Hegel's view of his moral theory in *The Philosophy of Right*. According to Hegel, his moral theory contained within it the partial truths ('approximate truths'), of its predecessors. Seen from the standpoint of *The Philosophy of Right*, previous substantive ethical theories were partial truths which converged increasingly toward Hegel's theory. Thus, there is no reason why ethical or aesthetic theories, or theologies or legal codes, cannot instantiate that same sort of dialectical development, in which a successor is an improvement upon its immediate predecessor such that the predecessor is preserved but surpassed by the successor, which Putnam calls *convergence* when it occurs in the natural sciences. Yet, even if we find an analogue of convergence in these sorts of cases, hopefully this is not going to commit us to a realist interpretation in all these cases. There are prescriptivist meta-ethical theories, for instance, which do not offer a realist interpretation of ethical theories, on which they would *refer* to moral properties and hence be capable of truth or falsity. Surely the 'convergence' alone in moral theories, if it systematically occurred, would not by itself rule out this, or similar, non-realist interpretations of moral theories. Similarly, development and convergence in theology need not commit us to a realist, referential interpretation of religious language. Those philosophers who sought an alternative, non-realist analysis for theological assertions are not going to commit themselves to a realist analysis merely upon finding theological convergence. Why would Putnam's arguments be at least initially plausible for convergence in natural science, and not in these other sorts of areas? In science and in ethics we may find convergence. In the former but not the latter case, we could be tempted to argue from convergence to realism as an explanatory hypothesis. What makes the difference in these two sorts of cases?

[65] Putnam, Hilary, 'What is Realism?', p. 179.
[66] Maxwell, Grover, 'The Ontological Status of Theoretical Entities', *Minnesota Studies In The Philosophy of Science*, Vol. III, University of Minnesota Press, Minneapolis, 1962.
[67] *Ibid*, p. 11.

CHAPTER V

MATERIALISM AND REFLECTION THEORY

It is now time to ask how materialism, and especially the reflection theory which it requires, fare when they are assessed by the six criteria which I have said that any plausible or adequate theory of knowledge must pass. Much of what is relevant in answering this question had already been incorporated into my discussion of the six features or characteristics. For example, I have already spent some time arguing that materialism can be dialectical, and that it is wholly consistent with the conception of man as doer of physical deeds or actions. This point is important. It is sometimes said, for example, that Lenin's appreciation of dialectics in *The Philosophical Notebooks* marks his rejection of reflection theory. Thus Lenin argues: 'Cognition is the eternal, endless approximation of thought to object. The *reflection* of nature in man's thought must be understood not "lifelessly", not "abstractly", not devoid of movement, not without contradictions, but in the eternal process of movement, the arising of contradictions and their solution' [from the 'Conspectus of Hegel's *Science of Logic'*, 1914]; and '. . . here we have an immeasurably rich content as compared with "metaphysical" materialism, the fundamental *misfortune* of which is its inability to apply dialectics to *Bildertheorie,* to the process and development of knowledge' ['On The Question of Dialectics', 1915].[1] How this could be read as a rejection of reflection theory by Lenin is something of a mystery, especially since Lenin explicitly criticises metaphysical materialism for failing to apply dialectics to reflection theory, and carefully distinguishes between two kinds of reflection theory, an unacceptable kind which views the reflection 'lifelessly' and the other, acceptable sort which does not. I have already argued that dialectics, understood in a way which allows both reciprocity *and* asymmetry, is perfectly consistent with materialism. Similarly, in Chapter III, I have discussed the compatibility between materialism and man's physical activity and criticised Korsch for failing to see this compatibility. I do not propose to say any more about how these things, dialectics and the notion of man as a physical doer of deeds, are consistent with reflection theory as well, since my remarks on their compatibility with Marxist materialism should be sufficient for this purpose. Since man can change the world, his thought can correspond to whatever he has made the world like. If he further changes or transforms the world, his beliefs can then reflect the changed circumstances. Change, transformation, revolution, and dialectics are no more incompatible with a correspondence theory of knowledge than they are with Marx's materialism. Finally, I will not say more about how a reflection theory can be consistent with the latest results of science. In the way in which I have stated a (theoretical) reflection theory, it should be clear that it is not saddled with any outmoded beliefs about the actual psychology of perception, acquisition of knowledge, etc. We distinguished the questions of how a man came to have his beliefs and what the relation was between his beliefs and reality. We insist on an answer to the latter question, a realist answer, but what we answer to that question will be compatible with whatever answers the special sciences offer to the first question.

The first feature I discussed was that an adequate theory of knowledge must respect the reality of the external world. It is obvious that a reflection or correspondence theory can do this. Any theory of knowledge which gives to thought a wholly interpretive role must compromise the reality of the external world by maintaining that an *essential* relation exists between any known object and thought. It is the contingency of the relation between thought and object on a reflection theory of knowledge which is crucial for preserving the integrity of the external world. Thus, only a reflection theory of knowledge can be a materialist theory of knowledge, although as I explained in a footnote in the Introduction, a reflection theory of knowledge is not by itself sufficient to insure materialism. A reflection theory of knowledge only assumes the contingency of the relation between an object and *its* concept, or a state of affairs or event and the thought of *it,* and not the contingency of the relation between the object, state of affairs, or event, and *any* thought whatever. But, although insufficient, a correspondence theory is certainly 'epistemologically' necessary for any credible materialism. For reality to be independent of all thought, it must be independent of any particular thought.

Throughout our preceding discussions of Kant, Hegel, Feuerbach, and Marx, we have time and time again used such metaphors as *creation, procreation, positing.* To extend the metaphor, I think we could say that a materialist theory of knowledge is a theory of knowledge appropriate to a situation in which either the existence of the object of knowledge is given or, the object of knowledge, although created by human labour, is 'embedded' in something which is given—men do not always *create* or *posit* those objects, or that in which those objects are embedded or materialised, and that it is for that very reason that those objects are independent of, in no essential relation to, men. The moon, the sun, the stars, to rehearse Kolakowski's examples, are not made by us. We can, *perhaps,* change some of them in various ways. We do not create them. This is equally true for social objects, products of praxis. There is an obvious sense in which we do create chairs, tables, the State, a market economy and science. But they are created always in a matter which is given (for even something as abstract as science must be 'materialised' in some way), a matter which therefore limits or constrains what we can do; and created often also in an 'unconscious' act of creation, like the market economy, so that we do not *know* or *understand* what we have created.

God, if he had created matter, the world, *ex nihilo,* would not need a materialist theory of knowledge. His creations would be wholly a projection of his own, conscious, intentions, and to know matter he would need merely to examine his own intentions. Equally, if we were like the Beatles in *The Yellow Submarine,* if we could deliberately produce flowers *ex nihilo* wherever we walked, we too would need no reflection theory of knowledge to understand those flowers, for we would have been consciously and knowingly responsible for whatever they were like. Of course, we are not like the Beatles because for us, unlike for them, there is an 'other', an inescapably 'other-than-ourselves', which we must come to know about by having our thought 'grasp' it, 'an intransitive object of science', in Roy Bhaskar's happy formulation,[2] to which our thought can correspond. This is where Schmidt goes utterly wrong when he claims: 'The question of the possibility of knowing the world only had meaning for Marx on the assumption that the world is a human "creation".'[3] This seems to me to be utterly false, and one is reassured by seeing that Schmidt here quotes not Marx, but Horkheimer and Ernst Bloch. It is true that, formally, God's knowledge would correspond to reality, but only *because* he would have first made the reality correspond to it. Nor would we need a correspondence theory for our cultural creations if they were not also part of the natural order, creations embedded in a material nature. Neither such a God nor ourselves would have need for a materialist theory of knowledge. Unfortunately, unlike the deity of orthodox theology, we are not in such a happy position. We do need a materialist theory of knowledge, even when the objects of knowledge are social or cultural, because such objects have a natural dimension as well. There is no Kantian noumenal realm in which the laws of nature cease to hold sway, and membership in which confers an escape from the 'determination' of the natural order. All our creations are subject to the constraints of nature, and it is because of this that we insist on both the moment of praxis and the moment of correspondence. However extensively we have created, changed the face of nature, we need our thought to correspond to reality in order to gain knowledge about what we have done in it.

It follows, then, that Vico's epigram that human history must be easier to understand than natural history, because the former but not the latter is our creation, must be treated with some degree of caution. Marx cites the epigram in a footnote to *Capital:*

Darwin has interested us in the history of nature's technology, i.e. in the formation of the organs of plants and animals, which organs serve as instruments of production for sustaining their life. Does not the history of the productive organs of man, of organs that are the material basis of all social organization, deserve equal attention! And would not such a history be easier to compile, since, as Vico says, human history differs from natural history in this, that we have made the former, but not the latter?[4]

It is true that human history is 'easier to compile' insofar as it is the effect of planned, deliberate decisions about its course. Of course it is not now 'easier to compile', because, as Marx shows, it does not now take a planned, deliberate course, but a course which unfolds despite the intentions and wishes of its human 'actors'. In any case, so it has done and will continue to do until the advent of socialism. After the advent of socialism, history will become a truly human history, because of its deliberate nature. To that extent, it would then become easier to know. But because it is a history which embraces man in his material situation, because even social and cultural objects, the creations of man, are *materialised* objects, embedded *in* the natural 'stuff' of the world, there is always an uncreated, recalcitrant dimension, the existence of which can always frustrate or foil our plans. The knowledge of that dimension and how it affects and limits human plans and purposes, cannot be dispensed with. 'Freedom in this field cannot consist of anything else but the fact that socialised mankind. . . regulate their interchange with Nature rationally, bring it under their common control. . . Nevertheless, this always remains a realm of necessity. . .'[5] For this reason too, a reflection theory is as appropriate for social knowledge as it is for knowledge of physical nature. Social things have natural aspects too. When we make watches, we do not suspend the laws of physics, but rather utilise them.

The existence of that 'other', material dimension must mean that a materialist, reflection theory of knowledge will always be in order. Unless we become gods and can eliminate that recalcitrant dimension, 'the material conditions under which they live', we shall always have to make it our task to harmonise our beliefs with that reality, so that in the end, they may come to reflect the real structure, the inherent properties, that reality has. We did not 'create' the subatomic structure of reality, nor the naturally given material from which cultural objects are made, and our coming to know that structure or those objects is a process in which our beliefs must come to correspond with how that reality is, what it is like apart from any interpretive structures which *we* 'create' or impose upon it. We can certainly know what we do not create, *pace* Schmidt.

Can a reflection theory meet the constraints that it be able to provide an account of the role of human activity in the acquisition of knowledge (where this is understood now as *mental* as well as physical activity) and that it be able to distinguish between the world as it is and the world as it appears? I wish to deal with these two points together and I will discuss the issues they raise through some brief remarks on Lucio Colletti's recent contributions to a Marxist theory of knowledge.[6]

Unlike the other Marxist or Marx interpreters we have been looking at so far, Colletti has stressed, more consistently than any of them has done, the duality of thought and being.[7] Nor has anyone done more to de-Hegelianise Marxism, to remove some of the idealist distortions that we found in our survey of other writers. Still, Colletti has not been wholly successful. Colletti, it is true, stresses the duality of thought and being, and therein locates Marx's alliance with Kant and opposition to Hegel: 'any attempt to evade this twofold process, in which reality and thought appear alternatively as limiting conditions and that which has limiting conditions placed upon it, is only an illusion. Reality is that which is *objective,* and the objective—contrary to idealism—is precisely that which is external to and independent of thinking subjectivity'.[8] But the problem lies in Colletti's understanding of the *nature* of this duality, a duality which Colletti describes using various pairs of oppositions: the logical process and the process in reality, deduction and induction, *ratio cognoscendi* and *ratio essendi.* Colletti says that although external reality is a condition for the very existence of thought, thought remains the *ratio cognoscendi* of being; '. . . just as reality is anterior and independent, and thought in relation to it is something on which limiting conditions are placed, so it is also true that we can only arrive at a *recognition* of that reality *deductively,* i.e. through a process from which reality emerges as the *result* of a sifting and a selection carried out by thought'. Or again: 'Reality or the concrete is first; materialism remains, in this sense, the point of departure. On the other hand, insofar as we can only arrive at the *recognition* of what is concrete through thought. . . the concrete itself, as Marx says, "appears in thought".' Since 'what is "thought" *(pensato)* is inevitably a product of thought *(pensiero)',* our comprehension of the real process must be a function of thought.[9]

Whatever Colletti's intentions may be, he has in fact produced a theory of knowledge incompatible with materialism as we understand it. If our recognition of reality is wholly determined by our *a priori* concepts (and herein is supposed to lie Marx's affinity with Kant), then we can give no description of, nor justification for, our beliefs about the other side of the supposed duality, the being which remains a 'limiting condition' or 'the cause' of thought. All such claims would merely reflect *our* interpretation of reality—for there could be nothing we could say which did not reflect the logical process of recognition—and hence it is not easy to see how such claims could set out the 'other side' of the duality, the determination of thought by being. Rather, they seem to witness only the determination of being by interpretive thought. This is, as we saw, 'Kant's problem'. Thus, I am attributing to Colletti the same sort of interpretive thought claim, (IC), that we earlier ascribed to Kant. It is quite true that what Colletti says also suggests the ascription to him of the much more banal claim that our comprehension of reality is always mediated through concepts, the sort of banality that we earlier saw Goodman confusing with the non-trivial Kantian claim about interpretive thought. Of course, if Colletti only has in mind the relatively banal claim that all knowledge is conceptual in character or that reality, to be 'recognised', must be 'recognised' by thought, there is no disagreement between his epistemological claims and the materialism which he also espouses. But there is also, on this interpretation of Colletti, no interesting comparison between Colletti's Marx and Kant. On the other hand, if we do ascribe to Colletti the very non-banal interpretive thought claim, then there is an interesting comparison between Colletti's Marx and Kant, but an interesting comparison bought at the price of making the epistemology of Colletti's Marx inconsistent (in the sense that I have described) with materialism, and bought at the price of making Colletti's Marx different from the real Marx.

On the assumption that he is projecting onto Marx a Kantian interpretive thought claim, what Colletti has attempted to do is to combine an idealist epistemology *(ratio cognoscendi)* with a materialist ontology *(ratio essendi)*. It simply won't work. In his claim for the logical process, 'that we can only arrive at a *recognition* of that reality' through the logical process, he has incapacitated his theory from being able to *say* anything about, or justify belief in, the real process, independently of its determination by and relation to the logical process. Once again the logical has managed to swallow the real. The *only* way a theory of knowledge can prevent this from happening is to insist that there are things that we can recognise about the real process, about reality, which are not just the product of our *a priori* 'recognition of that reality'. There must be as we have insisted, another *ratio cognoscendi* for any consistent materialism—the structure of the real world, both the natural and social worlds—in order for us to 'recognise' reality, or come to have true beliefs about it.

Not surprisingly it is Colletti's own preoccupation with a critique of positivism which is responsible for his total neglect of the moment of correspondence in our knowledge. This can be seen in his conflation of *being* and *observable fact* (in the sense that positivism gave to that latter expression). Colletti, in an earlier discussion, rightly criticised the positivist notion that there can be a level of observable facts which are logically independent of all theory and which serve as a solid foundation, certain and secure, for the construction and justification of theory.[10] 'Theory must be *a priori* for without ideas there can be no observation. We only see that our preconceived ideas prepare us or predispose us to see'; and then, citing Gunnar Myrdal; 'Theory . . . must always be *a priori* to the empirical observation of the facts. . . (since) facts come to mean something, only as ascertained and organised in the frame of a theory.' There is no level at which one can describe objects of observation or perception such that they are independent of all theory. Presumably it is the denial of the theory-neutrality of observations that Marx has in mind in *The Economic and Philosophical Manuscripts* when he asserts:

The senses have therefore become directly in their practice theoreticians.[11]

Colletti's insistence on the dependence of observation on theory seems acceptable, and compatible with Marx's own views.

But, having emphasised the 'theory-dependence' of all *observations,* Colletti does not distinguish this from the more general claim which he goes on to make: 'thought remains the *ratio cognoscendi* of *being*' [my emphasis]. Colletti is not entitled to the general claim about theory interpreting being, reality, merely on the grounds that theory interprets observational facts. Colletti neglects the fact that theory has *both* an interpretive and a reflective role to play. Against positivists, Colletti is correct in stressing the interpretive role of theory in its relation to observable facts. We agree with Colletti if what he is claiming is that there are no 'facts' which are logically independent of a theoretical setting, no neutral descriptions of the world which are free of theoretical commitments and presuppositions. Indeed, on any Marxist theory of knowledge, as we have already seen in our discussion of essence and appearance, the phenomenal 'facts' of our daily lives cannot stand alone, let alone be the solid foundations for theories. Facts are, at the phenomenal level, appearances only, and it is the role of theory to interpret and characterise those appearances by revealing the essential structure of the natural or social reality from which they arise. But, although theory may be interpretive with regard to observations, its intention is to be reflective about those real structures which are responsible for the appearances. We need a theory with which to 'interpret' the appearance of exchange-value and its magnitudes, for example, but the theory which correctly interprets those appearances can only do so by accurately reflecting the commodity structure in capitalist social reality which explains the occurrence of those appearances. Such claims about reality at the level of theory, if correct, reflect rather than interpret that reality. Such claims are unlike claims at the level of observation or observable fact.

‘ Thus, we can make a distinction which Colletti fails to make between what we can call facts of theory and facts of observation. Like Colletti we can reject all forms of positivism, which attempt to make facts of observation sovereign, and which are therefore committed to the acceptance of the world as it appears. With Colletti, we can say that our theories are *a priori,* interpretive, with regard to empirical observations. But unlike Colletti, our anti-positivism is consistent with a materialist theory of knowledge, for we hold that the function of theories is to reflect, not interpret, essential reality, knowledge of which is available to us not by observation alone but only by theory and theory-informed observation.

The inappropriateness of all images and metaphors of mental passivity in the acquisition of knowledge on reflection theory as we understand it can now be easily evidenced. Our theories may attempt to reflect reality rather than interpret it, but they cannot do so if the mind is inactive, a passive receiver of the signals of sense. A passive mind, should there be such a thing, could only receive *appearances* of observation, phenomenal 'facts'. As long as there is a distinction to be drawn between essences and appearances, as long as man stands in need of science *as such,* whose function it is to go beyond appearance, for that long no passive mind could ever come to know what reality is essentially like. Now, there is a sense in which constructing a theory must be the work of an active mind. It is only as a result of mental (and physical) labour that one comes to have a theory. But that the mind must be active in its discovery of a theory, that it must disregard or discount whatever might come to it in a purely passive way as misleading, does not prevent that theory from reflecting rather than interpreting. It is true that 'corresponding' may be less misleading here than 'reflecting', because of the associations with passivity that the latter apparently has. But the intention behind the two expressions is the same. We can actively create theories which reflect or correspond to the world. Thus, we also distinguish the questions of how a man comes to have a theory, and what the relation is between theory and reality. It is perfectly consistent to accept that the answer to the first question involves mental activity of certain sorts, and that the answer to the second is that the relation is one of correspondence or reflection, at least between the theory and what is essential about reality (but which may not *appear),* and this by itself shows that there is no passivity necessarily involved in a *(theoretical)* reflection theory. What I hope this discussion of Colletti will have brought out is the extent to which a (theoretical) reflection theory can account both for the distinction between essence and appearance, and the role of mental activity in the acquisition of knowledge. A theoretical reflection theory is adequate, when tested against our agreed criteria, in a way in which the positivists' (observational) reflection theory was not.

The claim that a reflection theory necessarily involves an element of mental passivity is one made by friends of reflection theory as well as foes. Sebastiano Timpanaro, for example, in his spirited defense of materialism, has this to say:

This emphasis on the passive element in experience does not, it is true, pretend to be a theory of knowledge. . . But it is the preliminary condition for any theory of knowledge which is not content with verbalistic and illusory solutions. This implies a polemical position towards a major part of modern philosophy, which has intangled and exhausted itself in the setting up of 'epistemological traps' to catch and tame the external datum, in order to make it something which exists solely as a function of the activity of the subject.[12]

But, as we have already seen, the reflection theory we have proposed, which does not make the external datum a function of subjective activity, does not commit us to a *passive* comprehension of experience either. Timpanaro's heroic decision to pay the price of passivity for his materialism is simply unnecessary. We can have both materialism, and a reflection theory of knowledge, without paying this price.

Colletti, in support of his claim that thought interprets rather than reflects, quotes a lengthy passage by Marx from the *Introduction to the Grundrisse.* In that passage Marx speaks not just of observable facts 'being a product of thought', but of 'the contemplated world as such'. Is this statement of Marx's consistent with a (theoretical) reflection theory? Does thought produce or generate the whole of the *contemplated* world at least? Marx does not seem to restrict his claim to observations, but extends it to the whole of (contemplated) reality:

Hegel fell into the illusion, therefore, of conceiving reality as the result of self-propelling, self-encompassing and self-elaborating thought; whereas, the method of advancing from the abstract to the concrete is merely the way in which thought appropriates the concrete and reproduces it as a concrete that has assumed a mental form. This is by no means, however, the process which generates the concrete itself. For consciousness, then—and philosophical consciousness is such that contemplative thought is conceived as real man and thus the contemplated world as such is conceived as the only reality—for this consciousness the movement of categories appears as the real act of production (which unfortunately receives only a stimulus from outside), the result of which is the world. All of this is correct, insofar as—and here again we have a tautology—the concrete totality, *qua* totality made up of thought and concrete made up of thought, is in fact a product of thinking and comprehending. In no sense, however, is this totality a product of a concept which generates itself and thinks outside and above perception and representation; rather, it is a product of the elaboration of perception and representation into concepts. The whole, as it appears in our minds in the form of a whole made up of thought, is a product of a thinking mind, which appropriates the world in the only way possible for it. The real subject still remains outside the mind, leading an independent existence. . .[13]

Marx, of course, insists that the concrete object exists externally to us, and this is materialism, as we have explained it. But it looks as if he is also saying that the concrete thought object, the object of knowledge, is 'in fact a product of thinking and comprehending'. Is Marx holding here an interpretive, non-reflection, theory of knowledge, as Colletti would have us believe?

Colletti has, I think, wholly misinterpreted the import of this passage. In order to interpret these remarks properly we must be clear about what question it is that Marx is attempting to answer. Although the references to Hegel may mislead us into epistemological corners, it is clear that Marx is discussing the method of political economy. Marx is asking the essentially methodological question: in our studies of society, how shall we proceed in order to gain a concrete understanding of social reality? Marx's answer is that we begin with abstract definitions and, by way of them, proceed 'to the reproduction of the concrete subject in the course of reasoning'. Marx contrasts this approach with the one used by political economy at its inception. But Marx is *not* raising Colletti's epistemological problem of whether known, or 'contemplated', reality is a product of *a priori* theory— the problem which was Kant's and Hegel's and which Marx's reference to Hegel might tempt us to conflate with the methodological question. Thus, when Marx says, for example, that 'the concrete, as a thought aggregate, the concrete subject of our thought, is in fact a product of our thought, of comprehension', he is only making the perfectly acceptable methodological claim that our understanding of reality proceeds by taking simple definitions and building them up successively into a full picture of concrete reality. Marx does not seriously intend to suggest that we *create* or *produce* even the reality we contemplate. Nor is Marx taking the unacceptable Kantian epistemological position that those simple definitions are only what the mind brings *a priori* to reality, and do not describe what is in reality as it is, independently of our conceptualisations of it. Indeed, Marx reminds us in the same passage that the concrete 'is the real starting point and, therefore, also the starting point of observation and conception'. The simple definitions with which we methodologically reproduce reality are, naturally, themselves derived or abstracted *from* that reality, so of course we can speak of what reality is like apart from our conceptualisation of it.

Indeed, the concrete concept 'produced' from the abstract definitions is 'the way in which thought appropriates the concrete and reproduces it as a concrete that has assumed a mental form', and this conceptual production is by thought which itself 'is the product of the elaboration of perception and representation into concepts'. Thus, insofar as there is an underlying epistemological claim, in addition to the methodological claim, in the passages which Colletti uses, it seems actually to be contrary to the one which Colletti purports to discover in the text. *Methodologically,* the concrete concept at which we arrive is a product of the abstract definitions with which we began. But Marx is *not* saying that *epistemologically* the concrete reality that becomes an object of our knowledge is wholly a determination of thought (rather than of reality), since Marx holds that the abstract definitions are themselves derived from reality—although it is true that the reality from which they are derived is one of which we can, at first, have only a 'chaotic notion'. The underlying tenor of the passage, then, is one of both ontological *and* epistemological realism—the existence of a realm independent of thought *and* a reality which is 'a starting point of observation and conception'. There is no reason to think that Marx has changed his earlier view that 'Sense-perception (see Feuerbach) must be the basis of all science',[14] and it is from perception of that reality that man begins the process of coming to a scientific understanding of that reality.

I do not think that, ultimately, methodological and epistemological questions can be separated, but it is important to see that the methodological question Marx is discussing in this passage is not identical with the epistemological problem we, and Colletti, have been discussing. Marx is here discussing the logic of scientific inquiry, *not* the epistemological question of whether thought is interpretive or reflective, whether, in Kant's words, our knowledge conforms to objects or objects to our knowledge. Using the distinction we made above between the two different questions of how a man comes to have a theory and what the relation is between theory and reality, we can say that, in this passage from *The Grundrisse,* Marx is answering the question: how do we arrive at an adequate theory of concrete reality? The answer Marx offers to that question is not Kant's answer to the other question: does our thought interpret or reflect the reality which it reveals? These are the two different questions which we earlier disentangled. That is, we distinguish the questions of how a man comes to have a theory, and what the relation is between theory and reality. The first question, which I have called a methodological question, is the one Marx is discussing in the passage cited. Colletti misinterprets Marx as offering a Kantian answer to the second question. It is Colletti's failure to distinguish these two questions which accounts for his misinterpretation of the passage from *The Grundrisse.* Since Colletti misidentifies the question being asked, it can hardly be surprising that he misunderstands Marx's answer.[15]

The conflation of these two different questions is not at all uncommon in discussions of Marx's methodology. In his discussion of Marx's method,

Maurice Godelier first notes that for Marx ideal logic, the logic of concepts, 'reproduces' the logic of reality.[16] Godelier then footnotes this with the following remark:

> This fundamental point is analysed by Marx in his *Introduction to the Critique of Political Economy*. The idea of 'reproduction' is to be distinguished from that of 'reflexion', which, however, it presupposes. It is *this* idea, and not that of reflexion, that lies at the heart of the theory of cognition implicit in Marx's work.

It is not clear precisely what to make of Godelier's remark, since he obviously thinks that in some way Marx embraces both the ideas of reflection and reproduction, since the latter is said to presuppose the former. But Godelier has not apparently seen that reflection and reproduction are ideas which are part answers to the two *different* questions I have discussed. Methodologically, the concrete concept is *reproduced* through mental activity. This is part of the answer to the question of how a man comes to have a correct theory and the image of reproduction here is accurate insofar as it serves as a reminder of the mental activity involved in theory construction. One does not obtain knowledge in a state of passivity. Epistemologically, if the theory or concept is 'correct' or 'accurate', then it *reflects* reality. That is part of the answer to the question of what is the relation between knowledge and reality, or an adequate or correct theory and reality. These questions must be kept distinct.

Lenin's remarks on Kant in his *Materialism and Empirio-Criticism* seem equally applicable to Colletti's Kantian interpretation of Marx. Kant's philosophy held within it certain unresolved tensions, since its epistemology was essentially idealist, whereas in its retention of the thing-in-itself, its ontology attempted to be materialist. We made a point parallel to Lenin's in Chapter I, about the tension in Kantian philosophy between idealist epistemology and pre-conceptualised intuitions. We called that tension 'Kant's problem', and we gave a short sketch of how that tension was resolved in two diametrically opposed ways after Kant in the philosophies of Hegel and Feuerbach.

Thus, Kant could be criticised, as Lenin indicated, from Left or Right. Those like Mach, Avenarius, and Bogdanov (and we could add Kolakowski to the list), who jettisoned the thing-in-itself, were attacking Kantianism from the right. As such, their 'refined' or 'purified' Kantianism was a rejection of materialism. In his imitation of Kant, Colletti's views have that same unresolved tension between materialist or realist ontology and idealist epistemology. Either we take his epistemology seriously, and go down the idealist road with Hegel and the latter day Hegelians, or we take the materialist ontology seriously, and travel the materialist road, replacing or supplementing Colletti's epistemology with something like the much despised *wiederspiegelungstheorie,* suitably refined and made plausible.

Finally, I want to consider whether or not a reflection theory allows for a social conception of knowledge. It might at first be thought that it does not do so. After all, thus far our discussion has been couched in terms of a man's thought or knowledge and its relation to reality. For instance, I earlier distinguished the questions of how a man comes to have a theory and the relation between his theory and reality. Such formulations seem individualistic rather than social, and so far nothing appears to have been said about the role of society in the acquisition of knowledge.

If the account I have given so far is to be considered individualistic, this can only be in a thoroughly acceptable sense of that term. Whatever mediating role society plays in the acquisition of knowledge by individuals, it is ultimately only individual men who can be said to have or possess knowledge or theories. Knowledge is unlike truth. There can be truth in a world without men, even though trivially there would be no one to realise or recognise what is true. But there can be no knowledge in a world in which there are no individual men to have that knowledge. Individuals are the sole thinkers of thought; there is no social mind which can do the thinking for the individuals.

What I am claiming, though, is not just the rather weak thesis that there can be no thought or knowledge unless there are individual men. Rather, I am claiming something stronger, viz., that any statement that a certain theory or body of knowledge exists in a society is equivalent to *(says no more than)* the statement that there are some individuals in that society who hold the theory, possess the knowledge, or whatever. The concept of social knowledge can be wholly reduced to the concept of a set of individual knowers. Methodological individualism may well be wrong as a general account of the reduction of sociological concepts to non-sociological (psychological or individualist) ones. 'Sociological concepts cannot be translated into psychological concepts *without remainder*. . .'[17] To say that any social 'institution' exists, that under capitalism there is a working class, for example, is not *just* to say that there exist individuals who have certain relations to one another and to other individuals, where those relations themselves are specified in 'non-sociological', individualistic terms. The sociological terms and concepts, like 'working class' or 'party', are 'richer' than the non-sociological ones; it is not surprising, then, that such attempts at reduction fail. But methodological individualism about the existence of theories or knowledge in society is not similarly mistaken.

Why should there be this difference between social structure, for example, and social knowledge? Both the methodological individualist and the methodological wholist would admit that statements about both social structure and social knowledge imply the statement that there are some individuals who stand in specifiable ('non-sociological') relations, or that there are some individuals who have or possess the theory or knowledge in question. Both agree that there can be neither social structure nor social theory without men. The debate is not whether the sociological statement implies the statement about individuals, but whether the statements are equivalent.

It is, as I have said, plausible to deny the equivalence between the statement about individuals and the sociological statement about structure, class, state, party, etc., because the concepts used in the formulations of these sorts of sociological statements appear to be richer than any set of concepts which occur in purely individualistic statements. Hence, no reduction of one set of concepts to the other seems possible. But such an argument would not be plausible when applied to the concept of the social existence of a theory and individualistic concepts. There is *nothing more* to saying that a certain theory exists in a society than saying that there are some individuals who hold that theory. But if statements about the existence of knowledge in society are no richer than statements that knowing individuals exist, then the reduction of the former to the latter is possible. Such statements about the social existence of knowledge imply and are implied by statements about knowing individuals, and hence they are reducible to them without remainder.

Thus, we are claiming not only that, unlike truth, there can be no social knowledge without men, but somewhat more strongly, that *all there is* to there being social knowledge or theory is that there are some individuals who know certain things. In this sense, we are happy to have an individualistic conception of knowledge. Now, there is no reason in principle why a reflection theory could not be stated in a non-individualist manner. If there were social minds or *Volkgeist* or whatever, then their theories would be true when they reflected reality. There is nothing intrinsic to the idea of correspondence or reflection which would preclude it being stated in a way that was irreducibly social, if it were desirable to do so. But the reflection theory I have developed was stated in an individualistic manner since there are no social minds and since social knowledge is only the knowledge of individuals. There may be nothing intrinsically individualistic about a reflection theory, but the version I have sketched certainly is individualistic to this extent, since it is right that it should be so.

I have been careful to say 'individualistic in this sense' or 'to that extent', for in other ways the theory is not individualistic. Nothing of what I have said denies that society necessarily plays a mediating role in the acquisition of knowledge. It certainly is a very deep fact about men that their knowledge, like their language, is acquired in social situations. As we said in the last chapter, the biological transmit that an individual man receives is insufficient for him to make much epistemological progress on his own. We have also spoken in this chapter and the last of human physical and mental activity. It may have appeared that these formulations too were individualistic. Both however are forms of *social* activity. In terms of physical activity, praxis, there is nothing in reflection theory which disallows in any way our comprehension of praxis as *social*. Reflection theory can certainly agree that

the subject of our discussion is first of all *material* production. Individuals producing in society, thus the socially determined production of individuals naturally constitutes the starting point. The individual and isolated hunter or fisher who forms the starting point with Smith and Ricardo belongs to the insipid illusions of the eighteenth century.[18]

More important for our present discussion is the social dimension of mental activity. I spoke earlier of the absurdity of attempting to imagine a man erasing *everything* which he in fact learns by way of social transmits in order to readmit only secure and certain knowledge. Reflection theory can provide a fully adequate place for those social transmits, the 'transitive objects of science' in Bhaskar's equally happy formulation. The acquisition of knowledge presupposes a social mode of intellectual production, and ultimately a mode of material production, in which that acquisition occurs. We can agree that knowledge acquisition may well occur only in a social setting with other thinkers or scientists, a setting which has both breadth, because it includes a multiplicity of thinkers at a time, and a depth because it has a history of past intellectual labourers over time. Individual contributors to that intellectual mode of production are dependent for making their contributions on a theory which is at least in part transmitted to and acquired by those individual contributors. But still each individual thinker holds a true theory only when, and to the extent that, *his* theory corresponds to reality.

Because we have separated the questions of theory acquisition and the relation between theory and reality, because we have distinguished Godelier's 'reproduction' and 'reflection', we can admit to all of the above and still insist that the relation between any piece of *knowledge* held by an individual (whether it represents an acquisition of his own or something he has received by way of transmit) and reality is one of *reflection*—an individual man's knowledge, however acquired, reflects reality. Thus reflection theory has no difficulty whatever in agreeing that

language *is* practical consciousness that exists also for other men, and for that reason alone it really exists for me personally as well; language like consciousness, only arises from the need, the necessity, of intercourse with other men . . . Consciousness is, therefore, from the very beginning a social product, and remains so as long as men exist at all.[19]

In whatever ways it *is* plausible to argue that knowledge is social, reflection theory has no special or peculiar difficulty in accounting for this. The conception of knowledge I have advanced is individualistic only in the sense in which knowledge simply *is* individualistic, because it is always and only the knowledge of individual men, albeit individual men in social settings whose acquisition of that knowledge has been mediated through society.

This now concludes the limited task I set for myself in this chapter. I have discussed several features or characteristics which I think that any adequate theory of knowledge must have. I have assumed that Marxists— and hopefully others too—would agree that it is reasonable to demand that these characteristics be possessed by any adequate theory of knowledge. I then argued, both in my discussion of those features in Chapter IV and subsequently in this chapter, that a version of reflection theory, which I called a theoretical reflection theory, can be formulated such that it meets the reasonable epistemological demands which Marxists commonly make.

I argued in the first chapter that a materialist must hold a reflection theory, on pain of epistemological inconsistency if he does not do so. That reflection theory, as I have stated it, avoids so many of the charges and accusations levelled against it by several generations of Marxist theorists, ought to strengthen confidence in my earlier argument. It is simply not true that reflection theory necessarily accepts the world as it appears, or has a mechanical, passive, undialectic, or a-social conception of the acquisition of knowledge. Some formulations of a reflection theory may well fall foul of these charges. Indeed, insofar as the positivists for example held a reflection (or correspondence) theory of knowledge, reflection theory in their hands often did suffer from many of these defects. But what is wrong with their reflection theory is not so much the reflection theory, but their commitment to some sort of principle of verifiability, and their attendant philistine attitude toward the existence of unobservables and commitment to theory reduction or elimination. In any case, the theory of reflection which we have formulated is not flawed in this way, and this is what the present and previous chapters have tried to show.

At least, then, the version of reflection theory I have described avoids these charges. But I wish next, in the sixth and final chapter of the book, to turn to Lenin's *Materialism and Empirio-Criticism,* which contains his statement of *a* reflection theory. To what extent does Lenin's formulation share the flaws that accompany a positivist formulation of reflection theory? Alternatively, are there suggestions and insights within Lenin's discussion which would justify us in ascribing to him, at least in his 'better moments', a version of reflection theory which also escapes the standard charges and accusations brought against it? In order to answer these queries, it is to *Materialism and Empirio-Criticism,* and to some of the many discussions of it, to which we shall turn in the next chapter.

In the *Introduction* I mentioned the problem that many philosophers might find the realism I was defending, and the idealism I was attacking, to be so obvious and uncontentious, and absurd and silly, respectively, that this book could appear to them as uninteresting and unmotivated. In a footnote to the *Introduction,* I recorded some rude remarks by a reviewer of Sebastiano Timpanaro's *On Materialism* which substantially made that very point. I said also in the *Introduction:* 'But most contemporary philosophers simply take realism for granted. Not since the phenomenalism of the logical positivists died a welcome death some decades ago have many orthodox philosophers argued that external reality is mind-dependent or questioned that, in Lenin's phrase, "the object exists independently of the subject".' It is time to note that this earlier, rather apologetic, judgement is not entirely true. The struggle between realism and idealism is as old as philosophy itself, and it continues to surface and resurface in ever new forms throughout the history of thought.[20]. Although we continue to accept that thought does not have its own, independent history, but that its course has a materialist basis, it is hard to spell out this connection in any plausible detail, since the appearance of idealism is such a 'universal' phenomenon, stretching across modes of production and historical epochs, and hence at least seems to defy being coupled with any particular concatenation of material or historical circumstances.

Idealism has surfaced again in contemporary orthodox philosophy, but in the new, fashionable garb of philosophy of language, rather than in the outdated dress of the theory of knowledge. True, it had never entirely disappeared.[21] But its recent rebirth has been in new apparel, itself in keeping with the also fashionable judgement about the shift of the centre of philosophy from epistemology to philosophy of language: '. . . the theory of meaning . . . is the foundation of all philosophy, and not epistemology as Descartes led us into believing.'[22] Thus it is that current forms of idealism have arisen out of these new emphases on language. What is curiously interesting is that the terminology of this idealism, which speaks of the essential, internal connection between world and thought, makes it much closer to the idealism that we traced through Kant and Hegel than to that of the subjective idealists who had surfaced meanwhile. This is, I think, because the neo-idealism in theory of language has learned well Wittgenstein's lesson concerning the publicity of language, the sociality of conceptual schemes, and so the idealism that emerges has far more in common with the socially oriented absolute idealism of Hegel than with the individualist phenomenalism of the logical positivists.

How does this linguistically motivated idealism arise?[23] The realist and idealist differ on whether objects are thought-dependent: 'An important question that may be raised here is whether or not what objects there are is something independent of language. Can we think of the construction of a language as involving the assignment of names to pre-existing objects? This would be the realist view. Consequently for the realist what is possible is language-independent.' What is wrong with such a realist philosophy? Isn't the world independent of thought or language? Phillips argues in the following way:

The (transcendental) realist believes that e.g. material objects have an existence 'by themselves and independently of the senses' and this can be taken to mean that he believes propositions about the senses and about the external world to be only contingently related and thus logically independent.

The realist must claim that statements about sense experience can constitute merely contingent evidence for the claims about the material world. The meaning of the two different claims are independent. But then how shall the realist answer the sceptic? Since the meanings of material object and sensation claims are independent, the realist must accept that there is a logically possible world in which the statements about sensations are true but (all) the statements about the material world are false. But how do we know that this logically possible world *isn't* our world after all? '. . . the realist position does, as Kant observes, lead to scepticism . . .' The realist, according to Phillips, cannot explain '*why* an instance of A [a sensation claim] provides evidence for a corresponding instance of B [a material object claim].'

The reply to the sceptic involves, for Phillips, adopting idealism or constructivism: '. . . transcendental idealism [is rooted] in constructivism' and constructivism is, to put it briefly, the assertion that 'I grasp the sense of a proposition if and only if I know what criterial evidence would justify asserting the material object claim. In that way, material object and sensory experience claims are logically, not contingently, related.' Thus constructivism leads to (transcendental) idealism. Material objects and sense-impressions are *logically* related. Phillips' rejoinder to the sceptic involves a logical insurance policy that, like love and marriage, you *can't* have one without the other. For the idealist, a decent reply to the sceptic can only be given on an idealist perspective. Once again, the objective world has become essentially dependent on the human.

Suspicion about the mind-independence of the material world has become widespread. 'The line between the subjective and objective, mind and its object, was not clear enough in early twentieth century philosophy to permit a clear formulation of the realism-idealism issue. Before anyone suspected that philosophy of language might be first philosophy, philosophers tried and failed to get clear about the sense in which there were "facts" and "objective relations" independent of mind. I do not think there *is* a clear and nontrivial sense to be given to this notion.'[24] Rorty attacks both the correspondence theory of truth and the 'transparent' sense of reference, which together comprise the materials out of which a realist theory of meaning could be constructed as an alternative to the constructivist theory of meaning. Rorty bids us to reject the notion of 'truth as "the accurate representation of reality" and that the truth of a sentence depends upon hook-ups between parts of the sentence and parts of the world . . .'[25] because both are 'linked to outworn philosophical projects. These projects arose in the context of the seventeenth-century image of mind as the Mirror of Nature . . .'[26] Milton Fisk succinctly summarises the metaphysical consequences of these, and related views: ' . . . the world is countenanced only in a sense that ties it closely to a common set of beliefs, while it is rejected in the sense that would make it other than thought . . . A need is felt [by the idealist] to overcome the obsession by pointing out that what had mistakenly been taken to be independent of thought is really just the other side of thought. The relation of aboutness [language is *about* the world] that holds from the fund of collectively acquired beliefs to the entities we regard ourselves as familiar with is not a relation external to those entities.'[27] For the idealist, ' . . . the world is not distinct from the set of true sentences.'[28]

Contemporary Anglo-American philosophy has, then, faced us with a new, linguistic variant of Absolute Idealism. The world becomes essentially dependent on, internally connected to, sets of publicly held beliefs, conceptual schemes, thought. Against such views, the realist must present a defense of the concept of correspondence and the notion of 'transparent' reference. Like Fisk, who as a Marxist realist is also concerned to expose these idealist tendencies in contemporary philosophy and to state a viable, realist alternative, we wish to adopt a notion of correspondence (or reflection) which has no pictorial associations, and I will elaborate on this in my discussion of the controversy between Lenin and Plekhanov in Chapter VI. It is a causal theory of correspondence, and reference which does seem to offer the best hope for the realist. I do not wish here to argue or defend that assertion, but merely mark it as part of the overall conception which a realist, and *a fortiori,* a Marxist, theory of language must elaborate.

Fisk's development of the notion of correspondence is one that he, too, wishes to make from an explicitly Marxist perspective: 'I conclude that one requirement for a consistent historical materialist approach to thought is that there be entities that are distinct from both thought and activities.'[29] Fisk also stresses the fact that the causal connection that exists between words and things is not 'natural', or personal, but socially mediated. An added advantage to Fisk's explication of correspondence, from a Marxist point of view, is that it involves not only causality but also practice. If correct, Fisk would make praxis perhaps more central in philosophy than I have thus far allowed it to be. Unhappily, I cannot see that he is right. It is not clear to me how causation and praxis are intended to mesh in his account of correspondence. Fisk argues that the condition that makes a thought true (the condition which 'corresponds' to the thought) is the condition which 'generates' the thought 'in the context of a practice.'[30] 'It is these activities that relate the condition and the thought . . .'[31] For instance, we might say that the thought that the moon is the earth's only natural satellite is related to (corresponds to) the condition that the moon is, in fact, the earth's only natural satellite, and it is in being causally related in appropriate ways to this condition that makes the thought true. Now, this condition is a constituent of human activity, both in the sense that it is studied, and in the sense that we do actually attempt active involvement with that condition—we attempt to land men on the moon. That the condition has this involvement with human praxis is what accounts for the interest we have both in the condition and in the thought which that condition makes true. But how does that activity help with *truth?* If Fisk thinks that causality plus activity explains correspondence, then it would seem that, really, causality by itself would be sufficient to explain correspondence; the causal connection between the thought and the condition seems sufficient for that accounting, without importing the notion of practice at all. Some true thoughts so explained may well be of little interest to us, because of their irrelevance to human activity, but still truth seems one thing, practice quite another. Moreover, causality alone would seem sufficient to steer between the conventionalist and idealist accounts of the relation between thought and object of which Fisk advises us to beware. Thus, although I can happily follow Fisk in the programme of devising a causal theory to underpin the notion of correspondence, a programme which will allow us to jettison whatever misleading pictorial associations 'correspondence' (or even 'reflection') might have, I cannot see that praxis helps us here in developing our understanding of truth by correspondence.

As for the constructivist argument against realism with which we began, several marks may serve to fix our sights on how we might wish to proceed. First, once again we see a philosophy adopted on the grounds that it alone is tailored to meet the demands of the sceptic. How better to show *why* our evidence is evidence for something than to devise a logical tie between the evidence and that for which it is evidence? We choose to ignore the sceptic. Our world *is* a world of uncertainty, of intellectual risk. Our evidence is contingent evidence. We *could* (logically) be wrong. Second, there is something between being logically entitled to a conclusion and not being entitled to it at all. Evidence can provide inductive support for a conclusion. There may be a *logically* possible world in which sensation statements are true and material object statements false, but inductive inference tells us that that world is *not* our world. Similarly, there is a *logically* possible world in which observation reports in science are true but theoretical statements are false; but induction assures us that we are entitled, on the observational grounds, to our theoretical beliefs. Indeed, what Phillips' argument rests on is a refined scepticism of its own, concerning the possibility of inductive inference. For a realist, induction itself is grounded in a view of nomological necessity that steers between logical necessity and sheer contingency. There is a law-like connection between things and the sensations they induce in us, and from this perspective, we are entitled to inferences from one to the other. The constructivist argument that we have been examining in many ways accepts all the weapons out of Hume's armoury: scepticism about induction, a denial of necessity *de re,* and a regularity analysis of causal connection. As realists, we wish to enforce a surrender of all these connected weapons.

Notes: Chapter V

[1] Lenin, V. I., *Philosophical Notebooks, Collected Works,* Vol. 38, FLPH, Moscow, 1963.
[2] Bhaskar distinguishes the intransitive and transitive objects of science. In addition to his *A Realist Theory of Science,* see also his 'Feyerabend versus Bachelard', *New Left Review,* No. 94, Nov-Dec 1975, pp.31-55.
[3] Schmidt, Alfred, *The Concept of Nature In Marx,* New Left Books, London, 1971, p.122.
[4] Marx, Karl, *Capital,* Vol. I, Progress Publishers, Moscow, 1965. Marx's footnote at the bottom of p.372.
[5] Marx, Karl, *Capital* Vol. III, Progress Publishers, Moscow, 1966. p.820.
[6] Colletti, Lucio, *From Rousseau to Lenin,* New Left Books, London, 1972, hereafter *FRL,* and *Marxism and Hegel,* New Left Books, London, 1973, hereafter *M&H*
[7] I have already agreed that the expression 'duality of thought and being' can be misleading if it leads one to assume that thought is not *also* part of reality. I said that one can speak of *total* reality, and of thought and being, where being is simply defined as all of total reality minus thought. The 'duality' of thought and being then simply means that the remainder of

reality could still exist even if that part of reality which is thought did not. This is important, for Roy Edgley has convinced me that it may well be that this expression in Colletti is a misunderstanding, symptomatic of Colletti's general 'extrusion' of thought from reality. Edgley conjectures that it may be this which accounts for Colletti's unwillingness to allow a dialectic of the real, for he confines contradiction to the realm of thought alone. Edgley may well be right about this. See Colletti's recent 'Contradiction and Contrariety' in *New Left Review*, No. 93, Sept-Oct 1975, pp.3-29.

8   Colletti, Lucio, *M&H*, p.119.
9   *Ibid.* pp.120, 119, 121.
10   Colletti, Lucio, *FRL*, p.75 and ff for subsequent quotes.
11   Marx, Karl, *EPM*, p.99.
12   Timpanaro, Sebastiano, 'Considerations on Materialism', *New Left Review*, No. 85, 1974, pp.7-8.
13   Cited in Colletti, Lucio, *M&H*, p.120.
14   Marx, Karl, *EPM*, p. 103. Ernest Mandel correctly emphasises the realism inherent in this passage from *The Grundisse*. See his *Late Capitalism*, New Left Books, London, 1975, p. 14.
15   Orthodox philosophy distinguishes between the context of discovery and the context of justification. For those who know the distinction, it might be helpful to say that, in this passage, Marx is dealing with problems of discovery of a theory. Reflection theory, since it offers a criterion for or definition of knowledge, is concerned with problems which arise in the context of theory justification.
16   Godelier, Maurice, *Rationality and Irrationality in Economics*, New Left Books, London, 1972, p.131. Consider also some of the Althusserian jargon of Barry Hindess and Paul Q. Hirst, in *Pre-Capitalist Modes of Production*, Routledge & Kegan Paul Ltd., London, 1975. In the 'Introduction', they criticise empiricist methodology, on the grounds that 'Empiricism represents knowledge as constructed out of 'given' elements . . . Unfortunately, for these positions, facts are never "given" to knowledge' (p.2). We agree with this, because we have maintained that the discovery of facts, theoretical facts, is the task of a theory, and arriving at a well-confirmed, plausible theory is a labour which demands intellectual and practical activity. However, Hindess and Hirst then proceed to conclude, from this denial that facts are given, that they are *produced:* 'They [these facts] are always the product of definite practices . . . Facts are never *given;* they are always produced. The facts of the sciences are products of scientific practices' (pp.2-3). This is a confusion. Facts may not be given—they must be uncovered or discovered. The antithesis to being 'given' is being *discovered.* We hold that the *discovery* of facts is a product of scientific practice. It certainly does not follow that the facts, themselves are also produced, which is a wholly idealist conception. The jargon of theoretical and scientific practices can be misleading if the analogy with productive activity is taken too literally. Manufacture *produces* objects which may not have antedated the manufacture; intellectual activity discovers that which is not usually created by the intellectual activity itself. Science itself is more like exploring than making, although if we consider science materialistically we can also see the close connections between science and productive needs.
17   Mandelbaum, Maurice, 'Societal Facts', *British Journal of Sociology*, VI, (1955) pp.305-317.
18   Marx, Karl, *Introduction to the Grundrisse* in *A Contribution to a Critique of Political Economy*, introduced by Maurice Dobb, p.188.
19   Marx, Karl and Engels, Frederick, *The German Ideology*, Laurence & Wishart, London, 1965, p.42.
20   This fact by itself makes Pannekoek's limitation of idealism to feudal conditions and materialism to the bourgeois struggle against feudal conditions seem rather silly. We shall examine this in some detail in the final pages of chapter VI.
21   Some examples would be: the continuing interest in the English idealists, as for example by Richard Wollheim in his study of Bradley; the 'neo-idealism' of Peter Winch in the social sciences and of Thomas Kuhn in the natural sciences; Nicholas Rescher's related

books on coherence theories of truth, conceptual idealism, and the centrality of practice to truth.

22	Dummett, Michael, *Frege: Philosophy of Language*, Duckworth, London, 1973. p. 669.

23	There are various, alternative methods for structuring the argument. With some changes, I am following the argument of Colin Phillips, 'Constructivism and Epistemology' *Philosophy* 53, Jan. 1978, pp. 51-69. For an attack on scientific realism by a philosopher of science, see the symposium 'The Underdetermination of Theory by Data' between W. Newton-Smith and S. Lukes in *Aristotelian Society: Supplementary Vol LII* (1978). Newton-Smith's strategy is to argue that there are cases in which there are alternative theories that can be constructed in science, and that the choice between them is underdetermined by all *possible* evidence. Either the realist must hold that one or the other theory is true, but we can never know which, or abandon his realist belief that there is any matter of fact that makes one or the other true.

	Newton-Smith chooses scientific examples, because he does not want to allow the possibility of the choice being made on philosophical but non-empirical grounds. His cases, though, turn on problems of temporal identity ('the same time') and spatial continuity, so it is not clear to me that there are not philosophical considerations for selecting between what are otherwise empirically equivalent theories.

24	Rorty, Richard, 'Realism and Reference', *The Monist*, July 1976, Volume 59, No. 3. p. 327.

25	*Ibid*, p. 330.

26	*Ibid*, p. 334.

27	Fisk, Milton, 'Idealism, Truth, and Practice', *The Monist*, July 1976, Volume 59, No. 3, p. 373.

28	*Ibid.*, p. 374.

29	*Ibid.*, p. 389. For a development of a causal theory of reference, see Hilary Putnam, 'Explanation and Reference', eds. Pearce and Maynard, *Conceptual Change*, Reidel, Dordrecht, 1973, pp. 199-221.

30	*Ibid.*, p. 386.

31	*Ibid.*, p. 387.

CHAPTER VI

LENIN AND HIS CRITICS

> ... there is a materialist line and an idealist line in philosophy, and between them there are various shades of agnosticism. The vain attempts to find a 'new' point of view in philosophy betray the same poverty of mind that is revealed in similar efforts to create a 'new' theory of value, a 'new' theory of rent, and so forth.[1]

We have agreed, in Chapters IV and V, that a reflection or correspondence theory of knowledge, 'suitably formulated', passed certain requirements which we claimed were essential for any acceptable theory of knowledge. In this chapter I propose to turn to a specific formulation of a reflection theory of knowledge, that of Lenin in his *Materialism and Empirio-Criticism*. It remains, thus far, an open question whether or not his particular formulation of a reflection theory of knowledge passes those tests of adequacy, and it is to that question which this chapter is meant to address itself.

It is *only* with Lenin's *Materialism and Empirio-Criticism* that I intend to deal in any detail. Many have claimed to detect an 'implicit' theory of knowledge in other of Lenin's published, non-philosophical writings. I have heard it claimed, for instance, that the theory of knowledge 'implicit' in *Imperialism: The Highest Stage of Capitalism* is 'undialectical'. More importantly, perhaps, Lenin wrote another, explicitly philosophical work, unpublished in his lifetime, *The Philosophical Notebooks. The Notebooks* are not so much a 'work' of philosophy, as Lenin's own extracts from, and marginal comments upon, a number of philosophical works of various philosophers, and above all on Hegel's *Science of Logic. Materialism and Empirio-Criticism* was written by Lenin during February to October, 1908, in Geneva and then London, and was aimed at a group of Russian Marxists, most notably Bogdanov, Bazarov, and Lunacharsky, who were attempting to underpin Marxism with the positivism of Mach and Avenarius. Subsequent to this philosophical intervention in the struggle going on within Russian Social Democracy, Lenin undertook, for the first time, a careful study of Hegel's philosophy, and it is the fruit of that study which forms the central core of *The Philosophical Notebooks* (Volume 38 of Lenin's *Collected Works,* Progress Publishers, Moscow), which were compiled by Lenin from 1914 to 1916.

Many have argued that *Materialism and Empirio-Criticism* and the *Philosophical Notebooks* are inconsistent. There is no doubt that certain emphases and insights can be discovered in the latter which only existed to a lesser extent in the former. One of these emphases is undoubtedly the whole question of dialectic. Lenin's later judgement that 'it is impossible completely to understand Marx's *Capital,* and especially its first chapter, without having thoroughly understood Hegel's *Logic.* Consequently, half a century later none of the Marxists understand Marx!' was no doubt meant to include within its scope the Lenin of *Materialism and Empirio-Criticism.* Nor can one easily imagine the Lenin of that earlier work proposing, as he later did, that Marxists form a society to be called 'the society of materialist friends of Hegelian dialectics'. But even if we admit to these changes and shifts that do undoubtedly occur in Lenin's thought after his study of Hegel, the task of a serious and balanced appraisal of *Materialism and Empirio-Criticism* still remains. Consider, for example, the rather untempered views of N. Valentinov, in his *Encounters with Lenin:*

This remark [from *The Philosophical Notebooks*] reveals that Lenin's earlier views on materialism were breaking up under Hegel's influence. This is confirmed by a phrase which would have been impossible on his lips earlier: 'Intelligent idealism is closer to intelligent materialism than is stupid materialism'. . .

. . . at that time [of *The Notebooks*] Lenin thought that materialism . . . was a very weak philosophical theory. Lenin had begun to understand quite well that the materialism he had propounded in his book with such fervour and confidence was also weak and vulnerable. In the years after the October Revolution he abandoned most of his previous views and certainties . . . and yet Lenin did not have the courage to say openly that he had thrown out, as useless, some very substantial parts of his philosophy of 1908.[2]

Where I willingly spoke of 'changes', 'shifts', new 'emphases and insights', Valentinov talks of Lenin's earlier views 'breaking up', of those earlier views being 'abandoned' or 'thrown out'. As my remarks at the beginning of Chapter V will have already indicated, no one has, I think, ever successfully substantiated these sorts of oft repeated claims of abandonment, rejection, etc. by Lenin of his earlier philosophical views of the period of *Materialism and Empirio-Criticism.* There are new emphases in the *Notebooks,* and it may even be, as Michel Löwy has recently argued,[3] that the new-found stress on dialectics in *The Notebooks* marks a crucial change in Lenin's revolutionary strategy, from a Menshevik 'stages' strategy for the Russian Revolution to a strategy of 'permanent revolution'. But I will argue that whatever change there may be between Lenin's philosophy of 1908 and 1914-1916, such changes do not amount to an abandonment, rejection, or throwing out of the earlier philosophy, as Valentinov claims.

Dialectics may, for example, be stressed in *The Notebooks,* but the topic is not missing entirely from *Materialism and Empirio-Criticism:* 'In the theory of knowledge, as in every other sphere of science, we must think dialectically, that is, we must not regard our knowledge as ready-made and unalterable, but must determine how *knowledge* emerges from ignorance . . .' (p. 127). In his discussion of 'relative' and 'absolute' truth, Lenin describes the way in which science *grows, develops,* proceeds. At any given moment we do not, he says, assume that we have the whole truth, or only the truth. At any moment in the ongoing scientific enterprise, our beliefs can fail to correspond. We can make mistakes, errors, and so on, which at least have the possibility of being corrected the next time around: dialectical materialism 'certainly does contain relativism, but is not reducible to relativism, that is, it recognises the relativity of all our knowledge, not in the sense of denying objective truth, but in the sense that the limits of approximation of our knowledge to this truth are historically conditioned' (p. 176). Science may 'aim at' reality; it does not always hit it. No one, I think, has ever had a finer intuitive feel for the dialectical development of science over time, the ways in which past errors have the opportunity to be replaced for present (or future) truths, and Lenin sees, as clearly as one can, how this appreciation of the dialectical history of science is wholly consistent with upholding, as a realist, the possibility of objective knowledge, true belief, about a reality essentially independent of thought or the human. None of the major themes of *Materialism and Empirio-Criticism* is, as far as I can see, actually contradicted in *The Notebooks*. In particular I claim that both materialism and a reflection theory of knowledge, however much developed and deepened, survive intact. As the quotation from *The Notebooks* cited at the beginning of Chapter V makes clear, Lenin carefully distinguishes between a dialectical and a non-dialectical theory of reflection. Both are theories of *reflection*. There is, then, no rejection of reflection theory in *The Notebooks*, but only an insistence that the sort of reflection theory adopted by materialists must contain a dialectical version of reflection. This I take to mean, essentially, that both science itself and the reality which it attempts to reflect should be seen in process, be seen to change and transform themselves over time, and should not be seen in some 'frozen', static form. 'The *reflection* of nature in man's thought must be understood not "lifelessly", not "abstractly", not devoid of movement, not without contradictions, but in the eternal process of movement . . .'; '. . . here [in Hegel's philosophy] we have an immeasurably rich content as compared with "metaphysical" materialism, the fundamental *misfortune* of which is its inability to apply dialectics to *Bildertheorie*, to the process and development of knowledge.' All of this certainly does not seem to add up to a rejection or abandonment by Lenin of his earlier views.

Valentinov's own argument for Lenin's subsequent rejection of materialism is both invalid and ill-informed. Valentinov begins by correctly pointing out that Lenin, in *Materialism and Empirio-Criticism*, closely identified materialism with the acceptance of Kant's thing-in-itself.[4] Thus, Lenin wrote: 'When Kant assumes that something outside us, a thing-in-itself, corresponds to our ideas, he is a materialist.'[5] Valentinov then concludes that 'If the thing-in-itself is discarded, a large part of materialism, epistemologically speaking, goes with it.'[6] Since, Valentinov continues, Lenin rejects the thing-in-itself in *The Notebooks*, then according to the identification of the thing-in-itself with materialism, Lenin thereby has signalled his rejection of materialism as well.

Valentinov's argument is invalid, since his evidence does not support the conclusion that Lenin, in *The Notebooks,* rejected the idea of the thing-in-itself. Valentinov's sole support for this conclusion is the argument that Lenin 'obediently writes out everything that Hegel says about the thing-in-itself . . .' However, from the fact that Lenin writes out everything Hegel says, in what, after all, is a 'conspectus' of Hegel's *Science of Logic,* a compilation of quotations from that book, it certainly does not follow that Lenin 'accepts it without reservation'. One cannot infer Lenin's acceptance of any random passage from Hegel simply on the grounds that he copies out the passage without comment in his notebook.

Valentinov's argument is, in addition, ill-informed. He correctly remarks that Lenin, in *The Notebooks,* 'praises the point made by Hegel that the "thing-in-itself" turns into a "thing-for-us".' Valentinov then insinuates that this implies Lenin's abandonment of the thing-in-itself: 'Before long he would have seen that *esse est percipi!'.* Valentinov seems ignorant of the fact that this was precisely the *same* stand that Lenin had already taken in *Materialism and Empirio-Criticism,* for in that book he, following Engels, had already accepted a *knowable* ('for us') version of the thing-in-itself, and it is the unknowability of Kant's thing-in-itself which there constituted Lenin's principle objection to Kant from his position 'on Kant's left'. Lenin continues, in the quotation above taken from *Materialism and Empirio-Criticism:*

When he [Kant] declares this thing-in-itself to be unknowable, transcendental, othersided, he is an idealist . . . The materialists blamed Kant for his idealism, rejected the idealist features of his system, demonstrated the knowability, the this-sidedness of the thing-in-itself . . .

The point that Lenin clearly enunciates is that, Kant notwithstanding, the thing-in-itself is knowable and becomes, with the growth of science, a thing-for-us. The point is one that Lenin insists upon repeatedly in *Materialism and Empirio-Criticism:* '. . . we shall find millions of examples . . . that illustrate the transformation of "things-in-themselves" into "things-for-us . . ."' (pp. 127-128). Lenin's praise of the point, in *The Notebooks,* that things-in-themselves become things-for-us, is not a rejection of some earlier, materialist understanding of things-in-themselves, but a continuation of it. As for Valentinov's insinuation that Lenin is on the road to adopting the slogan *'Esse est percipi',* it betrays a total confusion between ontology and epistemology. Both Hegel, and Marxists (Engels, Lenin, etc.), can accept the *knowability* of Kant's thing-in-itself, and both can criticise Kant on this score. It is true that for Hegel matter is knowable because it is a thought-product, and for Marxists matter is knowable because thought can correspond to it, but this difference, which involves ontological questions, does not detract from their agreement on the question of the knowability of the thing-in-itself.

As far as I can see, then, there are no important or major discrepancies or inconsistencies between Lenin's earlier and later views on materialism and reflection theory. There may be changes of emphasis, shifts in focus, but none of this is strong enough to bifurcate Lenin into a philosophically 'early' and 'late' Lenin. It is for this reason that, in what follows in this chapter, I intend to limit myself to a discussion of Lenin's views on these topics only as he develops them in his *Materialism and Empirio-Criticism*.

Materialism and Empirio-Criticism has never received, outside the Soviet Union, what one might call 'a good press'. It has been, literally, attacked from left, right, and centre, and its support has often come, embarrassingly, only from the orthodoxy imposed by anonymous Soviet censors. From the left of Lenin, Anton Pannekoek accused Lenin of 'concordance with middle-class materialism and his ensuing discordance with Historical Materialism',[7] which is, for Pannekoek, as it should be for someone who, in the pre-capitalist conditions of Russia, could only make a bourgeois revolution and introduce a régime of state capitalism. In respect of Lenin's philosophical views, Pannekoek claims that 'we cannot speak of a victory of Marxism, when there is only question of a so-called refutation of middle-class idealism through the ideas of middle-class materialism . . . Hereafter the révolution, under the new system of state capitalism . . . was, under the name "Leninism", proclaimed the official State-philosophy . . .'[8] Paul Mattick, in appraisal of Pannekoek's work, has this to contribute to a discussion of Lenin's philosophical talents: 'Lenin's philosophical ideas appeared in his work *Materialism and Empirio-Criticism* . . . Pannekoek not only revealed Lenin's biased and distorted exposition of the ideas of Mach and Avenarius, but also his inability to criticise their work from a Marxian point of view . . .'[9] Valentinov, to whose views on Lenin I have already made reference, describes *Materialism and Empirio-Criticism* with such complimentary phrases as 'crude abuse', 'the voice of a fanatical, die-hard conservative', and concludes his assessment of that book by saying that '. . . from this book a straight, well-bulldozed road leads to the official philosophy backed by the GPU-NKVD-MGB.'[10] Lyubov Akselrod, called 'Ortodox', a comrade of Lenin within the Social Democratic Party, had this to say about *Materialism and Empirio-Criticism* in an early and relatively favourable review of it: 'Unfortunately, Ilyin's book does not possess these qualities [of serious, thoughtful, and subtle argumentation]. The author's argument exhibits neither flexibility of philosophic thought, exactness of philosophic definition, nor profound understanding of philosophic problems . . .',[11] and 'Ilyin's polemics . . . have also been marked by an extreme coarseness . . . But when extreme, impermissible coarseness appears in voluminous work concerned with philosophical problems, then such coarseness is absolutely intolerable . . . It is beyond human comprehension how anyone could write such things, or, having written them, could have failed to cross them out; or, having failed to cross them out, could fail to seize the proof-sheets impatiently in order to delete all such absurd and coarse comparisons!'[12] Nor has Lenin's book found greater favour among professional philosophers than among those on the non-Stalinist left. In the main, orthodox philosophy has neglected Lenin's work. When it has come to consider his views, it has been politely dismissive:

What Lenin requires of philosophy is that it should deny neither established facts of science nor plain facts of common sense; but there are more ways of avoiding denial of these than he was aware of . . . he can hardly claim the merit of not going beyond 'the naive realism of any healthy person'. . .[13]

It is no exaggeration, then, to speak of a wide range of opinion highly unfavourable to *Materialism and Empirio-Criticism*. In more recent discussion it has been left to Louis Althusser to offer a spirited defence of that much maligned book.[14] What this chapter will attempt is to arrive at a balanced assessment of the strengths and weaknesses of Lenin's philosophy, and especially of his theory of reflection. Does Lenin's reflection theory pass any of the tests of adequacy that we have discussed in the previous two chapters? Are there any genuine insights in *Materialism and Empirio-Criticism* which we can credit to Lenin's favour? Or is the book as irredeemably awful as some of the critics have suggested?

Before we proceed to the substance of our discussion of Lenin's *Materialism and Empirio-Criticism*, it is important to clarify a change in terminology which our concern with Lenin necessitates. Lenin refers to phenomenalists who 'reduce' the world to complexes of sensations or experiences, as 'subjective idealists'. In Chapters I and II, we wished to underscore the contrast between Kant and Hegel on the one hand and the classical empiricist tradition on the other. We therefore distinguished between thought-independence and mind-independence, and we reserved the term 'idealist' for what some call 'absolute idealists', for those who denied the essential independence of the world from thought, and ultimately from Thought. Accordingly, we then referred to the classical empiricist tradition as a species of non-materialist realism, since the world, objects, however phenomenal or mentalistic they may be, are, for them, essentially independent of thought or idea. When, in Chapter III, we came to discuss Marx, we collapsed the distinction between thought and mind, treating them both as abstractions from the primary concept of man. We then spoke of idealism in a 'wider' sense, as a doctrine which tied the world to the *human,* whether that be thought, praxis, society, mind, sensations, or whatever. In this wider sense, the phenomenalist doctrine of the 'reduction' of the world to sense experience *is* idealist, since it ties the world, through such a reductionist analysis, to sensation or experience. The world is *nothing but* complexes of actual or possible sense experience, and is, in this sense, essentially dependent on experience. In this terminology, the classical empiricist tradition is a variety of idealism, in so far as it is reductionist, for it too ties the world to something recognisably human. Lenin calls this tradition 'subjective idealism'. In this Chapter, we intend to follow Lenin's terminology and speak of absolute and subjective idealism, referring by the latter term to those doctrines which we earlier called 'non-materialist realism'. For Lenin, then, 'idealism' refers both to the doctrines of Hegel, Kant, and Fichte, and the doctrines of Berkeley, Hume, Mach, and Avenarius, since both sorts of doctrines essentially tie the world, in one way or another, to human phenomena of some sort.

I want to begin my assessment with what I consider the greatest strength of Lenin's book. This is not, I believe, a strength widely appreciated as such. On the contrary, this strength has usually been considered a part of the book's main weakness. That strength is Lenin's clear perception of the intimate connection between materialism and a reflection theory of knowledge. The recognition of that connection already informed the philosophical outlook of Engels, and no doubt, far from it being original with Lenin, Lenin derives his own understanding of this nexus from Engels. Engels often speaks in one and the same breath of materialism *and* reflection theory; indeed, it is more accurate to say that Engels moves insensibly between an ontological and an epistemological theory, for the possibility of introducing any serious distinction between them is not one which would have occurred to him. For Engels, materialism 'automatically' includes a correspondence theory of knowledge. In *Ludwig Feuerbach,* Engels begins by distinguishing between materialism and idealism *ontologically,* by their different answers to the question of the primacy of nature over mind or spirit.[15] Engels then proceeds to speak of 'yet another side' to this same division between materialism and idealism, namely the epistemological question of 'in what relation do our thoughts about the world surrounding us stand to this world itself? Is our thinking capable of the cognition of the real world? Are we able in our ideas and notions of the real world to produce a correct reflection of reality?'[16] So the association, or even identification, of materialism with reflection theory is hardly something original with Lenin. It derives from Engels, and before him, from Feuerbach who, it may be recalled, termed his philosophy indifferently 'materialism' and 'sensationalism', the first of which denotes an ontological thesis and the latter an epistemological one.

Although correct and important, neither is the epistemological criticism of Kant's critical philosophy from a materialist perspective original with Lenin, for both Feuerbach and Engels had already expressed their dissatisfaction with the unknowability of the Kantian thing-in-itself. What one does find in Lenin's *Materialism and Empirio-Criticism* which does not derive, as far as I know, from Engels, or at least not in so clear and developed form, is the perception that it is Kant's interpretation claim, (IC), as I have labelled it, which is responsible for the unknowability of that which is essentially independent of thought, and which is therefore incompatible, 'epistemologically inconsistent', with any credible form of materialism. Lenin repeats many times that the choice is between materialism and the *a priori,* and that the choice of materialism 'epistemologically' necessitates the rejection of the Kantian, and the acceptance of a reflection, theory of knowledge. Lenin further correctly apprehends how variations on this Kantian interpretation theory of knowledge, all of which present themselves to him as 'enemies' of materialism, had surfaced in the philosophical interim between Marx and 1908, and especially in much of the work of Bogdanov and the other Russian admirers of Mach. Indeed, I think that the essential structure of the whole of my argument of Chapter I is to be found in *Materialism and Empirio-Criticism,* and that chapter is meant, in fact, to be only a recapitulation and elaboration of Lenin's argument.

It is especially in Chapter 3, Sections 3-5, and Chapter 4, Section 1, that Lenin develops this criticism of Kant. Causality, Space, and Time, either as categories of the understanding or forms of intuition, are some of that which Kant taught we synthesised 'into' our experience, and it is these three concepts which are singled out by Lenin in order to contrast the interpretive and reflective role that different philosophies have ascribed to them. Lenin throughout connects the choice between the reflective and interpretive (*a priori*) roles with the choice between materialism and idealism respectively: 'The question of causality is particularly important in determining the philosophical line of the recent "isms". Let us begin with an exposition of the materialist theory of knowledge on this point' (p. 198).

Lenin argues not only for the reality of an independently existing world but, like Feuerbach before him, whose views on natural kinds, causality, and necessity we had opportunity to mention in the concluding pages of Chapter II, Lenin is a realist about causality and necessity as well. Causal connections are real connections between things, and do not arise through Humean custom and habit, or through Kantian *a priori* rules for synthesising experience. Lenin argues for 'the recognition of objective law in nature' (p. 201). Lenin's understanding of causality is generally a realist understanding of causality: causal connections are necessary connections between things. Necessity is necessity *de re*. 'The recognition of necessity in nature and the derivation from it of necessity in thought is materialism' (p. 216). Lenin appreciates that for Feuerbach realism concerning the external world and realism about causal necessity go hand-in-hand, and both Feuerbach and Lenin are, I think, right about this:[17] 'Thus Feuerbach recognises objective law in nature and objective causality, which are reflected only with approximate fidelity by human ideas of order, law, and so forth. With Feuerbach the recognition of objective law in nature is *inseparably connected with the recognition of the objective reality of the external world, of objects.* [my emphasis-DHR] . . . Feuerbach's views are consistently materialist . . .' (p. 200).

Thus, causality and necessity are in nature, essentially independent of any cognising (or psychologically customary) activity of the human mind. They are, in short, *real.* They do not, for Lenin, arise out of the interpretive activity of thought. Since they are real, our causal beliefs can come to reflect or correspond to the way causal reality is. As realists or materialists, Lenin claims that we must hold a reflection theory and in particular a reflection theory about our causal beliefs:

All other views, or rather, any other philosophical line on the question of causality, the denial of objective law, causality, and necessity in nature, are justly regarded by Feuerbach as belonging to the fideist trend. For it is, indeed, clear that the subjectivist line on the question of causality, the deduction of the order and necessity of nature not from the external objective world but from consciousness, reason, logic, and so forth, not only cuts human reason off from nature . . . but makes nature *a part* of reason instead of regarding reason as part of nature. (pp. 220-201).

Lenin sees that the 'subjectivist line'—Kant's interpretation claim—leads to idealism, and proceeds therefore to identify this subjectivist or Kantian epistemology with idealism. On the other hand, Lenin connects the 'recognition of objective law in nature', which is materialism or realism, with 'the recognition that this law is reflective . . . in the minds of man', a reflection or correspondence theory. Thus, Lenin harnesses the two different ontological positions with the two different epistemological ones—interpretation and the *a priori* with idealism, reflection or correspondence with materialism—in a manner parallel to our argument in Chapter I; and at the end of the section from which we have been quoting, Lenin even adds an explicitly epistemological element to his definition of materialism and idealism: 'The recognition of necessity in nature and the derivation from it of necessity in thought is materialism. The derivation of necessity, causality, law, etc., from thought is idealism' (pp. 216-217).

The double wedding in Lenin's mind between materialism and reflection theory, on the one hand, and between idealism and a Kantian interpretation claim, on the other, is complete. Similar remarks, and similar assertions about such a double wedding, are made by Lenin when he comes to discuss the topics of space and time: 'Recognising the existence of objective reality, i.e., matter in motion, independently of our mind, materialism must also inevitably recognise the objective reality of space and time, in contrast above all to Kantianism, which in this question sides with idealism and regards time and space not as objective realities but as forms of human understanding' (p. 229). '. . . our developing notion of time and space *reflect* an objectively real time and space; that here, too, as in general, they are approaching objective truth' (p. 231).

What argument does Lenin use, or what insight motivates Lenin, to make this identification of idealism (the essential dependence of nature on thought) with a Kantian interpretation claim? In a shorter and more direct form, Lenin's remarks approximate the argument I attempted to offer in Chapter I: 'The subjectivist [Kantian] line . . . makes nature *a part* of reason . . .' (p. 201). On an interpretation claim, Lenin asserts, nature becomes a part of reason (or thought). I take 'a part' here to be equivalent to 'essentially related to'. On the Kantian theory of knowledge, Lenin is asserting, nature becomes essentially dependent on mind, and is in this sense a part of mind (or 'consciousness, reason, logic, and so forth').

It is clear from all of this that Lenin fully appreciated in Kant the tension between a residual materialism, (IpC), and an idealist theory of knowledge, (IC), which Kant attempted to inter-marry at the very heart of his critical philosophy. 'The principle feature of Kant's philosophy is the reconciliation of materialism with idealism, a compromise between the two, the combination within one system of heterogeneous and contrary philosophical trends' (p. 260). When Kant assumes, Lenin asserts, that there is something outside us, a thing-in-itself, Kant is a materialist. On the other hand, 'Recognising the apriority of space, time, causality, etc., Kant is directing his philosophy toward idealism' (p. 261, for this and the following two quotes). Lenin fully appreciates that, for Kant, ontology and epistemology sit in unhappy and contentious alliance. Thus it is, explains Lenin, that 'both consistent materialists and consistent idealists have mercilessly criticised Kant for this inconsistency'. We have also traced, in Chapters II and III, the fate of Kant's 'problem' at the hands of idealists and realists (or materialists). Lenin sees, correctly, that what materialists had to reject was the unknowability of reality (the thing-in-itself, as he calls it) and hence reject too the apriority that an interpretive role accorded to thought: 'The materialists blamed Kant for his idealism, rejected the idealist features of his system, demonstrated the knowability, the this-sidedness of the thing-in-itself . . . the need of deducing causality, etc., not from *a priori* laws of thought, but from objective reality'. In short, what materialists needed was a theory of reflection or correspondence, to underpin their claims to *knowledge* of a world essentially unrelated to mind, or thought.

Lenin, as is well known, was not (just) engaged in writing a theoretical tract about the philosophical errors of past philosophers. He was, rather, engaged in an intense struggle against the influence of Machism on the Russian party, especially through the philosophical works of Bogdanov, as well as others. Lenin calls Bogdanov and 'other Machists' 'empirio-criticists' (p. 16), and it is this school which provides the contrast to materialism in the title Lenin gave to his book. It is well outside the possible scope of this chapter, let alone its range of competence, to analyse carefully the writings of Mach (and Avenarius) to determine how far Lenin understood or misunderstood the significance of their work. Lenin also claims, about Bogdanov for example, that 'Bogdanov's . . . departures from "pure" Machism are of absolutely secondary importance . . .'[18] Whether this is so, or whether, conversely, Bogdanov has an important, original contribution to make to the history of positivism, is again an assessment well outside the scope of this chapter. What I do wish to point out, albeit briefly and only in passing, is how Bogdanov's philosophy, *assuming* that Lenin correctly characterises it by quoting fairly from Bogdanov, does in fact appear to contain within itself just those elements of an idealist theory of knowledge which Lenin had already criticised in the case of Kant.

Lenin quotes Bogdanov as saying that: 'The criterion of objective truth in Beltov's [Plekhanov] sense, does not exist; truth is an ideological form, an organising form of human experience . . .' (pp. 156-158, for this and the four following quotes). Although it is unfair to attempt to read the whole of a man's philosophy into a single, cryptic remark, Lenin is probably correct in what he supposes such a remark implies, namely, the 'humanisation' of truth and, with it, of known reality.

... if truth is *only* an ideological form, then there can be no truth independent of the subject, of humanity, for neither Bogdanov nor we know any other ideology but human ideology ... if truth is a form of human experience, then there can be no truth independent of humanity; there can be no objective truth.

For Bogdanov, there could be no truth 'independent' of humanity, no 'objectivity' independent of humanity, and hence no known reality not essentially dependent on humanity either ('no objective truth'), to put the matter in terms of our earlier discussion. Indeed, Kolakowski's views, which we discussed in Chapter III, seem strongly reminiscent of Bogdanov's remarks. Like Kolakowski's, Bogdanov's theory of truth is a rejection of the classical correspondence conception ('reflection') in favour of some socialised version of a Kantianesque conception. Bogdanov elaborates his theory of truth in the following way:

The basis of objectivity must lie in the sphere of collective experience. We term those data of experience objective which have the same vital meaning for us and for other people, those data upon which not only we construct our activities without contradiction, but upon which, we are convinced, other people must also base themselves in order to avoid contradiction. The objective character of the physical world consists in the fact that it exists not for me personally, but for everybody, and has a definite meaning for everybody, the same, I am convinced, as for me. The objectivity of the physical series is universal significance.

Another passage that Lenin selects from Bogdanov's *Empirio-Monism* is this:

The objectivity of the physical bodies we encounter in our experience is in the last analysis established by the mutual verification and co-ordination of the utterances of various people. In general, the physical world is socially-coordinated, socially-harmonised, in a word, socially-organised experience.

The world *is*, for Bogdanov, socially-organised experience. But it then follows that, if there were no social organising (compare: synthesis of the understanding), there could be no physical world. For Bogdanov, the world has become essentially tied to thought, to the human. Without wishing, then, to become embroiled in controversy about the correct, overall interpretation of Bogdanov's work, I think we can all the same quite safely affirm that Lenin had correctly identified certain Kantian themes in Bogdanov's theory of knowledge, themes which have the same incompatibility with materialism in Bogdanov's hands as they had in Kant's. The Kantian concept of the necessary, *a priori* forms of experience has been, in these quotations, both socialised and relativised. Bogdanov stresses that objectivity is to be found in 'collective experience', 'universal significance'. Experience has the 'same vital meaning for us and for other people'. The socialisation of the *a priori* forms is evident enough. Lenin is quick, and correct, to point out the relativisation latent in all this: 'If truth is only an organising form of human experience, then the teachings, say, of Catholicism are also true. For there is not the slightest doubt that Catholicism is an "organising form of human experience".' Different societies (groups, classes, or whatever) may well impose differing collective meanings on their experience. Objectivity and truth arise, for Bogdanov, only from *within* the meaning that a collective, a group, imposes on experience. Objectivity and truth, indeed, 'the physical world', have become something *internal* to such a collective interpretation, a collectivised act of synthesis, on which they essentially depend. Kant's interpretation claim has become collectivised and relativised, and there could be, as Lenin saw, as many conflicting 'objective truths' and 'worlds' as there are groups which can collectively interpret their experience.[19] Lenin is right to think that Bogdanov's views are idealist. In general, Lenin captures and criticises the Kantian epistemological themes within these passages he quotes, from Bogdanov and others, and sees that they too, because of their Kantian epistemology, are inimical to materialism. Lenin, throughout *Materialism and Empirio-Criticism,* watches for the appearance of idealism, in the precise sense in which we have been using that term: '. . . the fundamental philosophical line of subjective idealism . . . [is that] the non-*self* is "postulated" (is created, produced) by the *self;* the thing is indissolubly connected with the consciousness' (p. 80); he seizes upon elements in the epistemologies of post-Kantian philosophers like Mach or Bogdanov which, like Kant's, lead one to some variety of idealism. 'The "naive realism" of any healthy person who has not been an inmate of a lunatic asylum or a pupil of the idealist philosophers consists in the view that things, the environment, the world, exist independently of our sensation, of our consciousness, of our self and of man in general' (p. 80). Lenin tries to insure, by his adoption of a reflection theory of knowledge, that any suitably Marxist theory of knowledge retains its fidelity to that realism,[20] and he understands that no Kantian-inspired theory of knowledge can do so.

I have spent some pages elaborating what I take to be the principle virtue of *Materialism and Empirio-Criticism.* Whatever defects we may discover in that book, they do not outweigh this important virtue, which has been systematically overlooked in much of the unfavourable discussion of the book since its publication. But there are, to be sure, defects there as well, and I wish now to turn to what I regard as its main weakness, the conflation by Lenin of a correspondence theory of *knowledge* and a correspondence theory of *perception,* a conflation which was already adumbrated in Engels' writings. What, after all, is a reflection theory a theory of? In the *Introduction* we made it clear that our discussion was to be about the conflict between a reflection and interpretation theory of knowledge, or of concepts, and in Chapters I-V, we have dealt with that. Our discussion has centered around the truth of *beliefs* (knowledge) and the application of *concepts.* On a correspondence or reflection theory, (we also agreed to use these terms interchangeably), a belief is true if it corresponds to reality; a concept is instantiated or applicable if it corresponds to at least one thing. The contrast was between this and an interpretation claim, Kant's claim that some concepts and principles were *a priori,* and hence that such principles were true because the world accessible to our knowledge was structured by those principles. Thus, the discussion was in terms of 'beliefs', 'knowledge', 'concepts', 'principles', and 'truth', and there was little mention, until now, of 'perception', 'sensation', or other perceptual terms, and no mention at all of the strange-sounding idea that sensations or perceptions are somehow *copies* or *reflections* of their objects in a way analogous to the way in which a mirror image reflects or duplicates an object. Indeed, in so far as we mentioned perception at all, our remarks could be construed as being unsympathetic to any such claim. In Chapter V, for instance, we distinguished between theoretical and observational reflection. Against Colletti, we said that theories could have both a reflective and an interpretive role to play in knowledge. They might 'interpret' the observational base of the theory, so that all observation would be essentially theory-dependent. This might go some way to substantiate the claim often advanced against positivists that there could be no 'pure' experience, no observation which was not already informed by some theory. At the same time, theories might be reflective, in the sense that they might accurately (or approximately accurately) portray the real structures in nature or society through which the appearances, that which is open to observation, can be explained and accounted for. The appearance of value as an objective relation between things could be understood, for example, only when the theory we hold, in this case the labour theory of value, correctly reflects or portrays the non-appearing structures, the social relations of production, and the abstract labour of producers, which, in conditions of commodity production, are responsible for the appearance of value in the form of a relation between things.

These earlier remarks, and the distinction between theoretical and observational reflection, of which we have adopted only the former, already contain within themselves the distinction between a reflection theory of knowledge and of perception. To say that a theory reflects or portrays real structures is to make a claim about reflective beliefs or concepts. It is to make a claim about the correspondence between theories, beliefs, statements, on the one hand, and reality on the other. It is to imply nothing whatever about perceptual correspondence. Indeed, in so far as the theoretical entities referred to by such beliefs or statements are unobservable, there are no corresponding perceptions or sensations for them. Theories about subatomic particles, force fields, abstract labour, or social relations of production, are true when what they say is so. No theory of perception is implied, and in particular, no view that we have images of electrons, or impressions of abstract-labour or sensations of force fields, which reflect electrons, abstract-labour, or force fields, for there are no such direct sensations, images, or impressions of these things at all.

There is no doubt that Lenin does hold a reflection theory of perception, and has been criticised for so doing:[21] 'ideas and sensations are copies or images of those objects' (p. 21); 'sensations are images of objects, of the external world' (p. 161); '[The Machists err because they] do not regard sensations as a true copy of this objective reality . . .' (p. 164); 'Matter is a philosophical category denoting the objective reality which is given to man by his sensations, and which is copied, photographed, and reflected by our sensations . . .' (pp. 165-166). At one point Lenin explicitly builds this correspondence theory of perception into his definition of materialism: 'sensations are "symbols"—it would be more accurate to say images or reflections of things. The latter theory is philosophical materialism' (p. 40), and again, 'To regard our sensations as images of the external world, to recognise objective truth, to hold the materialist theory of knowledge—these are all one and the same thing' (p. 166). Lenin claims that the correspondence between perceptions and objects is the essential question of all epistemology: 'the fundamental question of the theory of knowledge' is, 'are our sensations *copies* of bodies and things, or are bodies complexes of our sensation?' (p. 234). It is clear that, in these quotations, Lenin is concentrating on questions of perception, and takes as his opponent the phenomenalist, who attempted to 'reduce' physical objects into sets of sensations.

Elsewhere, and especially when he comes to discuss Kant, it becomes clear that Lenin's interest has switched from the phenomenalist and the question of *perception* to the question of objective *knowledge*. The discussion of space, time, and causality, to which we have already alluded, does not necessarily involve a question of perception at all. Lenin is not really interested in a problem, if there be such, of whether our sensory perceptions of space, time, and causality correspond to space, time, and causality in themselves. Rather, Lenin is raising the question of whether our theoretical *beliefs* about space, time, and causality are *a priori,* or whether they correspond to an independently spatial, temporal, or causal reality. When Lenin argues that: 'The recognition of objective law in nature and the recognition that this law is reflected with approximate fidelity in the mind of man is materialism' (p. 200), he is worried about our *beliefs* about causality, independently of any problem about our perceptions of it. Lenin speaks of the status of 'the human *conception* of cause and effect [which] always somewhat simplifies the objective connection of the phenomena of nature . . .' [my emphasis—DHR] (p. 202), and of 'Human conceptions of space and time . . .' (p. 221); it is clear that his theory at this point is not a theory of perception at all, but a theory of concepts. Lenin explicitly claims that he is dealing with 'the question of the source and significance of all human knowledge' (p. 231), and tells us that we must realise 'that our developing *notions* [my emphasis—DHR] reflect an objectively real space and time' (p. 231). At another point he speaks of the external reality to which 'perceptions and conceptions of mankind' may necessarily agree (p. 245), and his insistence that 'the earth existed prior to man' is objectively true because it corresponds to the way things actually and independently of man were, underscores this concern about knowledge rather than perception, since for such theoretical truths as the pre-human existence of reality there *are* no relevant, corresponding perceptions. At several points Lenin speaks quite explicitly about *theories* reflecting, rather than perceptions doing so, as for instance when he says that 'it is nevertheless beyond question that mechanics was a copy of real motions of moderate velocity', and 'the recognition of theory as a copy, as an approximate copy of objective reality, is materialism' (p. 357), or 'old physics regarded its theories as "real knowledge of the material world", i. e., a reflection of objective reality' (pp. 344-345). Clearly, Lenin's focus of interest has changed substantially, for theories certainly cannot be said to *reflect* reality in any way similar to the way in which mirrors reflect, or in the way in which he presumably thought that perceptions did as well.

Perhaps one of the clearest single examples of this focus on belief or knowledge rather than on perception, is the case of alizarin, introduced by Engels in *Ludwig Feuerbach* and repeated by Lenin, but little appreciated by critics of either for its significance. Lenin quotes Engels' remarks on the subject (quoted on pp. 124-125):

If we are able to prove the correctness of our conception of a natural process by making it ourselves, bringing it into being out of its conditions and making it serve our own purposes into the bargain, then there is an end to the Kantian incomprehensible 'thing-in-itself'. The chemical substances produced in the bodies of plants and animals remained just such 'things-in-themselves' until organic chemistry began to produce them one after another, whereupon the 'thing-in-itself' became a 'thing-for-us', as, for instance, alizarin, the colouring matter of the madder, which we no longer trouble to grow in the madder roots in the field, but produce much more cheaply and simply from coal tar.

In changing from a 'thing-in-itself' to a 'thing-for-us', alizarin became *known*. It is immaterial whether or not it was perceived also, for we can know about many things which we cannot perceive. For Lenin, as for Engels, this example of alizarin is an illustration of their 'materialist' acceptance of a real world, the structure of which it is the aim of science to discover. Locke's real essences and Kant's things-in-themselves may not be known at a given period in the history of scientific inquiry, but they are knowable and become 'things-for-us' at the point at which they become known. Lenin enumerates some of the lessons which are to be drawn from the example of alizarin, and one of them is that alizarin exists 'independently of our consciousness . . . for it is beyond doubt that alizarin existed in the coal tar yesterday and it is equally beyond doubt that yesterday we knew nothing of the existence of this alizarin and received no sensations from it' (p. 127). Lenin's point is that theories refer to things, substances, whatever, whose existence is independent of the theory about it. More strongly, in the case of natural scientific theories, the things, substances, or whatever, are essentially independent of any human phenomenon, including sensation or perception. In the case of alizarin, Lenin, like Engels, is interested in the knowability of reality and the objectivity of that knowledge, not about the objectivity or otherwise of perceptions. Lenin was wrong, then, to say, as I have quoted him as saying, that 'to regard our sensations as images of the external world . . . to hold the materialist theory of knowledge, these are all one and the same thing'. Lenin can defend the objectivity of our knowledge about alizarin, without even introducing the question of a copy or image theory of perception. These are not 'all one and the same thing'.

Why does Lenin conflate these two very different sorts of theory, by lumping them under the same rubric, 'reflection theory'? In part Lenin is led to this conflation because of Engels' own failure to mark the distinction. Sometimes Engels, too, speaks of perceptions copying reality, but elsewhere, in *Anti-Dühring* for instance, his focus of interest is on knowledge rather than perception (quoted by Lenin on p. 41):

. . . But whence does thought obtain these principles? From itself? No . . . these forms can never be created and derived by thought itself, but only from the external world . . . it is not nature and the realm of humanity which conform to these principles, but the principles are only valid insofar as they are in conformity with nature and history.

However, there is another reason, I submit, which may explain why Lenin conflated these two very different kinds of 'reflection', the reflection of reality by beliefs (correspondence) and the reflection of reality by perception (images). Lenin, in *Materialism and Empirio-Criticism,* is arguing against at least two entirely different sorts of antagonists, and his failure to separate these antagonists may account in part for his failure to see the difference between the two different responses he should have offered to their philosophies. Lenin selects as objects of his criticism a range of classical philosophers, which included Berkeley, Hume, and Kant. Lenin does distinguish between the agnosticism of the latter two and the explicit 'subjective idealism' of the former, but he writes as if Hume's and Kant's philosophies are nearly identical, and both are mere half-way houses on the road to Berkeley's subjective idealism. What he overlooks is the very great difference between Kant and the empiricists on the question of the relationship between knowledge and perception. We have already seen, in Chapter I, how for classical empiricism all ideas (concepts, notions) are abstracted from impressions, and all empirical knowledge must be derived from perceptual experience. Empirical knowledge and perception are, for classical empiricism, ultimately one, and there can be no serious distinction between them. For Kant the matter is otherwise. *A priori* concepts are not derived from experience (although their range of legitimate application is limited to experience) and some of our knowledge is prior to all experience rather than arising from it. With Kant, there are concepts which are logically prior to experience or perception, but not so for the empiricist. Thus, in conflating a correcpondence theory of knowledge with a correspondence theory of perception, Lenin is essentially following the empiricists' own conflation of knowledge and perception. It is with Kant that one can begin to see a distinction between these two things, and it is certainly a distinction which any realist who is committed to the existence of unobservables must adopt. On a realist perspective, we can certainly have knowledge about that which we cannot perceive, and hence knowledge and perception *are* distinguishable. Lenin's conflation, then, is an empiricist conflation, and one which is inconsistent with his own materialist or realist perspective.

Lenin's error here can be seen in his mistaken acceptance of the philosophical terminology of a little-known, nineteenth century, French philosophical dictionary. In the passage in which Lenin refers to this dictionary, he begins by asserting that 'sensation reveals objective truth to man' (p. 167). Then, quoting directly from the dictionary, Lenin proceeds to speak of sensationalism: 'sensationalism . . . is a doctrine which deduces all our ideas "from the experience of the senses, reducing knowledge to sensations",' and he identifies materialism with an 'objective' variety of sensationalism. There is a very great difference, though, between claiming that all our knowledge is 'revealed' to us through experience, and claiming that all our knowledge can be reduced to experience; collapsing this distinction is what makes knowledge of anything other than experience an impossibility. It is ironic that Lenin, the opponent of positivism in philosophy, should himself have failed to detect one of the key assumptions in positivist philosophy which leads to the idealism he so detested. Our experience may lead us to or reveal to us knowledge of unobservables, but our knowledge of unobservables certainly cannot be reduced to those experiences on which it is (inductively) based. It is this strand in Lenin which then leads him to such remarks as that materialism 'teaches that nothing exists but perceptual being, that the world is matter in motion, that the physical world familar to all, is the sole objective reality' (p. 291). Such remarks are profoundly mistaken, and rest on this unwarranted conflation of knowledge and perception. This conflation, which does not represent Lenin at his best, has anti-realist implications, and make nonsense of Lenin's own realist understanding of the role of theory in science, as we shall soon see. If the 'physical world *familiar* to all is the sole objective reality', what possible use could we have for natural science, whose function it is to reveal to us the essential structure of a world which does not appear as it is?

Of course, even for a realist, knowledge about unobservables stands in some relation to perception, and is not *a priori* knowledge after the manner of Kant. Sometimes, to be sure, Lenin seems only to be asserting that, for a materialist, all knowledge must be grounded in experiences, as for example when he approvingly quotes Feuerbach's remark that 'sensation is the evangel, the gospel of an objective saviour' (pp. 166-167), which Lenin takes to mean that 'sensation reveals objective truth to man' (p. 167). But Lenin confuses this point, that all knowledge is based on experience, is *a posteriori,* with the claim that all knowledge can be 'deduced' from experience and, hence, can only be about what is perceived: 'fideism positively asserts that something does exist outside the realm of perception. The materialists . . . deny this' (p. 147). This latter claim, as I have argued, is mistaken. Its claim is that we can only know what we perceive. The point is that perception and knowledge cannot, for a realist, be directly identified in the way in which they were by the classical empiricist tradition. We need not, as Kant did, make some knowledge *a priori* in order to avoid collapsing the distinction between knowledge and perception. Knowledge can be inductively based on experience without being reducible to it. As realists, we can avoid the Scylla of the *a priori* and the Charbydis of direct perception by making some knowledge, knowledge which is about something 'outside the realm of perception', inductively grounded knowledge. Thus, for example, we can maintain the integrity of knowledge of unobservables, knowledge which is neither *a priori* nor directly observational knowledge. Knowledge of the world prior to human consciousness is such knowledge, as is a great deal of our other theoretical knowledge, and it is this sort of conception at which Lenin is aiming, but at which his empiricist confusion does not permit him to arrive. It is a confusion which, as realists, we certainly wish to reject. There is a sense in which concepts or beliefs can reflect reality, and another sense in which perceptions do. They might be the same sense only if we were to identify conceptions with sensations, as the empiricist tradition certainly did. We reject this identification, and criticise Lenin insofar as he was not alive to it. Lenin's remark, which we quoted earlier, concerning the 'perceptions and conceptions of mankind', itself bears testimony to the apparent ease with which Lenin moved between these two very different categories.

Is there anything to be said for a reflection theory of perception in its own right? I cannot even attempt a comprehensive answer to this question, but a few relevant remarks here may be in order. First, it is true that it would be consistent *both* to distinguish a correspondence theory of knowledge and a correspondence theory of perception, *and* to adopt both theories. As long as we admit, as realists, that we can have knowledge of things of which we had no perceptions, we might argue that, with regard to all the perceptions we do manage to have, these perceptions reflect or copy an independently existing reality. At the observational level at least, we might try saying that our perceptions are rather like photographs of objects.

However, there are many things wrong with a picture theory of perception and, in order to see at least some of them, it will be interesting to resurrect a debate which was current at the time of *Materialism and Empirio-Criticism* between Lenin and Plekhanov. Hitherto, we have tended to use 'reflection' and 'correspondence' interchangeably, taking 'reflection' in the sense of 'correspondence', without its pictorial associations. Some philosophers have been tempted into the absurdity that language, or the structure of language at least, in some pictorial-like way reflected the structure of reality.[22] There is no evidence whatever that Lenin had anything like this in mind, insofar as he is espousing a reflection theory of knowledge. 'Reflection' here is to be taken non-pictorially, in a sense which makes its use equivalent to 'correspondence'. But we also saw how, when Lenin espouses a reflection theory of perception, he does use 'reflect' in a pictorial sense, and uses such metaphors as 'picture' and 'mirror image'. 'Reflection' shifts its sense, from a non-pictorial to a pictorial one, when Lenin applies it to perceptions. In this usage, it is not *just* equivalent to 'corresponds', but has other associations and commitments as well.

In *Materialism and Empirio-Criticism,* Lenin attacks Helmholtz's 'theory of symbols (or hieroglyphs)' (pp. 310-318), a theory supported by Plekhanov. According to Lenin, the theory of hieroglyphs is 'the theory that man's sensations and ideas are not copies of real things and processes of nature, not their images, but conventional signs, symbols, hieroglyphs, and so on' (p. 310). Lenin objects to the theory that sensations give us *information* about things rather than *copy them,* on the grounds that the former theory leads to scepticism in a way in which the copy theory does not (p. 313):

If sensations are not images of things, but only signs or symbols, which have 'no resemblance' to them, then Helmholtz's initial materialist premise is undermined; the existence of external objects becomes subject to doubt; for signs or symbols may quite possibly indicate imaginary objects, and everybody is familiar with instances of *such* signs or symbols.

Of course, Lenin is quite wrong to suggest that a picture theory of perception has any advantage over a sign theory of perception on this score. If scepticism really were a worry, it would be equally a worry to both of them. It may well be that 'signs or symbols may quite possibly indicate imaginary objects', but so may pictures or images. Pictures of Snow White and images of Father Christmas may fail to 'indicate' anything. Lenin is simply wrong when he claims that '. . . an image is one thing, a symbol, a *conventional sign,* another. The image inevitably and of necessity implies the objective reality of that which it "images" ' (p. 314). Of course, one can use 'This is an image of x' in such a way that it does 'inevitably and of necessity' imply that there is an x, but one has as much, or as little, reason to treat 'This is a sign or symbol of x' in precisely the same way. To whatever extent failure of existence of the object affects 'This is a sign of such-and-such', it also effects 'This is a picture of such-and-such'. Precisely this point is made in the review of *Materialism and Empirio-Criticism* by Lyubov Akselrod, to which we have already referred. By this form of argument against the theory of symbols, Akselrod claims, Lenin

. . . all unawares, borrows arguments against the theory of symbols from Berkeley's philosophy. 'It is quite possible', our author declares, 'for signs and symbols to refer to imaginary objects'. Of course it is possible. But surely hallucinations, dreams, illusions, and delusions are not forms or copies of objects.[23]

Akselrod correctly points out that if Berkeley's arguments work, they work equally against both versions of a correspondence theory of perception, the sign version and the picture version.

Plekhanov explains his own sign or symbol theory in the following way:

Our sensations are in their way hieroglyphs which inform us of what is taking place in reality. The hieroglyphs do not resemble the events conveyed by them. But they can *with complete fidelity* convey both the events themselves, and—what is the main thing—the relations existing between them.[24]

Now, I think that the great advantage that Plekhanov's version of non-pictorial correspondence of perceptions to reality has over Lenin's pictorial version is that it is far more consistent with the naturalist perspective in philosophy than we espoused in Chapter IV. What, after all, are sensations, from a 'naturalist' point of view? They are complex neural events which take place in the brain and the central nervous system, by whose occurrence we can come to acquire information about the world around us. In complicated ways which we barely as yet understand, these neural happenings 'codify' information about the external world, and make such information available to us. In Plekhanov's words, these sensations, conceived as neurophysiological events, '*with complete fidelity* convey both the [external] events themselves and . . . the relations existing between them'. Sensations are neurophysiological occurrences by which we acquire information, and neurophysiological occurrences 'do not resemble the events', information about which they are able to convey to us. We can say that sensations, so conceived, *correspond* to the external world, in the sense that such sensations codify and permit us to acquire *information* which corresponds to reality. In this sense, a correspondence theory of perception becomes parasitic on a correspondence theory of knowledge. A sensation corresponds to reality only if the beliefs we acquire by those sensations correspond to reality. This sense of 'correspondence' for perceptions is wholly non-pictorial, and it is generally consistent with a naturalist approach to the theory of knowledge. It appears to have been Plekhanov's and Akselrod's sense.

The great disadvantage of Lenin's pictorial version of the correspondence of perceptions—perceptions as images or as literal reflections—is that it is not in keeping with the naturalist approach in philosophy. Akselrod criticised Lenin's pictorial version of reflection on precisely these grounds: 'Rejecting the theory of symbols . . . Plekhanov's critic takes his stand on a dualistic ground, preaching an inverted Platonism rather than materialism, since the latter rests on a single principle.'[25] If sensations are images or pictures, if they must actually *resemble* that to which they correspond, then one will be forced to adopt an ontological dualism, for the following sort of reason. There are in the world both tables and sensations of tables, chairs and sensations of chairs, clocks and perceptions of clocks, etc. Now, according to Lenin's pictorial version of correspondence, the sensations must resemble that of which they are pictures. However, no matter how hard one looks, using all of the techniques of science, one will never discover in the brain or nervous system anything that looks like or resembles a table, chair, or clock although one will find, of course, neurological occurrences. So, if there must be such things, and if they are inaccessible to the probings of science, the solution is bound to be the location of these little pictures in another ontological realm. They become mental things as opposed to physical things, and one is thereby committed to a full-blown dualism of an ontological, rather than just an epistemological, type. Ontological dualism and the pictorial version of correspondence are, then, closely connected. We have already distinguished, in Chapter III, the epistemological dualism inherent in any correspondence theory, itself necessary for any credible form of materialism, from the ontological dualism which we saw that Marx rejects.

The problem with Lenin's pictorial correspondence of perceptions with reality is that it commits us to the latter form of dualism as well as to the former. There is no doubt that Lenin did not *intend* to commit himself to any form of ontological dualism: 'Of course, even the antithesis of matter and mind has absolute significance only within the bounds of a very limited field—in this case exclusively within the bounds of the fundamental epistemological problem of what is to be regarded as primary and what as secondary. Beyond these bounds the relative character of this antithesis is indubitable' (p. 190). The problem, however, is to reconcile Lenin's intentions to keep the distinction merely 'epistemological' with the pictorial nature of the correspondence of perceptions to reality which he espoused.

Akselrod was clearly aware of this advantage of Plekhanov's non-pictorial correspondence over Lenin's pictorial version: 'The theory of symbols, *asserting the existence of both subject and object, unites both factors, regarding the subject as a special kind of object, and its sensations as a product of the interaction between two objects, of which one is at the same time also a subject.* Contemporary science accepts just this *objective* and *monistic* point of view'.[26] Epistemologically, we assert the existence of objects and subjects, while at the same time believing that they are, ontologically, the same sort of thing. Once we view sensations as natural phenomena, on a par with other natural phenomena, we can then explain perceiving in a scientific manner: 'the theory of symbols is thus related to the materialistic explanation of nature in the closest and most indissoluble way'.[27] On a pictorial view of sensations, such a naturalistic approach becomes unavailable: 'Materialism adopts the point of view that sensations, evoked by the action of different forms of moving matter, are not like the objective processes which generate them'. Akselrod's example of sensations of 'sound, colour, smell, heat, cold, etc.' which do not resemble that in objects which produce these sensations in us is to the point. Not only do sensations not *resemble* that of which they are sensations, but sometimes the information about the objects which they convey cannot be deciphered in the absence of a scientific theory. Not only do sensations of heat not *resemble* anything in hot objects, but what they tell us about those objects can only be fully deciphered with the aid of a theory of thermodynamics. Akselrod reminds us of all this by distinguishing materialism from naive realism. The decoding of the information contained in a man's sensory input sometimes happens 'naturally' or 'naively', but at other times a man needs an explicit background theory with which to break that code and decipher the information conveyed to him by his sensory experience. I think that we would probably wish to restrict the idea of perceptions *corresponding* to reality to those cases in which the decoding happens 'naively', without the aid of conscious, explicit theory.[28] Thus, if we perceive a man walking towards us, we might say that our sensations of this event do correspond to reality. Whatever decoding of the sensory input is necessary in this case occurs at an implicit, unconscious level. On the other hand, when we have sensations of heat, we might not want to say that our sensations of heat *correspond* to the high, mean kinetic energy of the object before us, since such decoding that occurs can occur only via a conscious, explicit theory of thermodynamics. The distinction, then, between perceptions which correspond and perceptions which do not would be relative to the explicit or implicit state of the background theory involved. But whether the decoding of our sensory input proceeds at an explicit or implicit, naive or informed, level, the idea of the sensory input, a neurophysiological event, *resembling* pictorially the things or event in the external world simply seems absurd.

The upshot of this controversy is, I believe, that in this debate Lenin was wrong and Plekhanov and Akselrod were right. The theory of hieroglyphs or symbols which the two latter advanced was more in keeping with a properly Marxist, naturalist approach in the theory of knowledge than was the pictorial theory. It is more in keeping with the overall naturalist perspective that Lenin himself claimed to accept: nature is 'the *immediately* given, . . . the starting-point of epistemology' (p. 301). We continue to use the term 'reflection' for the relation both between beliefs and reality and between perceptions and reality, but we wish to disassociate both of these uses from any pictorial implications. We can agree that 'true' or 'accurate' perceptions, whose decoding does not involve explicit theory, correspond to reality, but we take this 'naturalistically', after the manner of Plekhanov and Akselrod. We take this only to mean that we acquire true beliefs (which correspond to reality) by means of these sensations, sensations which we regard as complicated neurophysiological occurrences in our brains and nervous systems. There is no place in any of this for any pictorial metaphors to gain a toehold, metaphors which force us to a position of ontological dualism which we would prefer to avoid. Finally, as naturalists we can accept that the same sceptical difficulties can be brought against Lenin's pictorial theory as he argued could be brought against Plekhanov's non-pictorial theory. However, in keeping with the naturalist perspective we espoused in Chapter IV, we argued there that the sceptic should be ignored rather than answered. In so far as Lenin believed that his theory was preferable to Plekhanov's on the grounds that his, unlike Plekhanov's, was not susceptible to sceptical doubts, Lenin was wrong in thinking that he—or anyone—could answer a question that ought, in fact, to be ignored. In any case, we have already seen that Lenin's theory is no better at answering those sceptical doubts than was Plekhanov's, and, from our naturalist perspective on scepticism, such a result is hardly surprising.

In the concluding pages of this Chapter, I wish to return to some of the other strengths or virtues of *Materialism and Empirio-Criticism,* both in order to bring them out for their own sake and as a way of answering some of the standard criticisms of the book. I have already discussed at length Lenin's realism, but I have not yet mentioned explicitly his scientific realism. It will be recalled that I made this distinction in Chapter IV in the following way. According to realism (or materialism), the natural world exists essentially independently of all that is human. We could put realism thus: according to realism, beliefs or thoughts are about a world which is essentially independent of these beliefs or thoughts. Realism in the philosophy of science, or scientific realism as I called it, is a more specific doctrine, to the effect that scientific *theories* can refer to unobservables, are sometimes about such unobservables, which, as 'the intransitive objectives of science', are essentially independent of man's theoretical attempts to cognise them. Unobservables are that at which (some) theories 'aim', and are not creations of those theories, in the way in which Kuhn or Feyerabend might, for example, have us believe. I argued in Chapter IV that the commitment to realism or materialism itself already contained within it the commitment to unobservables, on the grounds that the contingent unobservability of unobservably small things for example was no different *in kind* from the contingent unobservability of any macroscopic material object in certain circumstances, and the contingent unobservability of things which *our* perceptual apparatus does not allow us to see (force fields, for instance), was no different in kind from the contingent perceptual unobservability of things to a blind man. As materialists or realists, we do not believe that things would cease to exist if we were to go blind, or if they were removed from our field of vision, and so *pari passu* we have no reason to doubt the existence of things too small to be seen or things which are not available to human perception of any sort.

Lenin is a realist in the philosophy of science, as well as a realist in the more general sense. Indeed, it is entirely to his credit that he does not even bother to distinguish these two things, if my argument about the connection between them is correct. In the quotations I have adduced so far from *Materialism and Empirio-Criticism,* Lenin speaks interchangeably about our beliefs reflecting reality, and our theories doing so. For example, he asserts that 'The theory of physics is a copy' (p. 373), because it refers to and describes some portion of reality. Lenin even expresses the distinction between materialism and idealism in terms of their respective views on the role of theory in science. The difference between them, he says,

is *only* that one recognises the 'ultimate'. . . reality reflected by our theory, while the other denies it, regarding theory as only a systematisation of experience, a system of empirio-symbols, and so on and so forth (p. 237).

On page after page of the latter part of the book, Lenin mocks mercilessly those anti-realist views of scientists and philosophers which we would call phenomenalist (or descriptivist), instrumentalist, and conventionalist. Lenin discusses, especially in Chapter V, those 'idealist' interpretations of science which had arisen as a result of the crisis in the physics of the early twentieth century. On such interpretations theories do not refer to essentially independent things in the world, but are human tools, instruments for predicting, or are summaries of observation reports, or are only human conventions, or some such. All such interpretations *humanise* the object of scientific inquiry in one sense or another, and *are* idealist in the way Lenin asserted. Duhem's conventionalism is rejected: 'Our concepts and hypotheses [according to Duhem] are mere signs, "arbitrary" constructions, and so forth. There is only one step from this to idealism . . .' (p. 422). Lenin approves the condemnation of instrumentalism and descriptivism advanced by an Italian physicist, Augusto Righi: 'For the positivist and utilitarian tendencies . . . a theory may serve in the first place only as a means of conveniently ordering and summarising facts and as a guide in the search for further phenomena. But while in former times perhaps too much confidence was placed in the faculties of the human mind . . . there is nowadays a tendency to fall into the opposite error' (p. 354). The theory of empirio-symbols, which bears much of the brunt of Lenin's invective, appears to have been committed to a descriptivist reduction of theoretical entities to observable ones; energy is 'a pure symbol of the correlation between the facts of experience . . .' (p. 367), according to the empirio-symbolist. Mach's physics, Lenin tells us, is a 'phenomenalist' physics (p. 390). Throughout *Materialism and Empirio-Criticism,* Lenin comes to discuss a wide range of philosophical views about the cognitive nature of scientific theory, and the reality it, naively anyway, appears to describe. These views are often complicated fabrications, composed in varying measures of instrumentalism, descriptivism, and conventionalism, but Lenin tars all of them with the same idealist brush. I have argued that Lenin was correct to do so, and correct in his staunch defense of realism in the philosophy of science, which is merely a part of an overall materialist or realist perspective in any case.

We noted in Chapter IV the complaint by Susan Stebbing that Lenin had attempted to impose *on* science, to predetermine or specify in advance the nature of scientific results. It is hard to imagine that she could have read *Materialism and Empirio-Criticism.* Lenin insists repeatedly that his materialism does not impose any special results on science. Lenin quite carefully distinguishes the epistemological concept of matter from any particular scientific concept of matter: 'But it is absolutely unpardonable to confuse, as the Machists do, any particular theory of the structure of matter with the epistemological category, to confuse the problem of the new properties of new aspects of matter (electrons, for example) with the old problem of the theory of knowledge, with the problem of sources of our knowledge, the existence of objective truth, etc.' (p. 165). 'Matter', in the sense in which Lenin is interested in it, 'is a philosophical category denoting the objective reality which is given to man by his sensations . . . while existing independently of them' (pp. 165-166), '. . . the *sole* "property" of matter with whose recognition philosophical materialism is bound up is the property of *being an objective reality,* of existing outside the mind' (p. 350): '. . . the concept matter, as we have already stated, epistemologically implies *nothing but* objective reality existing independently of the human mind . . .' (p. 351). Scientific theories about matter, or its disappearance, may come and go, and Lenin has no strictures to place on any of them. The object of his scorn are those scientists and philosophers who *confuse* the scientific and philosophical notions of matter, and who infer from the new physics that nothing whatever exists independently of mind: 'That "disappearance of matter" of which he [Valentinov] speaks, in imitation of the modern physicists, has no relation to the epistemological distinction between materialism and idealism' (p. 348). To say that the philosophical concept of matter 'can become "antiquated" is *childish talk'* (p. 166), because such a remark embodies a confusion between scientific results about matter and a philosophical doctrine! '. . . it is this sole . . . recognition of nature's existence outside the mind and perception of man . . .' (p. 353) in which Lenin is interested. Far from imposing doctrines *on* science, the brunt of Lenin's criticism of certain interpretations of the new physics is that they confused the results of a special science, physics, about matter, with philosophical materialism.

From the foregoing it would seem that, for Lenin, philosophical materialism retains a certain imperviousness to the results of the special sciences. We might then raise for Lenin the same questions we have already raised in Chapter IV: can science 'prove' philosophical materialism inductively, or are there any non-trivial, valid, deductive arguments the conclusion of which is the truth of philosophical materialism? Lenin seems to rule out the possibility of establishing materialism by deductive argument with the following remark: 'And Diderot, who came very close to the standpoint of contemporary materialism (that arguments and syllogisms alone do not suffice to refute idealism, and that here it is not a question for theoretical argument), notes the similarity of the premisess both of the idealist Berkeley, and the sensationalist Condillac' (p. 34). What then of the connection between science and materialism? Could the findings of science offer inductive support for philosophical materialism? Let us recall the argument that we produced in Chapter IV. We argued there that an 'absolute' idealist could always reconcile idealism and science by making the world essentially dependent on absolute spirit or mind rather than on human minds. Since, we claimed, talk about absolute spirit, mind, or whatever could ultimately be made intelligible only by theology, absolute idealism *was* a variety of theology. But theology itself was not inconsistent with science in the sense that science could 'disprove' faith. Similarly, the subjective idealists too had available to them a variety of techniques for making the reduction of the world to *human* experience or sensation compatible with science. By allowing their ontology to encompass both actual and possible experience, knowledge of a pre-human world could be made compatible with subjective idealism. Science disconfirms then neither absolute nor subjective varieties of idealism. But even though in Chapter IV we argued against an inductive relation between science and philosophical materialism, we did not despair of finding some other sort of connection, although a 'looser' one.

I think that one can find, in *Materialism and Empirio-Criticism,* among other positions, a position similar to the one for which we argued in Chapter IV: '. . . the views of natural science, which instinctively adheres to the materialist theory of knowledge . . .' (p. 46); 'The natural sciences *unconsciously* assume that their teachings reflect objective reality . . .' (p. 374); and '. . . the *inseparable* connection between the instinctive materialism of the natural scientists and their philosophical materialism' (p. 471). Lenin is clear that there is *some* connection between natural science and materialism, and chides bourgeois philosophers for denying that this is so. 'That science is non-partisan in the struggle of materialism against idealism and religion is a favourite idea . . . of all modern bourgeois professors . . .' (p. 178).

Sometimes, Lenin conceives of this connection as one between philosophical materialism and the *de facto* beliefs of an overwhelmingly large *numerical* majority of natural scientists— '. . . the materialist theory of knowledge, which the overwhelming majority of contemporary scientists instinctively hold . . .' (p. 54).[29] Lenin claims that only 'a minority of new physicists' (p. 487) are idealists, and that 'the temporary infatuation with idealism' is 'on the part of a small number of specialists' (p. 418). But this is not, or should not be, Lenin's considered view. In some of the above quotations, Lenin spoke impersonally of the views of 'natural science' rather than 'natural scientists'. He speaks at one point of the *unconscious assumption* of natural science, and elsewhere repeats that 'This materialist solution alone is really compatible with natural science . . .' (p. 95). He talks of materialism as being 'in full agreement with natural science' (p. 47), and in discussing the relationship between Avenarius' philosophy and geology, Lenin speaks of 'the impossibility of reconciling it [Avenarius' philosophy] with the demands of natural science' (p. 95). Indeed, Lenin's discussion in the latter part of the book of the way in which many scientists were misled by inaccurate interpretations of the new physics into varieties of idealism itself suggests the inappropriateness of arguing a connection between materialism and natural science merely by a head-count of the views of scientists. Lenin describes Helmholtz, for example, as 'a scientist of the first magnitude [who] was as inconsistent in philosophy as are the great majority of natural scientists' (p. 311). Such remarks do not strengthen confidence in the philosophical views of the majority of scientists, and Lenin marks this point by usually speaking of the views of natural science, rather than the views of natural scientists. Of course, natural science does not 'hold views' and Lenin marks this too by speaking of such views as 'instinctive' or 'unconscious': 'natural science holds an instinctive and unconscious materialist point of view' (p. 106). Elsewhere he does not speak of the connection between materialism and natural science in terms of any 'beliefs' or 'views' of natural science at all: 'This materialist solution alone is really compatible with natural science' (p. 95); 'Materialism, in full agreement with natural science . . .' (p. 47); and 'only such a philosophy [as materialism] is reconcilable with the natural sciences' (p. 374). I interpret the impersonal way in which Lenin speaks of the views or demands of *natural science* to mean that there is a connection between natural *science* and materialism, and not just between natural *scientists* and materialism. 'The demands of natural science' (p. 95) are not the demands of natural scientists. They are, rather, the methodological demands of science. I argued earlier that materialism is the philosophy *of* science, the diurnal philosophy, because it genuinely expresses the spirit of science. It is a philosophy which disallows our moving beyond science. Idealism, on the other hand, demands that we bifurcate the ways in which we approach the world, because the idealism we have earlier discussed was itself intimately connected with theological or quasi-theological beliefs about God, Absolute Spirit, Idea, or whatever. This is the sort of point, I believe, that Lenin is trying to make when he speaks of 'the demands of natural science'.

However, we are not so easily entitled to the fruits of our earlier argument in this discussion of Lenin, since he, as we have already noted in another connection, uses the rubric 'idealist' in our 'wider' sense, to include not only figures such as Kant and Hegel, who make the world essentially dependent on Thought, but also phenomenalists or positivists such as Berkeley, Hume, Mach, Avenarius, or the Russian empirio-critics, who by their reductive analyses make the world dependent on, because composed of, human sensations. Lenin was aware, and makes much of, the religious views of Berkeley. But there is no real connection between phenomenalism or positivism in general and theism. Lenin does assume that positivism and religious belief are intrinsically connected: '. . . our Machists have all become ensnared in idealism, that is, in a diluted, subtle fideism . . .' (p. 471); and 'Idealism says that physical nature is a product of this experience of living beings, and in saying this, Idealism is equating . . . nature to God' (p. 306). Lenin is not right about this. Kant and Hegel were 'absolute' idealists. Because they made nature, the object, essentially dependent on thought, they both tended to reify thought into Absolute Thought, The Thought of God.[30] Thus, a pre-human world could be essentially dependent on this Absolute Mind or Thought. But the phenomenalists, the Machian positivists, the empirio-critics, were 'subjective' idealists. They 'reduced' the world into a complex of human sensations. They did not *need* God in their philosophy, however much individual 'subjective' idealists may have imported him for other purposes. They had alternative devices such as 'possible sensations', 'permanent possibilities of sensations', counterfactual conditional assertions about sensation, and so on, to account for the pre-human existence of nature. As Lenin quotes Bazarov as saying about the pre-human existence of nature: 'Had I been there [on the earth, prior to man], I would have seen the world so-and-so' (p. 102). This range of philosophical techniques, counterfactuals, possibilities, etc., could be used to define a sense in which the world could be said to have existed prior to the advent of man, without postulating a reification such as God, Idea, or Absolute Spirit. In this way, this reductive, subjective idealism is not *necessarily* theological in the way in which absolute idealism is, and Lenin is wrong when he says that it is. Absolute idealism, then, imposes a bifurcation in our thinking about reality, for it demands that we think 'scientifically' about one part of reality, but non-scientifically, religiously, about another. Now, we have argued that subjective idealism—the phenomenalism of many of those whom Lenin attacks in *Materialism and Empirio-Criticism*—does not *necessarily* bifurcate our thinking in this way. However, it does not follow that these reductive analyses of reality into sensations— 'the earth is a complex of sensations . . .' (p. 92)—do not bifurcate our thinking in some other way, between science and something else. This bifurcation of methodology or approach may not take the form of *a posteriori* science and faith. Lenin describes, in a section entitled 'Did Nature Exist Prior to Man?', the moves made by various of the positivists and empirio-critics, Avenarius, Petzoldt, Willy, Bazarov, whose purpose it was to make philosophy compatible with natural science. It is revealing to note what Lenin says about these ploys. Bazarov had spoken in counterfactual terms: 'Had I been there [on earth, prior to man], I would have seen the world so-and-so'. Lenin's reply is: 'In other words: If I make an assumption that is obviously absurd and contrary to natural science (that man can be an observer in an epoch before man existed), I shall be able to patch up the breach in my philosophy!' (p. 102). In order to ascribe a pre-human past to nature, Avenarius spoke in terms of mental projection: 'how is the earth to be defined prior to the appearance of . . . man . . . if I were mentally to project myself in the role of an observer' (p. 91), and Lenin's rejoinder to this is that 'Avenarius graciously consents to "mentally project" something the possibility of admitting which is *excluded* by natural science' (p. 92). In both cases the phenomenalist must speak of what is logically possible but physically impossible. In the first case he must speak of the *logical* possibility of observing things at a time when as a matter of *natural* fact there were no observations, and in the latter case of 'mentally projecting', conceiving of myself as observer at a time at which natural science excludes observation. In short, these reductive analyses in terms of *counterfactuals* are just *that, counter-factuals;* they bifurcate philosophy and fact. Lenin appreciates that these reductions force us to speak of what is logically possible but physically impossible. Lenin does not want to allow us the realm of the logically possible; what could have happened, even in philosophy, should be restricted to what was physically possible: 'No man at all educated or sound-minded doubts that the earth existed at a time when there *could not* have been any life on it . . .' (p. 92). Such philosophical manoeuvres are 'mysticism' (p. 90), 'philosophical obscurantism' (p. 92), for although they are neither deductively nor inductively inconsistent with natural science, they demand the same kind of break with the method of the *a posteriori* sciences that religion demands. Counterfactuals, or contrary-to-fact conditionals, can be 'about' physically impossible states of affairs, as were Bogdanov's and Avenarius'. However, they do not assert or postulate such states as actual. Rather, they are more akin to suppositions than to assertions—'Suppose or imagine, although it is actually physically impossible, that I had been an observer on the earth before the time at which sentient life in fact arose. If so, I would have seen . . .' Now, such 'suppositions' or 'imaginings' are not inductively disconfirmed by the *fact* of the physical impossibility of my having been such an observer, since such suppositions do not *assert* that I was such an observer. It cannot be inductively inconsistent with the facts to suppose or imagine a situation which is different from the way things factually were, as long as I do not assert that the state of affairs which I imagine or suppose was actual.

However, Lenin does, I think, ask us to limit our suppositions in philosophy to what is physically possible. This demand is a demand for methodological continuity between science and philosophy rather than a demand for, strictly speaking, the *inductive consistency* of science and philosophy. The logically possible but physically impossible, is a no better philosophical basis than the Absolute Idea. Materialism, which resorts to neither, which shies away both from religion and the methodology of the *a priori,* is the approach of the sciences writ large, or anyway writ larger. It is in this spirit, then, that we interpret Lenin's remarks about 'the demands of natural science'. At his best, Lenin is not making claims about the majority views among groups of natural *scientists.* Rather, he is claiming that there is a method, an approach, appropriate to science, and that our philosophy ought to be methodologically continuous with that approach. Our philosophy, materialism, is a philosophy of the *a posteriori,* even if not precisely an *a posteriori* philosophy. Lenin rejects both forms of idealism as being discontinuous with that approach, both the idealism of Kant and Hegel and that of positivism and phenomenalism. This is, roughly, the same view we took about the nature and epistemological status of materialism in Chapter IV.

Finally, these remarks on religion and religious belief bring me to the threshold of a criticism of *Materialism and Empirio-Criticism* advanced by Anton Pannekoek. Pannekoek's own position on the nature of Lenin's philosophy is almost embarrassing in its simplicity. Pannekoek distinguishes sharply between middle-class materialism and historical materialism. Middle-class materialism expresses, for Pannekoek, the fight of the bourgeoisie against the old order, underpinned as it was by religion. 'The fight of the bourgeoisie against feudal dominance was expressed by middle-class materialism, cognate to Feuerbach's doctrine, which used natural science to fight religion as the consecration of the old powers'.[31] The 'scientism' of the bourgeoisie was a weapon at their disposal in the struggle against the feudal order and the religious ideology which was its expression and its legitimisation in the realm of thought. On the other hand, 'The working class in its own fight has little use for natural science, the instrument of its foe; its theoretical weapon is social science . . . To fight religion by means of natural science has no significance for the workers; they know, moreover, that its roots will be cut off anyhow first by capitalist development, than by their own class struggle'.[32]

These intellectual judgements fit well into Pannekoek's overall political judgements of Bolshevism. By the latter half of the nineteenth century, we are informed, middle-class materialism had disappeared in Western and Central Europe. The bourgeoisie was there victorious, and no longer stood in need of a militant, atheist materialism with which to combat feudal absolutism. 'In Russia, however, matters were different. Here the fight against Czarism was analogous to the former fight against absolutism in Europe. In Russia too church and religion were the strongest supports of the system of government . . . The struggle against religion was here a prime social necessity.'[33] However, the absence of a bourgeoisie forced the leadership of this struggle on the Russian intelligensia. This intelligensia, scorned by a 'now reactionary and anti-materialist' bourgeoisie in Western Europe, could only appeal to the working class. Thus, in Russia, under the banner of Marxism, the intelligensia, in lieu of a bourgeoisie, lead a revolution which supplanted the Czarist absolutist state by a state capitalist régime. In this struggle, despite the banner of Marxism, its ideology was middle-class materialism, with its characteristic hallmarks of atheism and a glorification of natural science. 'So the Russian intellectuals, in adopting the theory to the local task, had to find a form of Marxism in which criticism of religion stood in the forefront'.[34] This they found by returning to Marx's early writings, which themselves suffer from being the product of the period 'when in Germany the fight of the bourgeoisie and the workers against absolutism was still undivided'. Lenin then made, by using the working class, a bourgeois revolution in Russia, and his philosophy is an expression of this. '. . . the alleged Marxism of Lenin and the bolshevist party is nothing but a legend . . . Russian bolshevism cannot be reproached for having abandoned the way of Marxism; for it was never on that way. Every page of Lenin's philosophical work is there to prove it.'[35] Lenin's philosophy, for Pannekoek, is only 'a so-called refutation of middle-class idealism through the ideas of middle-class materialism'.[36]

Pannekoek's too easy identification of religion with feudal absolutism and natural scientific atheism with the bourgeois struggle against feudalism is not only appallingly simple, but strangely contradictory with other details of this story which he tells. Why, according to Pannekoek, were the bolshevik 'intelligensia' forced to turn to the working class for its support? Pannekoek's answer is that they were forced into this alliance because the Central and Western European bourgeoisies had become 'reactionary and anti-materialist'. But what would be the philosophy 'characteristic' of a reactionary and anti-materialist bourgeoisie? Clearly, on Pannekoek's account, it would be idealist and religious in tone, and he speaks, in the last quote above, of 'middle-class idealism'. Thus, idealism and theism even for Pannekoek, *can* be the philosophy either of a feudal nobility or of a bourgeoisie, and are not confined to either particular epoch or mode of production. Whether the bourgeoisie adopts a materialist or an idealist stance, on such a view, might depend on its stage of development. When it is a progressive class, struggling to free the forces of production from feudal constraints, it could be expected to adopt a progressive, materialist philosophy. When, on the other hand, it has become a reactionary class, struggling to maintain a mode of production inimical to the further growth of the social force of production, its philosophy would be expected to become a reactionary, idealist one.[37] Now, from the fact that a revolutionary is a materialist whose materialism is characterised by a strongly anti-theist and anti-idealist tone (as was Lenin's), it does not follow that such a revolutionary would be a bourgeois revolutionary upholding 'merely middle-class materialism' against a feudal enemy. He might, on this natural extension of Pannekoek's own remarks, just as well be a proletarian revolutionary upholding historical materialism against the resurgence of theist and idealist modes of thought amongst the bourgeoisie, against a 'reactionary and anti-materialist' bourgeois enemy. In our view, this is precisely what Lenin was doing.

Had *Materialism and Empirio-Criticism* been written by a Frenchman, to combat the rise of idealism among the members of the French party, Pannekoek's thesis would have had no initial credibility whatever. What Pannekoek might have replied to my above remarks is that they may serve to deflect such accusation from hitting the target of a hypothetical *Materialism and Empirio-Criticism* written in ·the conditions of an advanced capitalist country. In France, Germany, Britain, or the USA., one could argue that idealism and theism had become bourgeois phenomena, and hence legitimate objects of attack by a spokesman of the working class. But Pannekoek could argue perhaps that this same defense is not available in the context of Lenin's Russia. *There* the idealism and theism *was* the idealism and theism of the feudal aristocracy, and hence its attack was, essentially, a bourgeois task rather than a specifically proletarian one.

Such a possible reply, placed in the mouth of Pannekoek, does bring out the extraordinary nationalist compartmentalisation latent in his thinking. The structure of Lenin's book, as well as the content of his argument, stresses time and time again that the attack is directed firstly against a general, idealist, European cultural phenomenon, and then secondly against a particular, idealist, Russian version or application of that phenomenon. Throughout *Materialism and Empirio-Criticism,* Lenin criticises not only Bogdanov, Bazarov, and Lunacharsky, but the Belgian Duhem, the Germans Hermann Cohen, Eduard von Hartmann, F. A. Lange, the Austrian Mach, the Englishmen James Ward and Karl Pearson, the Frenchmen Poincaré, Le Roy, and Leclair, and the American journal *The Monist,* among many others. Idealism, Lenin correctly saw, was rampant throughout the academies of advanced capitalist societies: 'anyone in the least acquainted with philosophical literature must know that scarcely a single contemporary professor of philosophy . . . can be found who is not directly or indirectly engaged in refuting materialism' (p. 15). Russia may not itself have been a developed capitalist country, but yet it was firmly locked into the sphere of the capitalist mode of production. However many local variations there might have been, its cultural life was shaped by the capitalist mode of production too. Lenin argued that the Russian idealists were importing 'Western' and 'Central' European fashions. 'There can be no doubt that we have before us a certain international ideological current . . . which is the result of certain general causes lying outside the sphere of philosophy' (p. 410). Russian idealism was, for Lenin, essentially connected with this European cultural phenomenon: 'A true-Russian philosophical idealist, Mr. Lopatin, bears about the same relation to the contemporary European idealists as, for example, the Union of the Russian People does to the reactionary parties of the West. All the more instructive is it, therefore, to see how similar philosophical trends manifest themselves in totally different cultural and social surroundings' (p. 406). Lenin's overall assessment is that, far from making any original contribution, Russian idealists actually managed to confuse and confound otherwise clear divisions in their inept transposition of European idealism into Russian conditions: 'It was only the Russian Machists who brought confusion into this perfectly clear question, since for their West-European teachers and co-thinkers the radical difference between the line of Mach & Co. and the line of the materialists generally is quite obvious' (p. 322).

Once we situate Russian idealism into its European context, Pannekoek's thesis tends to collapse. Russian idealism, like its counterparts in Germany, France, Britain, and elsewhere, was a bourgeois phenomenon, *not* a feudal one. To attack this idealism, and the fideism which often tended to accompany it, was a genuine proletarian task, a task of historical materialism. It is, then, simply absurd to say that 'the working class in its own fight has little use for natural science, the instrument of its foe . . . To fight religion by means of natural science has no significance for the workers; they know, moreover, that its roots will be cut off anyhow first by capitalist development . . .'. Pannekoek simply overlooked, in such judgements, the extent to which further capitalist development can itself lead to idealism, and hence overlooked the possibility of a proletarian defence of materialism and natural science. Recent history certainly seems to have proven Lenin's vision to be more certain and steady than Pannekoek's. When one considers the forms of irrationalism to which the capitalist mode of production has given birth since Lenin wrote—and one must number Fascism as the best and worst example of the irrational denial of natural science, with its absurd genetic and racial theories—the idea that any form of truth, and especially the truths of natural science, have 'little use' for the proletariat in its struggle is itself a 'reactionary and anti-materialist' conception. Nor is the fight against religion completed in the capitalist epoch. Pannekoek is mistaken in restricting religion to the role of being a narcotic to the feudal masses; it works its soporific effect within bourgeois society too. Bourgeois or middle class idealism is also

a subtle, refined form of fideism, which stands fully armed, commands vast organisations and steadily continues to exercise influence on the masses, turning the slightest vacillation in philosophical thought to its own advantage. The objective, class role of empirio-criticism consists entirely in rendering faithful service to the fideists in their struggle against materialism in general and historical materialism in particular (p. 488).

It is with these words that Lenin concludes the tasks he set for himself in *Materialism and Empirio-Criticism.*

Notes: Chapter VI

1   Lenin, V. I., *Materialism and Empirio-Criticism,* Progress Publishers, Moscow, 1970, p. 189. All further page references in the text, unless otherwise indicated, refer to this edition of Lenin's book.

2   Valentinov, N., *Encounters with Lenin,* Oxford University Press, London, 1968, pp. 254-256.

3   Löwy, Michel, 'From *The Greater Logic* to the Finland Station', *Critique* No. 6, 1976. Löwy's argument may be found unconvincing for other reasons, but my point is only that it is not necessarily *in*consistent with my own views on the relation between *Materialism and Empirio-Criticism* and *The Philosophical Notebooks.* I have argued that nothing of importance in the latter contradicts the former. But it could be that the new 'additions' or stresses or emphases in the latter were sufficient to make a difference to Lenin's political practice.

4   Valentinov, N., *op. cit.,* p. 255.

5   Lenin, V. I., *op. cit.,* pp. 260-261.

6   Valentinov, N., *op. cit.,* p. 255 for this and the following unnumbered quotations.

7   Pannekoek, Anton, *Lenin As Philosopher,* Merlin Press, London, 1975, p. 86.

8   *Ibid.,* pp. 99-100.

9   *Ibid.,* pp. 130-131.

10   Valentinov, N., *op. cit.,* p. 260.

11   Akselrod, Lyubov (Ortodox), 'Review of Lenin's *Materialism and Empirio-Criticism',* first published in *Sovremenny Mir,* July, 1909, No. 7. Reprinted in *Russian Philosophy* Vol. III, edited by James Edie, James P. Scanlan, and Mary-Barbara Zeldin. Quadrange Books, Chicago, 1965, p. 458.

12   *Ibid.,* p. 463.

13   Paul, G. A., 'Lenin's Theory of Perception', first published in *Analysis,* 1938, and reprinted in Margaret Macdonald, ed. *Philosophy and Analysis,* Blackwell, Oxford, 1954. Chapter X, pp. 278-286. The quote is from p. 286.

14   Althusser, Louis, *Lenin and Philosophy,* New Left Books, London, 1971.

15   I quoted this remark by Engels in the Introduction.

16   Lenin quotes this on p. 122 of *Materialism and Empirio-Criticism.*

17   'Van Fraassen remarks that, historically, realism includes the doctrines that there are real necessities in nature. He offers to ignore that aspect of realism in his paper, but one gets the impression that he believes that realists are stuck with defending an account of natural necessity other than the eliminative account offered by Hume. If he thinks that, then, I believe, he is right. The verificationist arguments that can be advanced against taking scientific theories to be accounts of causal powers or accounts of the nature of natural necessity are so similar to the arguments that can be advanced against other realistic interpretations of theories that it is hard to see how a realist can accept the former and reject the latter. It would appear that realists must defend a non-Humean account of causal powers and natural necessity . . .'. Richard N. Boyd, 'Approximate Truth and Natural Necessity', *Journal of Philosophy,* Vol. LXXIII, No. 18, 1976, p. 634.

18   Very little of Bogdanov's writings have been translated into English. In the *Russian Philosophy* volume mentioned in footnote II, extracts from Bogdanov appear, taken from *Priklyucheniya Odnoy Filosofskoy Shkoly,* St. Petersburg, 1908. Other than that, I am unaware of anything in English by Bogdanov. This, if correct, is a pity; some of his work needs translation, for it is an important document in the history of Marxist thought. S. V. Utechin has an article on Bogdanov in *Revisionism: Essays on the History of Marxist*

Ideas, ed. L. A. Labedz; Gustav Wetter's *Dialectical Materialism*, trans. by Peter Heath, devotes a small number of pages to him. In *Proletarian Science? The Case of Lysenko*, New Left Books, 1977, Dominique Lecourt has included an appendix, 'Bogdanov, Mirror of the Soviet Intelligentsia', taken from his introduction to a selection (in French) of Bogdanov's writings. James White, 'The First "Pravda" and the Russian Marxist Tradition', *Soviet Studies*, Vol. 26, 1974, is of considerable interest on this era. For an example of the impression Mach was making on the Left at the time, see Friedrich Adler's 'The Discovery of the World Elements', in *The International Socialist Review*, Vol. III, No. 10, April 1908, translated by Ernest Untermann.

[19] For a view of this kind, see R. G. Collingwood, *Essay on Metaphysics*, Oxford University Press, 1940, and his discussion of the 'absolute presuppositions' of different views and outlooks. There is an interesting discussion of Collingwood in Stephen Toulmin, *Human Understanding*, Oxford University Press, 1972.

[20] Lenin, however, did not like the term 'realism', and preferred 'materialism', because of what he considered the debasement of the former term by philosophers: 'Let us note that the term "realism" is here employed [in Cauwelaert's exposition of the shifts in Avenarius' philosophy] as the antithesis of idealism. Following Engels, I use *only* the term materialism in this sense, and consider it the sole correct terminology, especially since the term "realism" has been bedraggled by the positivists and the other muddleheads who oscillate between materialism and idealism' (p. 68). My uses, however, of 'realism' and 'materialism' (in a non-reductive sense) are equivalent, as I have already explained in Chapter III.

[21] See for example G. A. Paul, *op. cit.*

[22] Some of the logical positivists were tempted by this doctrine, that somehow the logical structure of language was able to 'picture' the logical structure of the world. For example, in the *Tractatus* 4.03, Wittgenstein says that statements are 'logical pictures of facts'. For a development of the idea of correspondence which avoids any crude notion of picturing, and for a plausible development of the sorts of ideas found in Wittgenstein and others, see Wilfred Sellars, *Science, Perception and Reality*, The Humanities Press, New York, 1963, ch. 6, pp. 197-224. For Sellars, language 'pictures' the world in a sense that expressions, linguistic inscriptions, are 'linguistic projections' of non-linguistic objects. '. . . in the case of matter-of-factual statements . . . their role is that of constituting a projection in language users of the world in which they live'. (p. 223). Sellars does not, I think, make it sufficiently clear, at least in this chapter, what he intends by his notion of projection.

[23] Akselrod, Lyubov, *op. cit.*, p. 459.

[24] Plekhanov, G. V., *Selected Philosophical Works*, Vol. I, Progress Publishers, Moscow, p. 536. The quote is from Plekhanov's own remarks in the first Russian edition of Engels' *Ludwig Feuerbach and the End of Classical German Philosophy*, Geneva, 1892, for which he wrote a foreword and notes.

[25] Akselrod, Lyubov, *op. cit.*, p. 459.

[26] *Ibid.*, pp. 459-460.

[27] *Ibid.*, p. 460, for this and following quotation.

[28] However, Lenin does not restrict 'corresponds' in this way. For instance, 'The sensation of red reflects ether vibrations of a frequency of approximately 450 trillions per second. The sensation of blue reflects ether vibrations of a frequency of approximately 620 trillions per second' (p. 409). In this usage, it is difficult to see how, for Lenin, 'reflection', even in cases of perception, could retain any real pictorial implications whatever. Our sensation of blue is certainly not a picture or image of an ether vibration of a frequency of 620 trillions per second! In cases like this, one begins to feel that Lenin did not himself take the pictorial associations of 'reflection' at all seriously.

[29] Or again, '. . . the instinctively materialist theory of knowledge to which . . . the vast majority of natural scientists adhere' (pp. 431-432), or 'the very firmly implanted . . . tendencies of the overwhelming majority of the scientists' (p. 477).

[30] At one point, Lenin criticises O. Ewald for claiming that the idealists tie the object to *human* sensation with the following rejoinder: 'The term is incorrect; he should have said

subjective idealism, for Hegel's absolute idealism is reconcilable with the existence of the earth, nature, and the physical universe without man, since nature is regarded as the "other being" of the absolute idea' (pp. 85-86). Lenin expresses here his awareness that only subjective idealism, had need for a 'co-ordination' of world and sensation, object and subject, through phenomenalist, reductive analyses in terms of counterfactuals and possibilia, since the absolute idealist has God to help with the existence of an earth without man. Lenin also indicates his view that even absolute idealism is not, strictly speaking, 'irreconcilable' with the findings of science.

31 Pannekoek, Anton, *Lenin As Philosopher*, Merlin Press, London, 1975, p. 92.
32 *Ibid.*, pp. 92-93.
33 *Ibid.*, p. 93.
34 *Ibid.*, p. 94.
35 *Ibid.*, p. 97.
36 *Ibid.*, p. 99.
37 For an interesting study of this shift in the thought of one spokesman for the bourgeoisie, the nineteenth century legal theorist John Austin, from a 'progressive' phase marked by the offence of the middle-class against the aristocracy, to a 'reactionary' phase marked by the defence of the middle-class against the new challenge of the working class, see Eira A. Ruben's article on Austin in *Perspectives in Jurisprudence*, Glasgow University Press, 1977.

POSTSCRIPT

In this postscript I wish to answer several criticisms of the book which have been raised, and to say a bit more, and more lucidly, about some of the topics which were touched on rather quickly in Chapters IV and V. There are also a few matters of textual clarification, and additional supporting references, which I should like to take this opportunity to offer.

Professor J. W. N. Watkins has suggested to me that I write as if all reflection theories are true ones, and wondered whether, in addition to reflection theory, I might not need another category to cover false (what would otherwise be) 'reflection' theories. For example, I say that 'For the empiricist tradition, we could say that thoughts, concepts, ideas are reflective of the world or correspond to the world . . .' (p.13). Watkins' impression arises from the unhappy way in which I expressed myself. A reflection theory is a theory about how we are to *construe* theories (or beliefs, concepts, etc.). According to such a view, our theories or beliefs, the empirical ones at least, are to be construed as *aiming* or *intending* to refer to and describe real entities, structures, objects, or whatever. In the case of true or approximately true theories, they successfully refer and successfully or approximately successfully describe those things. In the case of false theories, either they successfully refer but fail to successfully describe, or (as in the case of aether or phlogiston) they fail even to successfully refer. But even in the cases of failure, their *function* is to refer and describe, a function not fulfilled in those cases. I cannot see that one needs a separate category other than 'reflection' for false theories, as long as the 'reflection' is taken in the sense of 'aim to reflect' or 'attempt to reflect', as indeed I suggested on p.167.

Perhaps the most sustained criticism of some of my arguments comes from Roy Bhaskar, in the *Postscript* to the new edition of *A Realist Theory of Science*.[1] This criticism concerns both rejoinders to my criticism of his particular transcendental arguments, and replies to some general remarks I made on the status of transcendental arguments.

Let me take Bhaskar's particular arguments first. I dealt with two of his transcendental arguments, one for the intransitivity of the objects of experience and the other for the structured nature of the objects of knowledge.[2] Bhaskar's argument for the intransitivity of the objects of experience runs as follows: 'scientific change (and criticism) is only possible on the condition that there are (relatively) unchanging objects' of experience.[3] My original criticism was that, in the argument Bhaskar offered, his description of the pre-change theory and post-change theory assumes without argument that in the standard case they refer to intransitive objects of experience, which is precisely the point he needed to prove.[4]

Bhaskar's reply, I take it, occurs in his answer to the question, 'But what are my grounds for the major premise in this case?',[5] because he is certainly right that that is the question at issue. Now, to begin with, I am not sure *which* argument Bhaskar takes as a transcendental argument. He sets out the following, which I shall call argument A:

(1) 'Scientific change (and criticism) is only possible on the condition that there are (relatively) unchanging objects' of experience.
(2) 'Scientific change and criticism occurs'.
(3) Therefore, there are relatively unchanging objects of experience.

Bhaskar calls argument A a 'transcendental argument' and says of it that it is deductively valid.

But Bhaskar also says, rightly, that this argument A is trivial, and that the interest lies 'in the production of the knowledge of the major premiss (i.e. in the analysis)'.[6] He then offers an 'analysis' or argument, which I shall call argument B, for the truth of the major premiss of argument A. Now, since all the examples of transcendental arguments from Kant to Strawson resemble more closely argument B rather than the trivial argument A, I am going to call argument B a 'transcendental' argument. Whatever we call it, it clearly is the one that is doing all of the philosophical work, and is alone of any interest. Bhaskar's argument B might be reconstructed thus:

(1) Theories which account for scientific change and criticism include realist theories, theories which posit 'Kuhn-loss', and theories which posit 'incommensurability'.
(2) A theory which posits incommensurability presupposes 'a field of real objects with respect to which the *rival* theories are incommensurable', and hence it is indistinguishable from a realist alternative.
(3) A theory which posits 'Kuhn-loss' cannot account for change or criticism, because 'Kuhn-loss' 'involves neither transformation nor discursive intelligence'.
(4) A realist theory can account for scientific change and criticism.
(5) Therefore, scientific change and criticism are possible only if realism is true (viz., if there are unchanging objects of experience).[7]

In the first edition, we heard nothing of 'Kuhn-loss' and almost nothing, except in the closing pages of the book, of incommensurability. So I gather that this is a genuine addition to, rather than development of, the argument I criticised.

Argument B, which is of course the crucial argument for Bhaskar's intransivity conclusion, is not, even according to Bhaskar, deductively valid, because there may be more theories to choose between than those offered for choice in premiss (1): 'Thus it is certainly the case that there is no way of demonstrating the uniqueness of the conclusion of such an argument in advance of every possible theory.... Further it should perhaps be stressed that I have not demonstrated that transcendental realism is the only possible theory of science consistent with these activities; only that it is the only theory *at present* known to us that is consistent with them'.[8] Argument B is *not* deductively valid, and Bhaskar does not hold that it is.

There are two points I wish to make concerning Bhaskar's new position. First, my criticism was against the possibility of 'non-question-begging, valid deductive arguments for the conclusion' of transcendental realism. If we take argument B as an example of a transcendental argument, as I think would be normal, I believe Bhaskar has conceded my point. Of course, argument A *is* deductively valid, but as an argument *for* transcendental realism, it would be question-begging unless we could independently establish the first premiss. Second, I dispute that Bhaskar has even achieved the rather limited aim of showing that transcendental realism is the only theory at present known to be consistent with scientific change and criticism. In argument B, premiss (3) for example assumes two things without argument; (b) and (c):

(a) If there is Kuhn-loss between two theories, then the two theories have no objects in common.

(b) If two theories have no objects in common, the change between them must be neither rational (no 'discursive intelligence') nor occur by a process of any sort taking time (no 'transformation', but accomplished 'in a single synthetic act').

(c) If the change between two theories is neither rational nor occurs by a temporal process, no sense can be given to the concept of scientific change and criticism.

(d) Hence, if there is Kuhn-loss between two theories, no sense can be given to the concept of scientific change and criticism.[9]

Whatever the details of Kuhn's position may be, and whatever else Kuhn may himself be committed to, Bhaskar offers no reason whatever for thinking, concerning two theories which do not 'share' objects in common, that (a) there are no other standards of rational choice for choosing between them, (b) even if the change from one to the other is non-rational, it cannot be one of the nature of a temporal process, (c) no notion of criticism can be given sense if the ultimate foundations of criticism must rest on non-rational choices or options,[10] and (d) no notion of change between theories can be given sense if the 'change' is instantaneous and does not take time. All four assumptions seem to me to be dubious, and if they are, premiss (3) in argument B cannot be upheld. Moreover, I think that similarly unargued assumptions can be detected in premiss (2). Since there can be rival but incommensurable formal or non-empirical theories which do not 'posit' 'a field of real objects', Bhaskar needs to say much more in defence of (2). So I cannot see that Bhaskar achieves even the less ambitious task of being able to *show* that, *of all currently known theories*, only transcendental realism can explain the possibility of scientific change and criticism.

The other transcendental argument of Bhaskar's that I criticised was the argument for the structured nature of the objects of knowledge.[11] My claim was that although the Bhaskarian experimenter produces an event a, which would not occur naturally, and indirectly produces an event b, he does not produce *that* a is followed by b. Bhaskar claims that this is precisely what he does show, under the notion of 'experimental control', because without the experimenter a would not be followed by b. Hence, the experimenter produces causal sequences but not causal laws, so Bhaskar concludes that these cannot be the same thing.

Now, it seems obvious to me that the experimenter produces only the event a, and indirectly the event b, but not *the fact* that b follows a. However, the argument for this is rather complicated, and it is not surprising that Bhaskar did not see my argument, given the very compressed treatment I gave to this.

It is not easy to see what precisely are the points of disagreement between Bhaskar and contemporary, sophisticated versions of a regularity thesis, Davidson's or Mackie's, for example.[12] Bhaskar argues in the *Postscript* that

My argument is that without our causal activity, given a, b may not occur, and in general, will not occur. Patently, if it is the case that our causal activity is necessary for the realisation of the consequent of laws, they just cannot be glossed, without absurdity, as empirical regularities.[13]

Bhaskar's argument is that, if, *given* that the antecedent a occurs, 'our causal activity is still necessary for the realisation of the consequent of laws, they just cannot be glossed without absurdity as empirical regularities'. I take it that neither Bhaskar nor the empiricist must hold that the antecedent itself should occur naturally, without causal activity.

But the question that is crucial is what 'a' or 'the antecedent of laws' refers to. Suppose that we have to experimentally introduce oxygen into a particular match's environment in order to get it to light. If it is true that striking *this* match, given what was done in *this* experiment, caused it to light, Bhaskar seems to presume that the relevant causal law is 'If matches are struck, then they light'. Bhaskar then argues that, since given the striking, 'our causal activity is necessary for the realisation of the consequent of laws', and hence our causal activity produces the fact that the sequential relation holds between events described in that way.

But Bhaskar is aware, as his discussion of Davidson makes clear,[14] that no sophisticated modern version of the regularity thesis holds such a simple-minded thesis. All that a regularity thesis need subscribe to is that if it is true that the striking of *this* match caused it to light, then there is a causal law which establishes an empirical regularity between two event-types, let us call them 'C' and 'D', and that striking this match a, is a token of the type C, and the lighting of this match, b, is a token of the type D. However, what the descriptions are which are involved in the names of the causally relevant types, C and D, will certainly be extremely complicated, perhaps as yet unknown. In particular, it is unlikely that they will be anything as straightforward as a simple generalisation from 'a' and 'b' to 'a-type events' and 'b-type events'. Our ordinary descriptions of the tokens are unlikely to give us clues as to the relevant type descriptions, *viz.*, it is not going to be 'strikings of matches generally' and 'lightings of matches'. For example, in the case we imagined, a causally relevant description of the antecedent will certainly include reference to the presence of oxygen.

Bhaskar's argument only works against a regularity thesis of the simple kind, where the type descriptions are simple generalisations from the common token descriptions. Strikings are not always followed by lightings, so it might seem as if the experimenter has, at least sometimes, to produce the sequence even after he has produced the antecedent. But if we use the more complicated descriptions for the antecedent events, the problem turns out otherwise. Given the more complicated event-type descriptions, whatever they may be, there will be no cases in which, given the antecedent, it remains necessary to experimentally *produce* that the consequent follows. What there is, though, is the truth that events of that rather complicated antecedent type might almost never occur naturally. We can view an experiment as a situation in which *antecedents* of true empirical regularities, which almost never occur naturally, are artificially produced.

Thus, there is something, I grant, artificial about the question of whether the experimenter *produces* the antecedent event or, given the antecedent event, *controls* what consequent it will have. Which we say will depend on what description of the event we use. But what a regularity theorist will hold is that there *exist* descriptions on which all experiment is the production of non-naturally occurring antecedent conditions. On those descriptions, the sequential relation is *not* something that has to be produced after the antecedent is produced.

One last remark about this. Bhaskar does produce several criticisms of the Davidsonian position. But, again, I cannot see how his position finally differs from it. This concerns the understanding of talk of tendencies,[15] and I regard this question as very much an open one. I offer the following only tentatively.

Bhaskar says, of the case of what he calls 'open systems':

If a system is closed then a tendency once set in motion must be fulfilled. If the system is open this may not happen due to the presence of 'offsetting factors' or 'countervailing causes'. But there must be a reason why, once a tendency is set in motion, it is not fulfilled . . . Once a tendency is set in motion it is fulfilled unless it is prevented.[16]

Bhaskar is no indeterminist; he certainly thinks that for everything that happens, there is a sufficient condition of its happening ('there must be a reason why . . . it is not fulfilled . . .'). But this seems close to saying that, for whatever there is a tendency to occur, there is some compendious statement which gives the sufficient condition for its occurring. No doubt, one would have to mention both the relevant underlying mechanism and the absence of offsetting factors and countervailing causes. But Bhaskar seems committed to there being the possibility of there being such a statement.

Now, this does not seem very different at all from Davidsonian laws. Is the only outstanding problem to do with Bhaskar's reluctance to call such non-tendency, sufficient condition statement 'laws'? Is there, in the end of the day, anything more between Bhaskar on the one hand and Mackie or Davidson on the other than the question of whether tendency statements are 'fully' laws or only proto-laws, or whether sufficient-condition statements are true-but-not-laws or really are laws? It begins to appear as if the controversy is a quibble. If there are statements which express sufficient conditions for whatever happens, then there are statements of *empirical regularities*. Does it matter if they are called 'laws' or not? Such statements might still differ from their more standard Humeian cousins in so far as they mention essential, unmanifest mechanism, but as far as their being only 'tendential', they will have become as 'regular' as those cousins ever were thought to have been.

Finally, there is the general question of the nature and status of transcendental arguments.[17] Of course, I agree with Bhaskar that deductively valid arguments can have surprising conclusions, as the proofs of many theorems in formal systems show. However, as far as Bhaskar is concerned, I take the impossibility of deductively valid transcendental arguments to have been conceded. Of course, if we think of Bhaskar's argument A, the trivial argument, as transcendental, then the conclusion is not even surprising relative to its premisses. But on Bhaskar's own account, argument B, whose conclusion is surprising, is not deductively valid.

Still, the question of deductively valid transcendental arguments is interesting in its own right. Let us consider those transcendental arguments which argue for the reality of the external world, or other minds, or the past, in general for anti-sceptical conclusions, through an examination of the necessary conditions for there being a language, or some part of language making or having sense, or the general conceptual scheme or framework which we employ, or some feature of that framework.[18] The general strategy of such arguments is to argue that, for example, if the distinction between waking and dreaming is even to be intelligible, then there must be the possibility of applying or drawing the distinction. That is, there must be the possibility of states which we can take to be waking and which we can take to be dreaming. Now, even if it were true that there must be the possibility of states of ours which we *take* to be waking in order to have the intelligible distinction between waking and dreaming, it does not follow that a necessary condition for the intelligibility of this distinction is that we *correctly* take such states to be states of waking. All the states we take to be waking states might in fact *be* dream states. So one can't argue, apparently, from the intelligibility of some feature of language, or of our conceptual framework, to there actually being things that the sceptic might deny, but only to our *believing* that there are such things.

Now, one obvious way to attempt to circumvent this difficulty is to adopt the sort of verificationist or criteriological theories of meaning that I mentioned in my brief discussion of Phillip's paper.[19] One might argue that to have a significant concept is to be in principle capable of verifying its *correct* application, or to be aware of the criteria for its correct application. Thus, following Barry Stroud, I would argue that no transcendental argument has any hope of being deductively valid unless it takes as one of its premisses one of these anti-realist theories of meaning. This is perhaps not the place to enter into a discussion of these anti-realist theories. But it is the place to suggest to Bhaskar that Kant's rejection of transcendental realism and his use of a transcendental mode of argument is no coincidence. In general, I think that because transcendental arguments would, in order to be valid, have to rely on anti-realist theories of meaning, their use is not available to a realist. I agree with Bhaskar that the objects of knowledge are structured and intransitive, but I cannot see any hope for the use of anti-realist transcendental arguments to establish these realist conclusions. About the realist analysis of causality, I am increasingly less clear. I can accept, happily, talk of underlying mechanisms; I think this is central to Marx's scientific programme. But I am genuinely worried that the tendency v. empirical regularity debate, if pushed hard enough, might well collapse into little more than a quibble about the use of the word 'law'.

On the question of the *a priori*, it seems to me now that my argument is pretty clearly a *non-sequitur*. I argue (p.102) or rather state a scepticism about the possibility of 'non-trivial, interesting, *a priori* truths which depend for their truth merely on the meanings of the words or expressions involved in their formulation'. I retain that scepticism. But then comes a non-sequitur:

Since there are, we claim, no such things as non-trivial, purely conceptual truths based on the meanings of words alone . . . no such truths on which the analytic philosopher could happily exercise his skill at *a priori* unpacking, then . . . [philosophy] has the same kind of *a posteriori* character that the fields of every other discipline have.[20]

There may be no *a priori* truths of the sort philosophy so conceived would need, *grounded* in analyticity or semantics, but it does not follow that there are no interesting, non-trivial *a priori* truths at all, ungrounded or grounded differently, and *a fortiori* it does not follow that philosophy cannot study them.

It used to be thought unproblematic, within the empiricist tradition at any rate, that all necessary truths were analytic, and conversely, and that all analytic truths were *a priori* and conversely. What has happened recently within orthodox philosophy is a general prising of them apart. Analyticity, due to the Quinian attack on it and perhaps also due to its utterly inflated overuse, seems to have fallen into general disfavour. With few exceptions, among which I would include very much to its detriment Peter Unger's recent *Ignorance*,[21] philosophers have seemed reluctant to use the alleged analyticity of a statement as an argumentative weapon. Necessity has become all the fashion, but most philosophers given to this way of speaking think that some things that are true in all possible worlds are knowable *a posteriori* and some *a priori*. But *a priori* itself has remained rather something of a forgotten stepchild, and here if anywhere seems a likely place for the next spurt of philosophical energy. The prising apart of these three notions has left 'a priori' systematically related to nothing else.

Insofar as the categories of the a priori and the a posteriori are still used, their use seems to rest on an as yet untheorised basis of brute intuition. I take this as unsatisfactory, not because there is anything wrong with using brute intuition. Indeed, many philosophical theories might correctly rest on such a basis. But the point is that such intuition needs to be theorised, as theories of analyticity attempted to do on the basis of our intuitions about analyticity and syntheticity. But there does not exist, as far as I am aware, any philosophical theory which sets out in systematic fashion these intuitions, or shows the connections between what is knowable a priori and anything else of philosophical importance. This is unsatisfactory for at least two reasons. Now, the first reason for which the under-theorisation of the distinction is unsatisfactory is that there is no reason to believe that we always draw the distinction correctly. What a theory about our intuitions permits is the possibility of holding some of the intuitions to be mistaken on the basis of the others. A systematic theory allows us to correct some of our judgements. There is no reason to believe that it is either a priori knowable, or infallibly certain, whether a particular truth be a priori or a posteriori. Second, there is always the possibility that every attempt at the theorisation of the intuitive distinctions some philosophers draw between things knowable a priori and things knowable a posteriori might come to grief. Although this would not show that there is no such distinction to be drawn, our inability to say anything deeper or more systematic or more revealing about it might make us suspicious of that distinction, and of the very idea of an a priori judgement. Thus, although my argument as I have set it out is not directed against any possible notion of the a priori, but only against any philosophically interesting one that is semantically grounded, the continuing failure to ground, explicate, or systematise it in any other way makes me deeply distrustful of the a priori tout court. However, I acknowledge this, too, as an open philosophical question.

I do not think that I have made very clear what my position on induction is. In reply to Phillips,[22] I claimed that 'Phillips' argument rests on . . . a refined scepticism of its own concerning the possibility of inductive inference. For a realist induction is grounded in a view of nomological necessity that steers between logical necessity and sheer contingency'. Yet, I seem to dismiss the possibility of an inductive reply to the sceptic on the question of establishing the reality of the physical world, and also of an inductive argument for the existence of unobservable, theoretical entities. Isn't my position contradictory?

In a narrow sense, induction is often identified with enumerative induction. In an enumerative inductive inference, the fact that objects of a certain kind, F, have a property G, makes probable the conclusion that all F's are G's. In this narrow sense of 'induction', clearly there can be no good inductive inferences from experience to a real world, or from observations to theory or theoretical entities. Typically, in these cases, the inference would not be from limited observations of a kind to universal generalisations about that kind, but from one 'kind' of thing to another 'kind' of thing altogether. These arguments 'ascend' levels rather than generalise from limited cases.

Now, I take 'induction' in a much wider sense than mere enumerative induction.[23] We do in fact argue in such a way that we 'ascend' levels. We do argue, in science for example, to theoretical conclusions from observational data, and we do think that the observational data probablifies our theoretical conclusions. I take this to be, simply, a fact about what we do.

There are at least two distinct questions that we can ask about this form of argument. First, what are the inference rules that we do use? Which theory out of an indefinitely large number of candidate theories is made probable, or more probable than the others, on the basis of the data? There has been some work on this question, which does begin to throw light on an answer. Here I can but gesture towards some of this literature.[24]

It also seems very likely that, whatever sorts of inference rules apply to inductive arguments from observational data to scientific theories will also apply at least partly or perhaps in a modified fashion, in setting out arguments from our sensory experience to the existence of an external world. At least two recent philosophers have argued along these lines. How, asks J. L. Mackie, are we to bridge the

... logical gap between ideas and reality, or between how we see things and how they are ...[25]

Mackie's 'solution' for bridging the gap by synthetic principles (and not by a criteriological or verificationist theory of meaning) has two parts. The initial part is to argue that 'the real existence of material things outside us is a well-confirmed outline hypothesis, that it explains the experiences we have better than any alternative hypothesis would, in particular better than the minimal hypothesis that there are just these experiences and nothing else .... What is essential in this outline hypothesis is that it fills in gaps in things as they appear, so producing continuously existing things and gradual changes where the appearances are discontinuous. Its resulting merit is a special sort of simplicity, the resolving of what would, on the rival, phenomenalist view, be quite unexplained coincidences',[26] and Mackie argues that this simplicity, the elimination of unexplained coincidences, is similarly 'of the greatest importance as a guide to the choice between alternative scientific hypotheses'.[27] If Mackie is right, we have a rule of inference, 'eliminate unexplained coincidences', which applies not only to the relatively straightforward cases of scientific inference, but also to the existence of material things from the appearances they help to explain, and 'while the existence of material things is not itself what we would ordinarily call a scientific hypothesis, being rather a framework within which the particular hypotheses that we so describe are formulated, it can, when the question of its justification is raised, be seen to be like a scientific hypotheses and to have in its favour this same sort of simplicity, this same elimination of unexplained coincidence'.

A final example of a purported rule of inductive inference which might, on the basis of sensory experience, problify or make it reasonable to believe in the existence of a material world which I would like at least to mention is put forward by Michael Slote.[28] Slote produces several such principles or rules, but the first one which he cites is what he calls 'the principle of Unlimited Inquiry'.[29] Slote argues that since the very point of science is to obtain more and more warranted explanations, it is unreasonable to adopt an hypothesis on which further warranted explanations of the matter to be explained become impossible. An hypothesis which rules out the possibility of further warranted explanations is an 'inquiry limiting hypothesis'. Thus, Slote claims that the principle of unlimited inquiry states:

(a) that it is scientifically *unreasonable* for someone to *accept* what (he sees or has reason to believe) is for him at that time an inquiry-limiting explanation of a certain phenomenon, other things being equal; and (b) that there is *reason* for such a person to *reject* such an explanation in favour of an acceptable non-inquiry-limiting explanation of the phenomenon in question if he can find one.[30]

We can think of such principles as inductive rules because by their application one can select one, or a small number of plausible explanatory hypotheses out of an indefinitely large number of candidates equally consistent with the evidence cited in the premises. The principles would offer criteria for theoretical choice, and conjoined with the evidential premises and a list of potential theoretical or explanatory candidates, ought to inductively imply a conclusion that states which one(s) of the candidates is preferable as an explanatory hypothesis. For Slote as for Mackie, such principles apply not only in scientific inferences from data to explaining hypotheses, but also in the case of the anti-sceptical inductive argument from experience to an external world. What Slote argues is that, in the anti-sceptical case, such a principle probablifies, on the basis of experience, the hypothesis of an external world, which is not inquiry-limiting, in preference to the Cartesian hypothesis of an Evil Genius, which is inquiry-limiting.

Let us for a moment accept Mackie's and Slote's principles as plausible rules of inductive argument, broadly conceived. Suppose also we conjoin these with other plausible candidates, for example the ones mentioned by Thagard: consilience, simplicity, and analogy.[31] Suppose further we make still more additions, whatever is in fact necessary, so that our list of inductive rules or principles does actually accurately characterise both the theoretical inferences scientists make from data to hypothesis as well as the anti-sceptical external world inference we should like to make in reply to the sceptic. Suppose we can get agreement on what rules go onto this list, and also agreement about relative weightings or priorities in case the rules do not always incline us to the same result (as will surely be the case). Finally, let's even suppose that, by application of these rules to the candidate hypotheses, the premisses of such inductive arguments yield one, or a relatively small number of, hypotheses in the conclusion.

Even if we could do all of this, we would have managed *only* to describe our inductive practices. But I began by saying that there were at least two distinct questions that we can ask about this sort of inductive argument. First, we can ask what are the inference rules that we do actually use, and, on all the suppositions above, we could answer wholly or anyway in good measure that question. But the second question we could ask is: what reasons do we have for believing that such rules are justified? The principles are, as Mackie said, 'synthetic', and we can ask what sort of evidence we could produce for their reasonableness or warrant, other than the intuitive appeal they may have. In a deductively valid argument, given true premisses, we know that the conclusion must be true. Deductive rules of inference preserve truth. What we require of an inductively good argument is that the inference rules preserve probable truth; given true premisses, inductive rules of inference insure that the conclusion is probably true. But how can we, in the face of the sceptic, show that these suggested inductive rules, such as elimination of unexplained coincidences or preference for non-inquiry-limiting hypotheses, or even simple simplicity, are more likely to lead to truth (than would the adoption of their denials)? Simplicity, elegance, and all the others may be more likeable, but it is not clear why they render conclusions inferred to by their use more likely to be true.[32]

So our sceptic can raise the same sort of doubts about inductive principles that he raised about unobservable entities in science and the external world. Still, this result is not trivial, for we might be glad to show that the sceptical burden can be shifted from realism and scientific realism to induction. If we were to grant the justification of our inductive practices in this very wide sense of induction, we can construct good inductive arguments which show that realism and scientific realism are probably true.

When I dismissed the possibility of an *a posteriori* or inductive reply to the sceptic in the book, when I claimed for example that 'both materialism and idealism are inductively consistent' (p. 108) with the empirical evidence, I probably was thinking of induction only in the narrow sense of enumerative induction. In any event, whatever may be the explanation of the way in which I there chose to express myself, my position is this. I still think that the particular considerations I brought against Putnam's *a posteriori* argument for scientific realism are telling. More generally, there may be a set of plausible-sounding inductive principles widely conceived (although this would need much fuller discussion and argument; I have limited myself to citing references which claim that there are such principles) by which one can argue to the conclusion of the essential mind-independence of the physical world and to scientific theories which posit unobservables, *from* premisses about sensory experience or empirical evidence, respectively, and a list of candidate hypotheses from which the choice is to be made. Such principles would be welcome to the realist, and no doubt would be part of the sort of inductive reply to Phillips that I had imagined. But of course, as I said in my discussion of Phillips (p. 162), 'a refined scepticism . . . concerning the possibility of inductive inference' is open to Phillips, or to the anti-realist, or to the sceptic. Thus, my main contention seems to me to still be correct. There are no non-question-begging replies to the sceptic. There are no deductive replies, and there may be inductive replies only if our sceptic isn't sceptical about inductive practices. These inductive practices rest on synthetic principles, whose truth must be contingent, and I have no doubt that Phillips, for example, would produce the same sort of anti-realist arguments about these inductive principles, because they can only be contingently true, that he produced against the realist at other points. On the other hand, if we argue for realism and scientific realism on the basis of these inductive principles, I would adduce the same sort of considerations of methodological continuity with the spirit of science on their behalf that I earlier adduced on behalf of realism itself. But I repeat that these considerations do not, in my view, 'answer' the sceptic in any non-question-begging way. There simply are, ultimately, no answers that can be given if our sceptic or immaterialist escalates his doubts far enough.

I have become increasingly aware of the large measure of agreement between Andrew Collier and myself on many issues.[33] But he, and others, have objected to what, ultimately, they see as a *prise de position* on my part. Of course, I do *not* say that Marxism must be adopted as a *prise de position*. I think that there are very obvious criteria of rational choice – like agreement with facts, explanatory power, absence of a comprehensive alternative as rival – which ought to incline any reasonable man to Marxism, and I think that the *failure* of the working class in large numbers to choose a Marxist practice is due not to their opting for some other equally valid *prise de position*, but because of their 'deception' by the way the social relations of production appear to them, and of course because of the non-rational influence exerted by the mechanisms of the bourgeois state through church, state, family, the media and other institutions of social control. The *prise de position* I take occurs at a very much greater level of abstraction – the adoption not of Marxism but of any realist theory about the world. And even then it is not *quite* a *prise de position*, for I do adduce certain methodological considerations in favour of it. But these considerations are not the sort that are going to impress the sceptic or immaterialist idealist. I hold that, if there is an epistemologically relevant distinction between experience and the reality the experience is of, if one does not collapse reality into thought or experience as does the immaterialist or idealist, and does not deny the knowability of external reality as does the sceptic, then that very epistemological distinction between experience and the reality the experience is *of*, must allow room for sceptical objections. We ignore those objections, because the price of rationally answering them is always and must always be a form of idealism. It is for that very reason that I suggested to any realist proponent of the method of anti-sceptical transcendental argument that there is a tension between realism on the one hand and transcendental argumentation on the other, for such anti-sceptical argumentation, to be successful, would depend on the adoption of an anti-realist theory of meaning of one sort or another.

I regret that I believe that there is, for human rationality, this impasse. It would have been intellectually more agreeable, for me at any rate, to be able to conclude that, ultimately, human reason did have the power of disproving scepticism while at the same time upholding a realist or materialist perspective on the world. Unhappily, I cannot conclude this, and, regretfully, holding fast to realism, I cannot see any rational means for disproving the sceptic, nor any non-circular arguments to convince the idealist or immaterialist of the truth of realism.[34]

At several points in my book, I argued for an epistemology which was individualist in at least one sense, namely 'that any statement that a certain theory or body of knowledge exists in a society is equivalent to (*says no more than*) the statement that there are some individuals in that society who hold the theory, possess the knowledge, or whatever' (p. 155). Thus, I claimed that *only* individual men could be epistemological subjects. I did not motivate my discussion in the book through citing real or fancied opponents, but it is not difficult to find opponents. Epistemological individualism in the sense in which I subscribe to it has been denied in Marxist circles by the Althusserian tradition and in orthodox philosophy by Popper and the Popperian school. Of course, along with the Althusserian tradition, I do not support in general an 'individualism' which reduces all social structures to the individuals which 'bear' them, but I do dispute the application of this valid sociological point to the question of the epistemological subject. Only individual men can be epistemological subjects, although of course these individual knowings are necessarily mediated by the social conditions in which such individual acts of knowledge occur.

Within orthodox philosophy, perhaps the most plausible attempt to dispense with individual knowing subjects is that of Karl Popper. In various of his essays, and especially in 'Epistemology without a Knowing Subject', 'On the Theory of Objective Mind', and 'Two Faces of Common Sense',[35] Popper has advanced the idea of the existence of objective knowledge in what he terms 'the third world'. The 'first world is the world of physical objects; the second the world of mental states; 'and thirdly, the world of *objective contents of thought*, especially of scientific and poetic thoughts and of works of art'.[36]

Among the inmates of my 'third world' are, more especially, theoretical systems; but inmates just as important are *problems* and *problem situations*. And I will argue that the most important inmates of this world are *critical arguments*, and what may be called – in analogy to a physical state or to a state of consciousness – *the state of a discussion*, or *the state of a critical argument*; and of course, the contents of journals, books, and libraries.[37]

What Popper seeks to show is that one cannot reduce the entities of the third world to entities of the second, as merely expressions of subjective mental states, or behavioural dispositions. Popper criticises traditional epistemology for its exclusive concern with knowledge in a subjectivist, second world sense.

This, I assert, has led students of epistemology into irrelevances. While intending to study scientific knowledge, they studied in fact something which is of no relevance to scientific knowledge. . . . While knowledge in the sense of 'I know' belongs to what I call the 'second world', the world of subjects, scientific knowledge belongs to the third world, to the world of objective theories, objective problems, and objective arguments.[38]

The concerns of theory of knowledge must be relocated: '. . . the study of a *largely autonomous* third world of objective knowledge is of decisive importance for epistemology'.[39]

The plausibility of Popper's argument, seems to me to rest on a significant sort of slippage. Let us grant, simply for the sake of argument, Popper's 'platonism' with regard to what he listed as the 'inmates' of the third world – problems, arguments, the state of a discussion. That is, let us suppose that the statement that a certain argument or problem exists is *not* equivalent to the statement that there are some individuals who are entertaining that argument or who have posed the problem. There may *be* arguments no one has yet entertained and problems no one as yet has come to realise as a problem. And when Popper adds 'the contents of journals, books, and libraries', I take him to be including propositions as denizens of the third world, and there is a sense in which there are propositions no one has as yet formulated, entertained, or considered.

Popper writes, though, as if his making good the 'third world' case for propositions, problems, and arguments would permit him to include, without further ado, theories and knowledge as similarly citizens of the third world. I dispute this. It does not follow that knowledge is a citizen of the third world if arguments, propositions, or problems are. Unlike propositions, problems, and arguments, knowledge *is* clearly relational. It is knowledge of an objective content – its 'object' is a proposition which may reside in the third world, but it is a relation between such contents and individual subjects. It is always somebody's knowledge of that content. In the third world, there may be intellectual objects, but within the territory of the third world alone there could be no knowledge of those objects. To assert that there is knowledge always invites the question 'Whose knowledge?' in a way in which the assertion that there is an argument does not necessarily invite the question 'whose argument,'. 'Knowledge' is clearly relational; 'x knows that p' is the essential locution. 'Argument' is not relational; 'the argument for p' is able to stand alone without any tell-tale incompleteness. When I wrote that 'Knowledge is unlike truth. There can be truth in a world without men, even though trivially there would be no one to realise or recognise what is true' (p. 155), perhaps the most charitable interpretation of my remark is that 'truth' is like 'argument' or 'problem'. Neither 'it is true that p' nor 'there is an argument for p' entail 'some individual holds that p is true' or 'someone argued for p', unlike 'it is known that p' which entails and is entailed by 'someone knows that p'.

Some critics have accused me of misinterpreting Lukacs. In a footnote to 'What Is Orthodox Materialism?' for instance,[40] Lukacs very explicitly asserts that the dialectical method 'is limited here to the realm of history and society . . . the crucial determinations of dialectics – the interaction of the subject and object . . . are absent from our knowledge of nature'. In 'Reification and the Consciousness of the Proletariat', Lukacs distinguishes the 'positive' dialectics of society from the merely 'negative' dialectics of nature:

. . . Hegel does perceive clearly at times that the dialectics of nature can never become anything more exalted than a dialectics of movement witnessed by the detached observer, as the subject cannot be integrated into the dialectical process . . .

From this we deduce the necessity of separating the merely objective dialectics of nature from those of society.[41]

But of course I did not *assert* that Lukacs did think that the identity of subject and object applied to the natural world. Rather, I think that there is a tendency in Lukacs to have it both ways, and so I presented him with a dilemma: either the identity of subject and object applies to nature as well as society, or it is restricted to society. If it were to apply to nature, Lukacs' position would indeed be idealist. On the other hand, if it is restricted to history and society, the identity of subject and object cannot be a solution to the problem of subject and object as it was understood by the classical German philosophers whom Lukacs discusses, since they certainly did not intend for it to be restricted in this way. Moreover, restricted to society, the 'identity' of subject and object *at the theoretical level*, which Lukacs says was an insoluble problem for classical German philosophy, is trivially simple, since social and cultural objects are precisely those bits of matter or nature which have been formed and transformed by human social praxis. There *is* another related question here, and Marxism is the *answer* to that question: Why is it the case that in a bourgeois society, men do not recognise social things (like value) as the expression of their activity (the relations of production into which they enter)? Marxism answers *this* question through its recognition that in a commodity-producing society such relations between men assume the fantastic form of relations between things,[42] and poses the praxis of the proletariat as the way in which a revolutionary transformation in society can bring about an epistemological revolution in which social creations no longer take on the objective, fetishised form of things. But this 'practical solution' is not to the problem of subject and object that puzzled classical German philosophy, but to the related but distinct problem of why it is that men do not always recognise their own social creations.

I think that my discussion of Marx's position in Chapter III, just as Lukacs' own discussion in 'Reification and the Consciousness of the Proletariat', displays an unfortunate choice of terminology. Sometimes I speak of the 'social world' and the 'natural world' as if these were two different worlds. Nothing could be further from my intentions, because I argued that social, human, cultural, or mental things are necessarily or essentially realised in or materialised in the natural world (although not 'reducible to' those natural things in which they are realised). Perhaps it would have been better to speak only of one kind of *thing* which can have two distinctive kinds of *properties* or *features*, natural ones and social ones. In this terminology, Marx's materialism is the assertion that (a) there can be things which have only natural properties and (b) if anything has a social or cultural feature, it is *necessarily* a thing with natural or material properties or features too. This position remains distinctive from reductive materialism, which could claim that the social or cultural features of things are identical to, or are nothing but, natural or physical features of things. Marx's materialism preserves the integrity of both the social and natural properties of things, but insists that there can be instances of things with the latter and without the former but *not* with the former and without the latter.

Perhaps using this terminology I can say again what I take to be Marx's position about thought and nature. If we consider human beings as bodies of a special sort located in space and time, Marx's position is not ontologically dualist for the following reason. These special spatio-temporal objects or bodies which we call 'persons' have two sorts of properties which can be attributed to them, mental or social properties and natural properties. Mental properties (like the property of being conscious, to use one of Marx's own examples from *The German Ideology*) are *necessarily* properties of these spatio-temporal bodies to which physical or natural properties are also attributed.

I was less than clear when I said that 'the essence of thought includes being' (p. 75). What I meant by this is that a mental or social or cultural property of an object (a person or an artifact) is necessarily the property of a physical being and *not* that a mental (or social, etc.) property is identical with (is nothing but) a physical property. The latter doctrine would be a variety of reductive materialism, and this, following Marx, has already been rejected.[43] Finally, Marx's view is that, in this one-world terminology, there can be bodies to which only physical but no mental (or social, or cultural) properties are attributed, but not conversely.[44]

Thus, there are two kinds of properties (not two kinds of 'worlds' or 'realms'), neither kind reducible to the other. But this is not, ontologically speaking, a dualist view, since it is impossible, for one set, for anything to have a property of that set without having properties from the other set or kind. Ontological dualism requires essential independence; there is a sense in which Marxian mental or social properties are not 'essentially independent' of natural properties, since *necessarily* anything with a mental or social property has natural or physical properties too. In order to stress the point that we are not speaking of two worlds or realms, expressions like 'the essential independence of nature from thought' and 'the essential dependence of thought on nature' would be better replaced by 'the possibility of things with natural but no mental, social, or cultural properties' and 'the impossibility of things with mental, or social, or cultural properties but no natural properties'.

In the first edition of the book, and especially in Chapter III, I contrasted 'thought' with 'object'. No doubt this was natural, because of the way in which I had traced these issues through Kant, Hegel, and Feuerbach. However, in this edition, I have altered the text at various places in order to change 'object' to 'natural object' and 'objective' to 'natural'. My earlier terminology lent itself to the unfortunate suggestion that thought or praxis was not 'objective' but merely 'subjective'. Of course, I do and did not think this, because thought is necessarily materialised and hence is as objective as nature is. The absurdity of this suggestion can be brought out even more clearly using the new terminology. There is no reason to think that the natural properties of a thing are more objective than its social, cultural, or mental properties, since these latter properties are necessarily properties of natural things. Mental, etc. properties are no less objective than are natural or physical ones.

Again using this terminology, one can restate again why materialism 'needs' a correspondence theory of knowledge. On a correspondence theory, 'correspondence' is a contingent relation. The relation between the objects of knowledge or true beliefs and the cognitive processes of which they are the objects is contingent in both directions,[45] and I said in Chapter III that we could, if we wished, talk of the epistemological dualism of experience and object (and *not* ontological dualism). Now, it is perfectly consistent to maintain, as Marx does, that ontologically speaking epistemological properties, which imply the existence of knowing or believing subjects, (such as the property of being known or of being truly believed about) are necessarily properties of an object to which physical or natural properties are attributed, *and* that the relation between the cognitive process and its object is contingent. Objects of knowledge may have epistemological properties only contingently (e.g. the property of being known), but if they have epistemological properties, then they necessarily have physical or natural ones too.

But if the epistemological relation between cognitive process and its object were necessary or essential, as I have argued it would be on a Kantian interpretation theory or its Hegelian offspring, then it could not be epistemologically consistent, in the meaning I gave to that phrase, to hold that there can be natural objects to which no epistemological (or, no mental or social) properties, such as the property of being known or about which there are true beliefs, are attributed. There might indeed *be* such natural or physical objects, but we could never have any knowledge of them. Every *known* object would have an epistemological property necessarily or essentially. Only if such epistemological properties are had by known things contingently would we be *entitled* to our materialist beliefs.

I admitted in the book to the absence of any real discussion of terms such as 'necessary' and 'essential'. To some extent, I have tried to rectify that omission in my forthcoming paper, 'Marxism and Dialectics'.[46]

Lastly, I want to offer additional textual support for my attribution to Marx of materialism, a supplementary passage from Hegel which further confirms, I think, my views on Hegel and intellectual intuition, and Hegel's relationship to Fichte, and to mention in passing one or two sources and texts which I have found useful and which have come to my attention since the publication of the first edition. First, for additional quotations from Marx concerning the essential independence of nature from man:

(1)'The soil (and this, economically speaking, includes water) in the virgin state in which it supplies man with necessaries as the means of subsistence ready to hand, exists independently of him.'[47]
(2)'Labour is *not the source* of all wealth. Nature is just as much the source of use-values . . . as labour. Labour is itself only the manifestation of a force of nature . . . Man's labour only becomes a source of use-values . . . if his relation to nature, the primary source of all instruments and objects of labour, is one of ownership . . .'[48]
(3)'The worker can create nothing without *nature*, without the *sensuous external world*.'[49]

It might also be of interest to consider some of Marx's remarks in the 'Doctoral Dissertation', although it is insufficiently clear how this early discussion by Marx of Greek atomism would be related to his own and to his mature position.[50]

Hegel, in the 'Introduction' to *The Philosophy of Nature*, has this to say about intellectual intuition:

In order to state briefly what is the defect of this conception of intellectual intuition . . . this unity of intelligence and intuition, of the inwardness of spirit and its relation to externality, must be, not the beginning, but the goal, not an immediate, but a resultant unity. A natural unity of thought and intuition is that of the child and the animal . . . But man . . . must have gone through the labour and activity of thought in order to . . . overcome this separation between himself and nature. The immediate unity is thus only an abstract, implicit truth, not the actual truth; for not only must the content be true, but the form also.[51]

This confirms, I think, the view that Hegel accepted the idea of intellectual intuition, and that his critique of the doctrine, at the hands of others, was methodological only, and not substantive.

As for additional sources or texts I wish to mention, I would like to cite Shlomo Avineri, *The Social and Political Thought of Karl Marx*,[52] as a negative example of a writer who, in the course of only a few under-argued pages, is able to get almost everything wrong about Marx's epistemology, the place of Engels and especially *Dialectics of Nature* in an authentic Marxist tradition, and the alleged 'mechanism' of *Materialism and Empirio-Criticism* and its relation to *The Philosophical Notebooks*. Had I remembered that Avineri had gone so wrong so often, I would have used him as an explicit whipping-boy in the text. In a much more positive spirit, it is a pleasure to mention the (in the English-speaking world) under-valued and under-discussed *Le Nouveau Leviathan* of Pierre Naville,[53] and especially his discussion of reciprocity in Vol. 4, *Les Echanges Socialistes*. Robert S. Cohen has a short discussion of Bogdanov in an appendix to an article on Ernest Mach.[54] Finally, a very long study of Feuerbach by Marx Wartofsky has appeared in English, filling a very large gap in the English literature. There is nothing that I said about Feuerbach in the book which that book has made me wish to review or qualify.[55]

In a recent review in *Radical Philosophy*, No. 21, Spring, 1979, the reviewer accuses me of the 'poor argument' that 'since the universe of physical objects did once exist without human beings, therefore *a fortiori* it can do so'. Since I explicitly reject that argument on p. 20, pp. 107-8, pp. 122-23, p. 126, and pp. 191-93, I cannot understand why that argument is ascribed to me. Consequently, I find much of the review subsequent to that misascription simply irrelevant as a criticism of my position.

[1] Bhaskar, Roy, *A Realist Theory of Science*, 2nd edition, Harvester Press, Hassocks, 1978. A 'Postscript' to the 2nd edition appears on pp. 251-262.

[2] Although I overlooked, as Bhaskar says, the fact that one of the arguments established something about the objects of experience, rather than of knowledge. Needless to say, I do not in general conflate these things any more than does Bhaskar, as my remarks in Chapter V about a theoretical rather than an experiential reflection theory, and my distinction in Chapter VI between a reflection theory of knowledge and of perception, should make abundantly clear.

[3] Bhaskar, *op. cit.*, p. 31.

[4] See above, p. 100.

[5] Bhaskar, *op. cit.*, p. 258.

[6] *Ibid.*, p. 257.

[7] *Ibid.*, p. 258.

[8] *Ibid.*, p. 260.

[9] *Ibid.*, p. 258.

[10] This would be especially contested by anyone of idealist sympathies. Quite a lot of room might be left for criticism, even if it fails at the most basic level. Consider for example R. G. Collingwood's views on 'absolute presuppositions' in *An Essay In Metaphysics*, Oxford, 1940.

[11] See above, p. 131.

[12] See for example Donald Davidson, 'Causal Relations', *Journal of Philosophy* 64 (1967), pp. 691-703, and reprinted in Ernest Sosa, *Causation and Conditionals*, Oxford University Press, Oxford, 1975; J. L. Mackie, *The Cement of the Universe*, Oxford University Press, Oxford, 1974, especially Chapter 3, pp. 59-87.

[13] Bhaskar, *op. cit.*, p. 256.

[14] *Ibid.*, p. 140.

[15] I have dealt at some greater length with the problem of tendencies in 'Marxism and Dialectics', in John Mepham and D.-H. Ruben (eds.), *Issues In Marxist Philosophy*, Harvester Press, Hassocks, 1979.

[16] Bhaskar, *op. cit.*, p. 98.

[17] *Ibid.*, p. 257

[18] I am following the extremely plausible argument of Barry Stroud, in 'Transcendental Arguments', *Journal of Philosophy*, Vol. LXV No. 9, 2 May 1968, pp. 241-256.

[19] The discussion of Phillips' occurs on pp. 158-162 above. A good introduction to, and bibliography for, criteriological theories occurs in W. Gregory Lycan, 'Noninductive Evidence: Recent Work on Wittgenstein's 'Criteria', *American Philosophical Quarterly*, Vol. 8, No. 2, April 1971, pp. 109-125.

[20] See above, pp. 102-103.

[21] Unger, Peter, *Ignorance*, Oxford University Press, Oxford, 1975.

[22] See p. 162 above.

[23] As is now customary. See for example Richard Swinburne, (ed.), *The Justification of Induction*, Oxford University Press, 1974, p. 5: 'There seem to be perfectly correct arguments to scientific theories which do not merely generalize the premisses'.

[24] Perhaps the first thing in this direction was Norwood Russell Hanson, *Patterns of Discovery*, Cambridge University Press, 1975, see pp. 85-92. Following C. S. Peirce, Hanson calls inferences from data to theory 'abductive inferences' 'retroductive inferences', and seems to have conceived of them as distinct from inductive inferences. The way in which he characterised the distinction *must* be erroneous, for he says that 'abduction merely suggests that something may be'. But one hardly needs an *inference* to establish a 'might-be'; abduction, like induction, better shows us that something probably is.

On the contrary, I am convinced by Gilbert Harman's article, 'Inference to the Best Explanation', in *The Philosophical Review* 74, 1965, pp. 88-95. Harman takes as the basic category 'inferences to the best explanation', which would include theoretical or abductive inferences, and shows how enumerative induction itself is best viewed as a special case of inference to the best explanation.

Finally, for a careful and interesting discussion of the criteria scientists actually use in determining, on the data, which theory is the most plausible, see Paul R. Thagard, 'The Best Explanation: Criteria For Theory Choice', *The Journal of Philosophy* Vol. LXXV, No. 2, February 1978, pp. 76-92.

Discussions of simplicity are also relevant; see, for example, Elliot Sober, *Simplicity*, Oxford University Press, Oxford, 1975, since a likely inference rule for moving from data to theory will be something like, 'Other things being equal, choose the simpler hypothesis or explanation'.

[25] Mackie, J. L., *Problems from Locke*, Oxford University Press, 1976, pp. 62-67.

[26] *Ibid.*, p 64.

[27] *Ibid.*, pp. 66-67.

[28] Slote, Michael, *Reason and Scepticism*, Allen & Unwin, London, 1970.

[29] See *Ibid.*, Chapter 2, especially pp. 67-69.

[30] *Ibid.*, p. 67.

[31] Thagard, Paul R., *op. cit.*,

[32] A similar point was made in a review of Slote's book by Fred Dretske in *The Journal of Philosophy* 69 (1972), pp. 47-53: '... what does ... Slote show? That if we can describe what we do, in our attempts to be reasonable, in a general enough way (so as to earn for the description the label 'Principle') we can ignore sceptical quibbling about the validity of what we do?" (p. 52).

[33] Collier has sent me a copy of his article, 'Truth and Practice' which appeared in *Radical Philosophy* 5. I have also had the opportunity to read two articles by him which will appear in John Mepham and D. H. Ruben (eds.), *Issues In Marxist Philosophy*, Second Volume, Harvester Press, Hassocks, 1979.

[34] Perhaps I should make clear that I take the difference between the sceptic and the immaterialist or idealist to be this. The sceptic denies that we can have knowledge of physical objects; the immaterialist or idealist says we can, but that physical objects are reducible to, or essentially dependent on, human experience.

[35] All collected in Karl Popper, *Objective Knowledge; An Evolutionary Approach*, Oxford University Press, Oxford, 1972.

[36] *Ibid.*, p. 106.

[37] *Ibid.*, p. 107.

[38] *Ibid.*, p. 108.

[39] *Ibid.*, p. 111.

[40] Lukacs, G., 'What Is Orthodox Marxism?', *History and Class Consciousness*, Merlin Press, London, 1968. Translated by Rodney Livingstone, p. 24, n. 6. Thanks to Tim O'Hagan for reminding me of this footnote.

[41] Lukacs, G., 'Reification and the Consciousness of the Proletariat', *op. cit.*, p. 207.

42   For the best Marxist discussion of this available, see I. I. Rubin, *Essays on Marx's Theory of Value*, Black & Red, Detroit, 1972.

43   Using the current philosophical distinction, Marx in denying reductive materialism, is denying property-identity and hence denying a form of type-type identity between mental and physical events. He accepts only that, necessarily, every individual thing of which a mental property is true is a thing of which natural or physical properties are true.

44   I am involved in stating Marx's view here, not defending it against all possible objections. In particular, it would be important to extend this to universals, abstract objects such as numbers and propositions, etc. Does everything to which mathematical or linguistic properties can be attributed also have natural or physical properties attributable to it?

45   The same philosophical fight is fought and refought. See for example, for a good, old-fashioned statement of a view similar to this, and a similarly motivated critical study of Kant, H. A. Prichard, *Kant's Theory of Knowledge*, Oxford University Press, Oxford, Chapter VI. Prichard was part of the school of Oxford realism which was led by John Cook Wilson. Many of the issues and themes I have been arguing turn up, not unsurprisingly, in their writings.

46   To appear in John Mepham and D. -H. Ruben (eds.), *Issues in Marxist Philosophy*, Harvester Press, Hassocks, 1979.

47   Marx, Karl, *Capital I*, Progress Publishers, Moscow, 1965, p. 178.

48   Marx, Karl, *Critique of the Gotha Programme*, in *The First International and After*, David Fernbach (ed.), Penguin Books, Harmondsworth, 1974, p. 341.

49   Marx, Karl, *Economic and Philosophic Manuscripts*, in Karl Marx and Frederick Engels, *Collected Works*, Vol. 3, Lawrence & Wishart, London, 1975, p. 273.

50   Marx, Karl, 'On the Difference Between the Democritean and Epicurean Philosophy of Nature' in Karl Marx and Frederick Engels, *Collected Works*, Vol. 1, Lawrence & Wishart, London, 1975. See pp. 70-73.

51   Hegel, *The Philosophy of Nature*, trans. by A. V. Miller, Oxford, 1970, p. 9.

52   Avineri, Shlomo, *The Social and Political Thought of Karl Marx*, Cambridge University Press, 1969. See especially pp. 68-72.

53   Naville, Pierre, *Le Nouveau Leviathan*, Editions Anthropos, Paris. See Vol. 4, *Les Echanges Socialistes*, 1974, pp. 122, 123, 128-130 for an extremely interesting discussion of the notion of reciprocity, Naville traces its lineage from Kant and Hegel through to Marx's use of it in a theory of exchange.

54   Cohen, Robert S., 'Ernest Mach: Physics, Perception, and the Philosophy of Science', *Synthese* Vol. 18, 1968, pp. 132-191. The appendix is entitled 'Appendix: Machists and Marxists: Bogdanov and Lenin', pp. 162-166.

55   Wartofsky, Marx, *Feuerbach*, Cambridge University Press, Cambridge, 1977. My review of Wartofsky's book is forthcoming in *Mind*.

INDEX OF NAMES

Names in footnotes are included in the index only if they are elsewhere mentioned in the text itself, or some discussion occurs in the footnote. Names merely cited in the footnotes alone have not been included.

INDEX OF TOPICS